THE NOBEL
LAUREATES

THE NOBEL LAUREATES

HOW THE WORLD'S GREATEST ECONOMIC MINDS SHAPED MODERN THOUGHT

MARILU HURT McCARTY

McGraw-Hill

New York   San Francisco   Washington, D.C.   Auckland   Bogotá
Caracas   Lisbon   London   Madrid   Mexico City   Milan
Montreal   New Delhi   San Juan   Singapore
Sydney   Tokyo   Toronto

Library of Congress Cataloging-in-Publication Data

McCarty, Marilu Hurt.
  The Nobel laureates : how the world's greatest economic minds shaped modern thought
by Marilu Hurt McCarty.
    p. cm.
  Includes bibliographical references.
  ISBN 0-07-135614-2
  1. Economics—History—20th century.   2. Economists.   3. Nobel Prizes—History.
HB87 .M337   2000
330—dc21   00-024447

McGraw-Hill

*A Division of The **McGraw·Hill** Companies*

1 2 3 4 5 6 7 8 9 0   DOC/DOC   0 9 8 7 6 5 4 3 2 1 0

ISBN 0-07-135614-2

This book was set in Fairfield by Impressions Book and Journal Services, Inc.

Printed and bound by R. R. Donnelley & Sons Company.

McGraw-Hill books are available at special quantity discounts to use as premiums and sales
promotions, or for use in corporate training programs. For more information, please write to
the Director of Special Sales, Professional Publishing, McGraw-Hill, Two Penn Plaza, New
York, NY 10121-2298. Or contact your local bookstore.

This book is printed on recycled, acid-free paper containing a minimum of 50%
recycled, de-inked fiber.

CONTENTS

THE NOBEL PRIZE WINNERS IN ECONOMIC SCIENCES

1969 Jan Tinbergen (1903–1994) and Ragnar Frisch (1895–1973)
1970 Paul Samuelson (1915–)
1971 Simon Kuznets (1901–1985)
1972 Kenneth Arrow (1921–) and John Hicks (1904–1989)
1973 Wassily Leontief (1906–1999)
1974 Friedrich von Hayek (1899–1992) and Gunnar Myrdal (1898–1987)
1975 Tjalling Koopmans (1910–1984) and Leonid Kantorovich (1912–1986)
1976 Milton Friedman (1912–)
1977 James Meade (1907–1998) and Bertil Ohlin (1899–1979)
1978 Herbert Simon (1916–)
1979 Theodore Schultz (1901–1998) and Arthur Lewis (1915–1990)
1980 Lawrence Klein (1920–)
1981 James Tobin (1918–)
1982 George Stigler (1911–1991)
1983 Gerard Debreu (1921–)
1984 Sir Richard Stone (1913–1991)
1985 Franco Modigliani (1918–)
1986 James Buchanan (1919–)
1987 Robert Solow (1924–)
1988 Maurice Allais (1911–)
1989 Trygve Haavelmo (1911–)
1990 Merton Miller (1923–2000), Harry Markowitz (1927–), and William Sharpe (1934–)
1991 Ronald Coase (1910–)
1992 Gary Becker (1930–)
1993 Robert Fogel (1926–) and Douglass North (1920–)

THE NOBEL
LAUREATES

INTRODUCTION

A man went to see his physician for what he thought was a minor ailment and was distressed to learn it was most serious and that, in fact, he had only six months to live.

"Please, Doctor, is there anything I can do?" he pleaded.

"Yes, there is one thing," came the reply. "You can marry an economist and move to North Dakota."

"Will that make me live longer?"—hopefully.

"No. But it will seem longer."

Of course, this is the way most people look upon economists. And if one economist is boring, 44 Nobel Prize–winning economists must be 44 times as boring. Right?

Well, maybe not.

My goal is to convince you otherwise—that, in fact, the Nobel laureates in economic sciences embody such rich human qualities as to justify our interest and investigation. When asked which of the 44 is my favorite, I am compelled to answer, "The one I'm studying at the moment." Studying each of these economists opens such a range of vistas that it is impossible to evaluate that person by any single standard. Brightest? Most imaginative? Most compassionate? Funniest? Yes, some are truly funny. It's impossible to choose.

One characteristic they all share, however, is their deep concern for the welfare of ordinary men and women, their drive to use their talents for the betterment of human society. And here emerges an unfortunate fact about most people's understanding of economics and economists. The idea that the pronouncements of economists might have some bearing on the circumstances in which ordinary men and women live out their lives has not crossed most people's

1

minds. We readily make that connection when a chemist is rewarded for developing a new vaccine or a physicist, for creating a new molecule. And, truth be told, those achievements may be no more life-altering than those of an economist who improves our understanding of the route to a better life.

The Nobel Prize in Economic Sciences is a rather recent addition to the Nobel series, not a part of Alfred Nobel's original plan but established by the Bank of Sweden in 1968 as a further memorial to the Swedish inventor of dynamite. U.S. economists have dominated the history of the prize, and the University of Chicago has dominated U.S. recipients, claiming a total of eight awards.

Still, the idea of economics as a "science," worthy of such an award, is alien to some people. After all, economics has no laboratories for carrying out controlled experiments: isolating organic or inorganic subjects, manipulating their physical environment, and measuring the results of change. Economists regard the world as their laboratory, however. This world provides the human guinea pigs whose behavior the economic scientist passively observes as the world changes. In this all-inclusive laboratory, the economic scientist proceeds much as the physical scientist proceeds: first, stating a theory (hypothesis) tentatively explaining human responses to certain stimuli; second, observing human behavior under various economic conditions, measuring effects, and recording data; third, organizing the data and evaluating their consistency with the stated hypothesis; and finally, if the data are not inconsistent with the hypothesis (the awkward phrasing here is intentional), proclaiming an economic law or principle as a useful explanation of how the world works.

Economic laws can never be as precise as those of the physical sciences, of course, in the absence of laboratories where two molecules of hydrogen always behave as expected when confronted with one molecule of oxygen—the laws of physics being unyielding to the observations of the lowly scientist. Human beings are never so predictable. Because human behavior seldom conforms precisely to the scientist's expectations, economic laws or principles are less than perfect. Nevertheless, Robert Solow, Nobel laureate of 1987, advises us not to grieve over the hole in the doughnut but to be thankful for the doughnut. We learn more about the "doughnut" by the sorts of endless probing, poking, and prodding carried out by the diverse minds that make up the community of economic scientists.

That community has been especially active in the years since the mid-twentieth century. Some of their findings are more valid, relevant, and usable than others; but most fit rather splendidly into what is becoming a fuller, more nuanced appreciation of the infinite possibilities human beings devise for themselves. This is especially true of the advances made by the 44 Nobel laureates described here. Not in any sort of chronology, not even according to any overall plan, more in the manner of fitting together the pieces of a very complicated jigsaw puzzle, the Nobel laureates in economic sciences are moving thinking people toward an improved understanding of the economic world around us.

The jigsaw puzzle will never be complete, of course. And some sections may develop at a tangent to the main picture, ultimately to be shoved to the side. Still, even when developments are outside the main thrust of economic understanding, they help economic scientists overcome the disadvantages they face through the lack of a scientific laboratory. Tangents from the main picture substitute in economics for the many laboratory experiments that turn out to be mistaken but must be carried out before the physical scientist finally identifies a concept worth further investigation.

To improve understanding of such a complex environment as human society requires minds that veer off the beaten path, that march to different drummers, that defy orthodox discipline. These sorts of minds are wont to disagree, giving rise to an entire body of humor at the expense of economists: "stretched end to end, they would never reach a conclusion; compelled to render an opinion, they will come up with more opinions than the number of economists asked; asked to change a lightbulb, . . ." well, you can make up your own ending. Actually, it is the disagreements among economists that help advance our understanding, as you will discover as you read about the eclectic blending of competing schools that constitute the community of Nobel economists.

Furthermore, whatever "school" of economics individual economists represent, they agree about much that is fundamental to economics. They agree about the problem of scarcity and society's compelling need for systems and institutions for allocating scarcity efficiently. Economists tend to harp on the problem of scarcity, which generally makes them unpopular and gives rise to much of the cynical humor about them. Often it is the task of the economist to bring the bad news, the news about the necessary trade-offs of wanted things for other wanted things. "There is no such thing as a free lunch" cannot be the motto of a loved profession!

We deal with scarcity every day. Scarce time spent commuting is not available for meeting with clients. Savings spent cruising in the Caribbean are not available for building a stock portfolio. Corporate earnings spent for advertising are not available for research and development. Tax revenues spent for defense are not available for training displaced workers. Even such intangibles as named Web addresses are scarce, ownership by a teenage hacker in Des Moines precluding ownership by a multinational corporation. It is in dealing with scarcity that we most often encounter limits in our ability to have our cake and eat it too. We want more of the things that enhance the quality of life, and we want to give up as little as is absolutely necessary in return. This is why we need economics. Economics helps ordinary men and women choose how to use what we have in such a way as to minimize the necessary sacrifices.

Understanding the contributions of the Nobel laureates in economic sciences leads to an understanding of the economic thought of the last half of the twentieth century. This is not to say that the Nobel economists were the only contributors to modern economic thought nor that their contributions were independent of the contributions of many others. Physical scientists describe their dependence on their monumental achievers as "standing on the shoulders of giants." The tremendous power of cumulating effort suggests a different metaphor from our jigsaw puzzle, with its discrete, precisely interlocking pieces. The cumulating contributions of the many associates of these 44 economists is more like the tiny coral animals that together build a complex structure, reflecting at the same time the diversity and the cohesion of their individual contributions. The Nobel economists have served as foci in erecting a structure that achieves its infinitely changeable shape through the fertile contributions of other scholars, each struggling toward improved understanding of the most fundamental of human institutions: our economic system.

PART 1
THE RATIONALISTS AND INDIVIDUAL CHOICE

*George Stigler • Friedrich von Hayek •
Gary Becker • Herbert Simon*

Anyone who has ever cut short a lunch with friends in order to keep a dental appointment is behaving precisely as the "rationalist" group of Nobel economists would expect. The rationalists expect us, in everything we do, to weigh the benefits of one choice against the costs, where the costs are the benefits of another choice we could be enjoying. The outcome from rational choice is maximum net benefits, the maximum difference between total benefits and total costs. When the benefits we enjoy from socializing with friends exact the cost of a flaming toothache, the choice is easy to make.

We describe the first group of Nobel economists as *rationalists* because they look to the rationality of ordinary men and women to effect the decisions that promote maximum social welfare. When all people behave rationally, they say, the result is a perfectly efficient society, one with the highest possible levels of living, on the average, and the greatest individual freedom. Because the rationalists derived their philosophy from the "classical" economists of the eighteenth and nineteenth centuries, they are often referred to as *neoclassical economists*.

The neoclassical economists describe the beneficial results of rational choice in terms of a serene metaphor, that of a stately Greek temple whose lines cut cleanly across a cloudless sky and meet in sublime harmony. Wow! Would that it were possible to arrange our lives to such perfection.

Chapter 1
RATIONAL PEOPLE DO GOOD THINGS

Human beings are born selfish, as is every other gaping, clawing fledgling. And we remain selfish, more or less, despite the blandishments of our moms—bless 'em. So it is fitting that this inherent characteristic should become the basis for organizing human society. Acknowledging our innate selfishness is *rational*, which is the term the neoclassical economists use to describe the governing principle of a market economy.

Probably the supreme rationalist of all economists is George Stigler. Even the most superficial dip into economics brings one into contact with his work. In fact, Stigler defined, articulated, and made comprehensible the concepts that make economics the fundamental discipline of the social sciences, an accomplishment that yielded for him the Nobel Prize of 1982. He translated and applied rational analytical tools to a variety of social decisions, ranging over such issues as the preservation of fish species in offshore fisheries, the proper terms and pricing of insurance policies, and the prospects for profitable investments in emerging market economies. People sometimes describe the social sciences as "soft" sciences because, without a firm foundation in analytical methods, they tend to dissolve into vague, unsubstantiated opinion. With analytical tools derived from economics, however, the social sciences enjoy a solid framework for scientific investigation.

The analytical concept with such wide applications in all the social sciences is *optimization:* the not-so-startling idea that people choose behaviors that yield the best possible outcomes for themselves. The most obvious applications of optimizing behavior occur every day as we choose combinations of products to buy—food and personal services, clothing and entertainment, rental housing and transportation services—each selected because of the way it contributes to our personal welfare. Stigler was the first economist to suggest another less obvious but perhaps more critical application of optimization, the job search. Here, we explore available jobs and the labor market, evaluate the positives and negatives associated with various job prospects, and eventually end our job search by accepting a job offer.

This is the sort of behavior the neoclassical economists describe as rational. Although this term is commonly used to distinguish thinking from nonthinking behavior, economists use it specifically to refer to self-interested behavior. When people behave rationally, the result of their behavior is maximum *welfare*—another term that is used differently in economics. Although in common parlance the word welfare refers to a particular kind of government program, to an economist maximum welfare means the largest quantity of income, wealth, or whatever else people might want.

Stigler was born to Eastern European immigrants to the United States and as a child spoke only German. He attended the University of Chicago for his advanced education, coming under the influence of the widely respected economist Frank Knight, who also influenced other Nobel economists, namely Milton Friedman, Paul Samuelson, and Theodore Schultz. Professor Knight was a precise and demanding educator, noted especially for his tendency to question sloppy thinking. Stigler later said that one of the words he heard most often while a student at Chicago was "nonsense," applied to opinions that were poorly supported by hard evidence. The influence of the "Chicago School" produced in Stigler a disdain for poorly supported opinions that he carried throughout his life.

All of Stigler's work demonstrates this tendency to question established beliefs and to seek objective information to support opinion—to move freely back and forth between theory and evidence. This is probably Stigler's chief contribution to economics: to examine critically the explanations of human behavior offered by other economists (past and present), discarding "nonsense" and explaining observed behavior using only those ideas that are well supported by evidence. Most new ideas are mistaken or useless, he admits, but this is not necessarily a bad thing. Indeed, society should welcome all sorts of new ideas; but it should also adapt them, patch up their weaknesses, and develop them further so that they can be applied in credible ways. To transform new ideas into usable guides to behavior requires valid information, information organized in such a way as to reveal likely cause-effect relationships. This is what economics does. And this is what we learn from George Stigler: to organize real world information toward choices that yield optimal outcomes.

The Mysterious Process of Optimization

Optimizing behavior begins with the assumption that whatever behavior we choose will yield offsetting results: some positive or beneficial results and some negative or costly results. The benefits of particular behaviors include all those changes in conditions that favor the tastes and preferences of the chooser, ranging from the immediate satisfaction of specific appetites (for such amenities as chocolate-chip cookies, urban housing, and even cultural enlightenment) to such broader tastes as, say, the value one places on global ecological balance. Costs include all the benefits not enjoyed when choosing one behavior requires the sacrifice of another and range from the immediate sacrifice of money, time, income, or attention that could be used for other things to such broader sacrifices as, say, the irreversible extinction of pandas, worts, or other irreplaceable species.

The goal of optimization is to choose from an almost infinite array of behaviors the particular behavior, or level of behavior, that yields the maximum difference between benefits and costs. In the language of economics, maximum net benefits or maximum personal welfare.

If it were possible to measure all the benefits and costs (here and elsewhere, now and forever) of all alternative behaviors, it would be a simple matter to calculate the sums and differences and choose the particular behavior that maximizes net benefits. This is not possible, of course, and if it were it would consume far more of our time than is feasible or desirable—rather like recomputing our income tax liability every day of our lives. Luckily, there is a practical route to the optimal choice: that is, by comparing the benefits and costs of one more unit of a particular activity and pursuing that unit only if the added benefits exceed the added costs.

The practical route to optimal choices is *marginalism*, decisions that take place at the margin or edge. Not all-or-nothing, but incremental, decisions that "edge" toward tentative answers to life's choices. Marginalism ignores past decisions (what's done is done and can be regretted but not changed) and considers only the next decision and, implicitly, the consequences of the next decision for our own interests.[1] Thus, marginalism is unabashedly selfish. As individual selfish beings we might compare the benefits of, say, a larger auto with the costs of a reduced stock portfolio. As a society of selfish beings, we might compare the benefits from, say, one more shopping mall with the costs of, say, increased traffic congestion and air pollution. For maximum net benefits we would pursue only those decisions that promise benefits greater than costs "at the margin." The fortunate result of decision making at the margin is to satisfy the objective of maximum net benefits without having to measure total benefits and costs of the things we choose.

Marginalism works because marginal benefits and costs change in opposite directions as we continue any sort of behavior. Sad to say, there is a natural tendency for the added benefits of a particular behavior to diminish as that behavior is continued. Sadder yet, the added costs of a particular behavior tend to increase. We shouldn't be surprised at this, since we naturally begin an activity where it will do the most good (yield the greatest immediate benefits) and cause the least damage (require the least immediate cost). As we continue any activity, however, our added enjoyment tends to diminish: for example, tastes for cookies are eventually satisfied; new shopping malls struggle to capture customers from established retailers. Moreover, added costs tend to increase: for example, sacrifices of time and money become more painful; increased shopper traffic makes commutes hectic and worsens quality of life for suburban home owners. With falling marginal benefits and rising marginal costs, additions to net benefits shrink. As rational beings, we begin and continue an activity only if marginal benefits exceed marginal costs. When additions to net benefits fall to zero, we have achieved maximum net benefits—maximum personal welfare—and there we stop.

The behavior of marginal benefits and costs appears to be an unfortunate fact of life. It is a fact of life that good things seem to peak and bad things seem to get worse. Good things gradually stop getting better, adding smaller and smaller benefits until ultimately total benefits are the best we can expect. Bad things start out barely tolerable and get increasingly intolerable. No matter how earnestly we adjust circumstances to reduce the costs of doing something, rising costs eventually take hold, which helps explain why an early philosopher labeled our subject the "dismal science." Economics, no less than life itself, requires us to recognize these inevitabilities: to compare the diminishing benefits of everything we enjoy with the inexorably rising costs so that finally we arrive at an accommodation that we regard as optimal.

Implications for Economic Efficiency

Without conscious thought, we all optimize when we do such basic things as select the combination of foods on our lunch trays, choose one television program over another, or walk rather than drive to the far end of the shopping mall. More consciously, we optimize when we allocate our incomes among current purchases and personal savings—having in mind some lifestyle preferences that we want to satisfy, including preferences for pleasures today and financial security tomorrow. In the same way, business firms optimize by comparing the benefits (sales revenue, market share, long-range productive capacity) and costs (labor and equipment time, capital outlays) of alternative types and levels of production. Then business firms choose, more or less rationally, depending on the quality of their information, the one alternative among many that maximizes net revenue. Or to use the more familiar term, profit.

Through our consumer purchases, we guide business firms toward the production decisions that, first, maximize our own net benefits and, second, maximize the supplying firms' net revenue. The exquisite result, as described most vividly by the first "modern" economist, Adam Smith, is a system that allocates a society's limited land, labor, and financial resources toward the kinds of production that most nearly satisfy the tastes and preferences of its people. What could be more democratic than that? And indeed Adam Smith articulated this fundamental principle in precisely the same year (1776) that Thomas Jefferson, and others, were articulating the democratic principles that would govern the world's first modern democracy.

A system that produces the most of what people want is described as "efficient." Efficiency is critical in all economic decisions, even more so as societies grow to include more people with more strongly expressed tastes and preferences, and as resources for satisfying those preferences become more strained. Resources are limited, at least for the foreseeable future, to those we find on this planet and include all the human and nonhuman species that breed and feed on it. On the other hand, human tastes and preferences continually grow, creating an inevitable conflict between the magnitude of human wants and the availability of resources for satisfying them. The tension between limited resources and unlimited wants makes the efficient use of resources especially critical and underscores the importance of optimizing behavior.

Perhaps the most wonderful thing about optimization is that it yields efficient outcomes without any sort of government control. It relies entirely on the decisions of ordinary men and women, who rationally balance off the benefits and costs of alternative decisions and selfishly choose the one alternative that adds most to their personal welfare. People don't have to be commanded, cajoled, or persuaded to behave marginally. It is an innate, inherent drive of humans (and, some evidence suggests, of other species as well). We all seem to want to accomplish the most with the least, and we do this incrementally.

Efficiency Requires Certain Conditions

Because efficiency is critical for maximizing welfare, society gains when it creates conditions conducive to efficient behavior. Ever since Adam Smith in the eighteenth century, and especially since the work of George Stigler in the twentieth, economists have come to value free, competitive markets for their contribution to economic efficiency. Free, competitive markets allow buyers and sellers to express, on the one hand, and to satisfy, on the other, our individual tastes and preferences. While it is often said that competitive markets determine prices, it is more correct to say that markets enable us to discover prices. We discover the price at which buyers' tastes and preferences value a product at precisely the cost of the resources sellers require to produce it. Rather marvelously, markets attach a number to a taste—a quality that we are unable, in the absence of markets, to measure.

Markets have another marvelous function, to respond immediately to such changes in tastes and preferences and changes in available resources that rearrange the benefits and costs of particular market decisions. Because changes occur constantly, markets are constantly adjusting, updating prices to reflect new information and shifting resources so that their allocation remains efficient even while conditions are changing. The capacity in free markets for efficient change is in stark contrast to resource allocation in an economy rigidly controlled by government. The former Soviet Union is the obvious example. Even the most diehard Soviet planners would admit the practical impossibility through central planning of recognizing and efficiently responding to such changes in tastes, preferences, and resources that occur continuously in a modern economy. Only freely competitive markets can do that.

Indeed, it is the efficiency of free, competitive markets that underlies Stigler's opposition to government involvement in market decisions.

Economists generally shrink from offering advice to governments. Once an economist openly advocates a particular government policy, her subsequent scholarly renderings become suspect. (Who truly believes the research on the minimum wage law offered by an economist employed by McDonald's?) The potential loss of credibility leads most economists to limit their policy contributions to estimating the benefits and costs of alternative decisions. The responsibility for matching estimated benefits and costs with society's goals is left up to the policymaker.[2] Fewer jobs for low-skilled workers because of a higher minimum wage? Or higher incomes for the working poor? The policymaker must decide.

The only policy advice Stigler would give governments is consistent with the neoclassical confidence in free markets: that is, no policy. No price fixing. No quotas or mandates. No more than the minimum absolutely necessary regulations and taxes. No interference with decisions made in free markets. Thus, Stigler remains truly in the neoclassical tradition, utterly convinced that decisions made by rational men and women, provided with information and unimpeded by government, work best to maximize welfare.

The difficulty of preserving competitive markets while limiting government involvement once presented Stigler with an intellectual dilemma. Like his predecessor Adam Smith, Stigler had noticed a tendency for small business firms to coalesce into large monopolistic firms or, paraphrasing Smith, conspiracies against the public. Large firms have certain advantages, of course. Indeed, Stigler admitted that some large firms charge lower prices than small firms can afford to do. Super-duper chain stores can generally underprice even the friendliest mom-and-pop grocer. But Stigler argued that large firms' lower prices are often a ploy to drive small firms out of business, after which there are no limits to a large firm's power to raise price.[3] Moreover, large firms' lower prices are generally not the result of their greater productive efficiency but of their power to force low prices from the small firms that supply their raw materials and parts. When firms grow so large as to achieve power over market prices and output, Stigler recommended government policies to break them up. Yes, break them up, the ultimate exercise of government power. Such massive government involvement in private businesses was contrary to all his no-government instincts; but, he probably said, "all in a good cause."

Although government policy to break up large firms might be associated with "left-leaning," "liberal" thinkers, Stigler regarded his conclusion as "conservative." It is conservative in the sense that it conserves the advantages of a free-market system, with the sorts of competitive pressure that forces firms to behave efficiently. It is conservative also in the sense that, once a competitive environment is restored, there is no further need for government involvement.

Stigler subsequently modified his opposition to large firms and his support for government policies to break them up. The growth of markets worldwide has rendered even giant firms small relative to global competition. (Even mighty Coca-Cola faces competition from imitators in markets around the world!) As markets grow, both geographically and in numbers of products, the power of large firms to set high prices fades. Government policies to limit business firm size are not as necessary today when competition from many suppliers and many different types of products weakens the power of the giants.

The U.S. Government Adopts Marginalism

The U.S. government now uses marginal analysis in a way you might never have expected and through its unorthodox method actually reduces the role of government in business affairs.

I am referring to recently developed policies for reducing environmental pollution. One way to reduce pollution is to pass a law prohibiting businesses from discharging pollutants into the air or water, then to monitor the businesses' performance and impose fines on businesses that fail to comply with the law. Revenue from fines can be used to repair the environmental damage. This is not a method that George Stigler would recommend, however, since such a "command-and-control method" looks to government to acquire information, hire enforcers, and generally intrude massively in business affairs. Command-and-control methods are not efficient either, since prohibiting all pollution requires cuts in some kinds of production that provide more benefits to consumers than the air and water saved by cutting production.

A better approach to this problem is to use marginalism to eliminate only the pollution that imposes more costs on the society than the benefits it makes possible. And this is what the U.S. government has been doing with respect to sulfur dioxide, SO_2.

SO_2 is released by certain electric power plants and combines with vapors in the lower atmosphere to produce smog and acid rain, both of which damage our lungs, buildings, forests and crops, and fish and other wildlife. A command-and-control solution to the SO_2 problem would require measurement of the benefits and costs of electricity produced by the offending plants and prohibition of production in excess of the amount that yields maximum net benefits. Even if this solution were possible, it would require an unacceptable level of government involvement in business decisions.

An alternative is to encourage power plants themselves to evaluate benefits and costs and identify the efficient level of output. The first step in this direction is to determine the maximum level of pollution the environment can tolerate. Say there are 10 power plants each emitting 10 tons of SO_2 during a particular period of time. Environmental scientists determine that a total of 50 tons can be safely absorbed by the environment, thus requiring that the plants reduce total emissions by half. Instead of requiring each plant to cut its emissions to 5 tons, government might issue each of the 10 plants licenses permitting emission of 5 tons. Now plants that can reduce SO_2 cheaply have an incentive to eliminate all their emissions and offer their licenses for sale. A plant whose costs for reducing SO_2 are higher can buy additional licenses and continue polluting. Ultimately,

50 tons of SO_2 will be emitted, meeting the goal established by environmental scientists.

This solution is efficient because the plants arrive at their emissions decisions by reasoning at the margin. The first reduction in emissions is the reduction that can be accomplished at lowest cost. That first reduction releases a license for sale to the plant whose first reduction would be quite costly. Likewise, the second reduction is the second lowest cost and releases a license to the plant with the second highest cost. And so forth until the lowest-cost plants have eliminated 50 tons of emissions, and the highest-cost polluters hold licenses permitting 50 tons. At this point, the market price of SO_2 licenses reflects the cost of eliminating the marginal ton of SO_2, which, interestingly, was approximately $100 in 1998.[4] Plants that can reduce emissions for less than $100 per ton do so and sell their licenses to plants that require more than $100. The $100 price was less than half the price that government policymakers expected, suggesting that the businesses found lower-cost methods of reducing pollution than was expected.

Polluting plants add the costs of acquiring licenses to their costs of production, and those costs are paid by consumers of electric power. Because consumers will agree to pay only as much for electricity as the value of benefits they enjoy from using it, we know we are producing only the quantity of electricity that maximizes net benefits.

A pollution-licensing program has another advantage in the encouragement it gives to technological advances in pollution control. A business that develops a cleaner method of producing electricity can sell all its licenses for a gain that offsets the cost of its technological advance. Moreover, a change in scientists' estimates of tolerable pollution can call for a change in the number of licenses issued, with consequent changes in total emissions, the price and production of electricity, and technological progress in pollution control. The government's licensing program for SO_2 has been judged so successful that plans are under way for more uses of such "market-oriented" methods of improving the environment.

Chapter 2

THE DANGERS OF BIG GOVERNMENT, FIRSTHAND

If George Stigler is the analytical mind of neoclassical theory, Friedrich von Hayek is its soul. The two economists have much in common, having attended conferences together on a Swiss mountaintop, where we might imagine them engaging in animated discussions regarding economic efficiency and social welfare. The Mont Pelerin Society founded by Hayek continues to meet 50 years later in Switzerland. Included in its membership have been other Nobel economists: Milton Friedman, James Buchanan, Maurice Allais, Ronald Coase, and Gary Becker, as well as Vaclav Klaus, Premier of the Czech Republic.

Hayek was awarded the Nobel Prize in 1974, along with Gunnar Myrdal, for their investigations into the interdependence of economic, social, and institutional phenomena.

To anyone who resists government involvement in free markets, Friedrich von Hayek is something close to a deity. Hayek understood well that a large, powerful government can become oppressive, having grown up in Austria before National Socialism propelled Germany and much of the world into World War II. Hayek's small book, *The Road to Serfdom*, appeared as World War II was drawing to a close and created a sensation that has not diminished much in the intervening years. The book attributed the rise of Naziism in Germany to the increasing involvement of Germany's government in that nation's economy.

From Liberalism to Totalitarianism

When Hayek was growing up, the dominant school of economic thought in Western Europe was economic liberalism, a term that had a different meaning then. Today, we think of a liberal as a person who welcomes government involvement in the economy, typically the sort of involvement that favors the interests of disadvantaged groups over the interests of the well-to-do. The liberalism that influenced Hayek's thinking was a carryover from the nineteenth century when liberalism had its original meaning, a meaning based on "liberty" or freedom. Instead of wanting help from government, nineteenth century liberals wanted freedom from governments that were generally oppressive. Indeed, nineteenth century liberalism was a reaction to the tendency of powerful governments to suppress individual liberties, to tax their workers oppressively, and to send workers' sons to war (wars that were intended to conquer other peoples whose liberties could be similarly suppressed).

Hayek's form of liberalism was strongly individualistic and laissez faire.[5] Like Stigler, Hayek favored only the minimum necessary government involvement in economic affairs and emphasized instead the importance of individual tastes and preferences for determining the goals of society. In a free society, he said, the rational, optimizing decisions of ordinary men and women promote economic efficiency— by shifting resources into the kinds of production that maximize welfare. Freedom to choose allows an economy to grow naturally, constrained only by the limits of available resources and evolving technological knowledge.

The problem with allowing the economy to grow naturally is that unplanned growth generally brings irregular and unequal improvements in living standards. Differences in living standards foment resentment and social conflict. Interest groups form and demand that the "impersonal and anonymous mechanism of the market," said Hayek, be replaced by the "collective and 'conscious' direction of all social forces to deliberately chosen goals."[6] Although disaffected interest groups might believe that collective decision making brings better living standards for everyone, Hayek warned that it sets the stage for totalitarianism.

Totalitarianism gives maximum power to government. It is "total" because it involves complete control of everyday life. Not just political and economic life, in the form of more laws and regulations, but also social and intellectual life, in the form of restraints on personal behavior, lifestyles, and even ways of thinking. This is what Friedrich von Hayek saw happening as Germany descended into Naziism.

Probably some of the public support for a powerful central government comes in response to advances in technology, especially the technologies that make possible mass production. On the one hand, mass production reduces unit costs and increases efficiency. On the other hand, it increases the power of large companies, which may require the kinds of restraints that can only be enforced by a powerful central government.

But hold on a minute here. If advanced technologies truly require government control, one might expect that the move in that direction would occur first in the world's most technologically advanced nations, and this is not what has actually happened. Instead of appearing in the most technologically advanced nations, tendencies toward greater government control have more frequently emerged in countries that are just beginning their technological development. For example, back in 1878 when Germany was just beginning to industrialize, the young German government put in place policies that increased its involvement in business—through trading cartels, corporate syndicates, and monopolies intended to speed the nation's industrialization. And, more ominously, to link the interests of businesses more firmly with those of government.

In today's newly industrializing economies, public support for strong government may be a reaction to the staggering complexity of modern technologies. Modern technologies require precise division of labor and intricate relationships among many buyers and sellers. Without government to plan production, say supporters of a strong central government, life in a rapidly changing, technologically advancing economy would dissolve into chaos. Hayek couldn't disagree more. What this notion fails to acknowledge, he says, is the fundamental purpose of free markets. In free markets all the intricate interrelationships that are necessary to make a modern economy function are handled by independent decision makers, each adjusting his behavior to facts that only he can know. No central planner can be as efficient as a system of freely competitive firms, each responding spontaneously to the changing requirements of modern technologies.

An even more serious disadvantage than the damage to economic efficiency, however, is the damage to individual liberty when a powerful central government sets a nation on a path to a single national goal. A nation with a single national goal ignores the "autonomous spheres in which the ends of the individuals are supreme"[7]—no mistaking Hayek's main concern here. None of us can fully understand and appreciate the goals of persons outside our own spheres, he declares. A decentralized government provides maximum possible freedom for ordinary men and women to set their own goals and pursue their individual preferences.

Interference With the Rule of Law

Perhaps the United States' revolutionary heritage has made us especially receptive to Hayek's warnings. Our Bill of Rights forbids constraints on certain fundamental rights, and even today we struggle to achieve a harmonious balance between individual choice and collective welfare—to identify the line between one man's fist and another's nose. We locate that and other invisible lines through laws decided through democratic processes.

Through democratically established laws, we set broad guidelines that govern behavior in frequently encountered situations, but leave us free within the guidelines to pursue our individual interests. A too powerful government cannot be bound by laws, however, because today's laws cannot predict all the conditions that might call for action tomorrow. Whereas citizens of a democracy are allowed to adapt their behavior to particular circumstances of time and place, such freedoms in a totalitarian society would disrupt progress toward national goals. Therefore, a totalitarian government must sweep aside mere laws and use its power arbitrarily to control people's behavior. For 70 years the people of Soviet-bloc nations experienced such arbitrary control by a government bent on serving a single national goal.

The Elusive Goals of Security and Fairness

Choosing individual decision making over a powerful central government is not always easy. Indeed, much of the support for a powerful central government comes from people who crave a more nurturing, more secure economic environment. For individual men and women, making economic choices can be painful, especially when resources are limited. Most of us would prefer not to make the painful choices nor to experience the resource limits. We tend to think that a powerful central government can relieve us of these onerous circumstances. We hope that centralized decision making can accomplish a more secure and more equitable distribution of the means to a good life. We tend to forget that the government's view of what is equitable may differ from our own. Ironically, citizens of East Germany, recently reunited with West Germany, are now expressing some of these same reservations about their move from strict government control to a free market economy.

True, free markets sometimes distribute income in ways that seem unjust or inequitable. But distribution by free markets is based on each individual's productive capacity (or, truth be told, luck) and not on some bureaucrat's opinion of who does or does not deserve a reward. The distributional inequities that flow from collective decisions are the result not of impersonal market forces but of deliberate policy decisions. In such circumstances, groups affected by distributional decisions attempt to influence government in their own behalf, regardless of the harm they inflict on other groups.

For meaningful freedom, a certain minimum standard of living and the opportunity to attain it are essential, and Hayek would not deny the need for some collective decisions to provide that basic minimum. But to guarantee individual incomes, government would have to guarantee against the sorts of declines in income that occur naturally in a market economy, irrespective of individual merit. When government controls the distribution of income, changes in income can no longer serve as signals to guide the allocation of resources. Then, resource allocation must be accomplished by direct order—including whatever penalties are necessary to ensure compliance. Hayek reminds his readers that "while the last resort of a competitive economy is the bailiff, the ultimate sanction of a planned economy is the hangman."[8]

Ideology and Leadership

To ensure popular support for its goals, a powerful central government must create a common ideology, or "world view." The German word for world view is *weltanschauung,* a word that seems at the same time both lofty and oppressive. Support for a government's world view requires not unbiased information, says Hayek, but rather indoctrination: that is, the active promotion of a state-sanctioned ideology, Naziism or Communism coming most readily to mind.

Indeed, subjects of a totalitarian state must adhere to a common state-sanctioned ideology, spontaneously supporting authorized beliefs even when truth must be sacrificed in consequence. A totalitarian government subordinates independent thought to the continuous creation of myths, most ironically the myth that by adhering to the official ideology one enjoys true freedom. (Recall the motto "Freedom Through Work" marking the entrance to forced-labor camps in World War II.)

The worst members of society rise to the top in a totalitarian state. The reason is that totalitarianism is most likely to emerge in a society whose people seek objectives that are impossible to satisfy immediately through free markets. Unless the leader is immediately successful, public pressures intensify. If he (occasionally, but rarely, she) is to avoid the loss of his position (occasionally his life), the leader must impose harsher and harsher penalties for nonperformance and dissent. Generally, he identifies a scapegoat to deflect the anger of dissatisfied members of the society. Civic violence and oppression increase, since "[t]o act on behalf of a group seems to free people of many of the moral restraints which control their behavior as individuals within the group."[9] Violence and oppression increase also against citizens of other societies. Hayek's ominous conclusion: the concepts of "humanity and therefore of any form of internationalism are entirely products of the individualistic view of man, and there can be no place for them in a [centrally controlled] system of thought."[10]

Chapter 3
EXPLAINING OUR SOCIAL RELATIONSHIPS

If Stigler and Hayek are correct—if free markets maximize society's net benefits and if powerful governments move inexorably toward totalitarianism—why would a nation allow any sort of government involvement in economic affairs? Are there any net benefits from making decisions collectively? Why would rational individuals ever choose to sacrifice individual interests for the sake of society as a whole?

Gary Becker is hardly an advocate of big government, but he does suggest some benefits to society of making some economic decisions collectively.

Becker was introduced to economics by reading the stock market reports and financial news to his father, who suffered from failing eyesight. At first he found the task rather boring, but eventually he applied his growing understanding of such matters in lively discussions about politics and justice. As a freshman at Princeton he accidentally enrolled in a course in economics and found in economics the means to combine his natural aptitude for mathematics with his desire to do something useful for society. He received the Nobel Prize in 1992 for his applications of economic theory to all sorts of human behavior, even sorts of behavior not typically regarded as economic.

Central to all behavior, says Becker, is our tendency to make decisions at the margin. Apparently, marginalism is inborn, extending back in time to explain the evolution of all human institutions. In other words, just as we optimize when we make our buying and selling decisions, we also optimize when we decide strictly social issues: how we marry and establish our families, how much crime we suffer, and—now the clincher!—how our optimizing decisions affect the evolution of the human species.

Even Altruism

And here we find one of Becker's most interesting applications of economic theory: to investigate a puzzle that has often challenged sociobiologists.[11] The puzzle relates to the biological process of natural selection, through which plant and animal species have evolved to their present state. According to the theory of evolution, if a species is to evolve to higher life forms, only the fittest members of the species can be permitted to survive and pass along their superior genes. To achieve the maximum survival of superior genes, members of a species must be selfish, pursuing their own self-interest even if their selfishness threatens other, less-fit members of the species. (A cynical reader can already spot the economics here.) In a word, if a species is to survive and evolve, its members must be "egoists." For egoists, to protect the bearers of the species' strongest genes is infinitely more rational than to nurture its weaker members.

(Scientists remind us, hurtfully, that our lives are not intended by nature to be satisfying but to be a means for transmitting genetic information. Or paraphrasing Samuel Butler, a hen is an egg's way of producing another egg. So much for all our philosophers' lofty cogitations about the meaning of life.)

In spite of our evolutionary compulsion toward selfishness, sociobiologists have found a puzzling tendency for individual members of a species to practice altruism toward other members of their species. Altruism is the opposite of egoism and means unselfish concern for others, even (or especially) the less fit: the young and disabled, victims of human and natural disasters, the unemployed and the homeless. The puzzle facing sociobiologists is that widespread altruism has not retarded the process of evolution but may instead have promoted it, ultimately raising the quality of life forms.

Before Becker, sociobiologists had observed one exception to egoism, which they called *kin selection*. As its name implies, kin selection promotes the fitness of a particular family. Fitness is defined in terms of numbers of surviving offspring, larger numbers being essential for passing on larger quantities of the family's genes. Altruism among family members increases the survival rate of that family's genes and promotes the dominance of its qualities in future generations. But Becker goes beyond the single family to suggest that rational members of one family have a reason for altruistic behavior toward members of other families as well.

He begins with the usual assumption that rational men and women increase their personal welfare by consuming certain products, those that satisfy their personal tastes and preferences. For an egoist, gains in welfare come from consuming the products purchased with his own income plus consumption made possible through fortuitous transfers of income from a fortuitously placed altruist. Altruists differ from egoists, gaining personal welfare both from their own consumption and from the consumption enjoyed by those who have received their altruism.

We might name our egoist Alfonse (Me-First) and our altruist Gaston (You-First). Both Alfonse and Gaston attempt to maximize their personal welfare, through increased consumption made possible by their own incomes and from transfers. Unlimited transfers are not possible, however, being constrained by Gaston's income. Thus, Gaston must decide how much of his income to spend for his own consumption and how much to transfer to Alfonse. With each transfer of income toward Alfonse, Gaston experiences a gain in personal welfare from Alphonse's increased consumption and a loss from his own diminished consumption. At first Gaston's marginal gains exceed his marginal losses, for net gains in his total welfare. Continuing to transfer income to Alfonse, however, diminishes the gain Gaston enjoys from the transfer, until finally the gain from providing more consumption to Alfonse falls below the pain he suffers from the reduction in his own.

Of course, a rational (optimizing) altruist would not let that happen. A rational altruist would transfer income only so long as the gain in personal welfare from altruistic transfers is greater than the resulting cost. Ergo, when the addition to Gaston's personal welfare from altruism is just equal to the additional cost, he has achieved maximum personal welfare.

Now let us move beyond our friends Alfonse and Gaston to see how optimizing egoists and altruists affect the welfare of society. We begin by defining society's total welfare as the sum of the individual welfare enjoyed by all its members, altruists and egoists alike. Maximum social welfare occurs where the optimum amount of income has been transferred from altruists to egoists, reducing altruists' consumption and increasing egoists' consumption until society as a whole enjoys maximum welfare from its total consumption.

Transfers from altruists to egoists are efficient not just because they yield gains in welfare but also because gains in welfare promote incentives to continue transfers. Here Becker envisions what might be called a virtuous cycle, a cycle in which good things lead to more good things. Altruists' vicarious satisfaction from transfers prompts them to continue transferring income to egoists. But at the same time egoists' enjoyment of transfers prompts them to behave in such a way as to increase the altruists' income (thus, indirectly both their own and altruists' welfare). We might suppose, for example, that low-income workers would oppose high taxes on high-income workers because they want members of the latter group to spend lavishly and secure the jobs of the former.

And this is the core of Becker's model: the suggestion that through their expectations of altruism, all members of a society are driven to behave so as to increase the income and welfare of others.

Species Survival

Finally, how does Becker's theory of altruism relate to biological evolution, survival of the fittest, and the puzzle facing sociobiologists? We've used Becker's model to describe the net benefits to society that come from shifting access to income. To convert Becker's basic model to a genetic fitness model, it is only necessary to describe the benefits to the human species that come from shifting access to fitness. We define genetic fitness as reproductive rates. The greater a species' reproductive rate, the more of its characteristics are preserved and the more viable—or more fit—the species becomes.

Again, altruists increase species fitness by performing acts that increase the fitness of other members of the species by more than what the altruists give up in their own fitness. Then, acts of altruism encourage egoists to respond in such ways as to increase altruists' fitness as well.

Thus, according to Becker, the tendency toward altruism among evolving species is not a puzzle at all. Altruism is not contrary to the principles of natural selection, but altruism promotes the evolution of species to superior life forms. In fact, to behave like altruists is consistent with the individual self-interest of all of society's Alphonses and Gastons.

Do you believe all this? Do you believe that altruistic behavior is natural or even likely in the real world? Probably not. Possibly in very small societies groups of altruists and egoists might agree only to take actions that increase the welfare of society as a whole. But worldwide increases in population have made it increasingly difficult to identify and understand the consequences for others of one's own altruistic behavior. Moreover, in the real world, interest groups have formed to advance the interests of egoists, occasionally to the detriment of the general welfare. Interest-group pressures and the high costs of acquiring information reduce opportunities for altruism that might increase society's total welfare but, instead, strengthen egoistic tendencies.

If spontaneous altruism is no longer practical, Becker suggests that government might use its power to create a kind of artificial altruism—through taxes and subsidies that redistribute income to achieve the greatest gains in genetic fitness.

Rationalism in Marriage

Few couples in love consciously consider the economics of marriage, but Gary Becker does—in much the same way that Stigler applies economic analysis to more mundane choices. Becker sees marriage as another free decision that promotes social welfare while requiring minimum government involvement.

Since the origin of humankind, for at least 50,000 years, marriage and the family have been the most fundamental institutions of human society. Marriage and family patterns are essential ingredients for economic growth and development, for population growth, income, saving and investment, especially investment in society's most valuable resources, its children. All these factors make marriage an appropriate focus for art, music, literature, and—not surprisingly—economic analysis.

Consider this: A married couple shares enjoyment of commodities produced in the market and commodities produced in the home, including meals eaten at home, children, shared recreation, improved physical and mental health, love, and companionship. Producing household commodities requires some use of market goods and some allocation of time by both parties to the marriage. Any allocation of a household's limited available time to production in the market or at home has its costs, defined as the sacrifice of production that would have occurred in the next-best allocation.

For an unmarried man or woman, deciding between time spent working in the market and time spent working at home is a straightforward choice. As in any other optimizing decision, the optimal allocation of time is determined at the margin, by shifting time to one or the other activity until the gain from a further shift is just equal to the cost. When a man and woman marry, the optimizing decision is somewhat different, since the partners might have different qualifications for market production and household production. One partner might be so much more productive in one type of production or the other as to promote specialization. The reason generally given for differences in productive capacity is the wife's biological suitability for rearing children and the husband's capacity for corporate or professional production, distinctions that have raised the ire of feminists and are no longer universally accepted.

Whatever the differences between the spouses, an efficient marriage yields greater shared satisfaction than the satisfactions enjoyed by its erstwhile unmarried parties.

Until now, we have paid little attention to love or "caring," although Becker does not disregard this essential product of marriage. In fact, Becker recognizes that love can cause marital satisfaction to exceed the satisfaction associated with the other more measurable commodities produced by the marriage. With love or caring, the marriage partners gain personal satisfaction from consumption enjoyed by the other partner (altruism again?), making possible a more equal distribution of commodities and reducing the need for policing the distribution. Marriages with caring may be efficient even when their material output is low, if the commodities consumed together provide greater satisfaction than the larger quantities of commodities that might be consumed separately or in noncaring marriages. (The partners spend more time enjoying the sunset together than working late at the office.)

Applying Rationalism to Crime

You might have wondered about the omission of moral values in Becker's analysis thus far, an omission that exemplifies the best (worst?) characteristic of economics. Some of us say "best" because Becker's efficient results do not depend on peoples' good intentions. The "best" believers are comforted by the prospect of good results from the acts of occasionally not-so-good people. Some people say "worst" because they believe their own moral values are so critical as to be required of all members of society, a result that Friedrich von Hayek would characterize as "worst of all."

Becker regards crime, like other types of social behavior, as a particular individual's rational responses to expected benefits and costs. Like all optimizers, criminals must decide if committing a crime is worth the risk of capture and punishment, a calculation not infrequently pondered by otherwise law-abiding men and women.[12] Who among us has never considered whether we might risk parking illegally when late for an appointment? Our ultimate decision is generally based on the likelihood we will be apprehended and the severity of the likely punishment.

Becker's emphasis is not so much on the optimizing decisions of criminals as on those of society, which must decide how much crime it wants to prevent. Your local parking authority, for example, must decide how much illegal parking to prevent. And that decision dictates further decisions regarding how much of society's scarce resources to devote to the apprehension and punishment of illegal parkers.

Essentially, the question for society's crime preventers is "What is the economically efficient level of crime?" Given that society will suffer some crime, what is the appropriate trade-off between the benefits from reducing crime and the costs of criminal deterrence?

Consider the usual factors. The benefits from reducing crime are the damages society avoids. The costs are the resources that must be shifted out of other types of production and into maintaining a criminal justice system—monitoring parking spaces, verifying violations, and following through with appropriate penalties. The optimal level of crime is that at which the cost of one more unit of deterrence is greater than the additional benefits in damages avoided. By comparing the marginal costs of deterrence with the marginal benefits, society achieves the efficient level of crime. Not zero crime, mind you, but an efficient level of crime. It is efficient because we deter crimes whose costs exceed the cost of deterrence, and because further acts of deterrence cost more than the damages avoided.

To guarantee efficient deterrence, a society must constantly reevaluate the marginal benefits and costs of deterrence and shift resources accordingly. Improvements in techniques for investigating crimes and convicting and punishing criminals might be expected to reduce the costs of deterrence and increase the efficient level. Case in point, the science of DNA and fingerprint identification is likely to yield more deterrence at lower costs, thus increasing the efficient level of deterrence.

Criminologists use an economic concept to describe how criminals respond to deterrence: *elasticity,* which means responsiveness. The concept is typically used in consumer markets, where it refers to the responsiveness of consumer purchases to differences in price. When used to describe criminal behavior, elasticity means the responsiveness of criminals to differences in the probability of arrest and conviction, on the one hand, and in the severity of punishment, on the other. Criminologists have found that criminals' elasticity of response is greater with respect to the former than the latter, suggesting that policies that increase the probability of arrest and conviction are more efficient deterrents than policies that inflict more severe punishments. (Supporters of mandatory sentencing laws take note.)

Becker suggests that society might achieve even more efficient deterrence by dividing the "market" for crime into submarkets according to different criminal's responsiveness to punishment. The objective is similar to that of business firms, when they divide consumer markets into submarkets according to different consumer's responsiveness to price. In markets with low consumer price elasticity, supplying firms set relatively high prices, expecting that consumers will continue to buy roughly the same quantities in spite of the higher price. For consumers of prescription drugs, for instance, price elasticity is relatively low, and suppliers can set relatively high prices without significantly reducing sales. Firms set lower prices where consumers would respond by buying significantly larger quantities (which explains why bars schedule happy hours). In consumer markets, setting different prices is called price discrimination, and it allows sellers to maximize their revenue from sales.

Similarly, dividing Becker's "market" for criminal offenses would allow law enforcement agencies to discriminate among criminals according to their responsiveness to punishment. Designing such a system would require grouping criminals according to age, mental competence, and criminal premeditation and estimating the responsiveness of each group to different sorts of punishments. Then the most severe punishments could be meted out only to groups with the least responsiveness to punishment. (It takes a heavy dose of punishment to get their attention.) By treating criminals that respond to punishment differently from criminals that do not, society might gain greater deterrence at lower cost.

Chapter 4

QUESTIONING NEOCLASSICAL THEORY

Economics abounds with skeptics. If you are skeptical about the neoclassicists' perfect Greek temple—that ordinary people always behave as rational optimizers—you should be comforted to learn that you are not alone.

Even laboratory sciences have their skeptics, of course. But laboratory sciences have—well—laboratories in which experiments are conducted under precisely controlled conditions. In such circumstances, it is much more difficult to question the scientist's conclusions. Moreover, conclusions reached in laboratories must be "refereed" before they are generally accepted, so that misrepresenting the results of experiments is well nigh impossible.[13] In a social science, on the other hand, controlled laboratory experiments are impractical—raising the possibility that investigations in the social sciences might be biased by the prejudices of the examiner, that they merely reflect the examiner's prior interests or beliefs.

Given these limitations, it is understandable that even the most minor pronouncement regarding the social sciences brings skeptics out of the woodwork. Herbert A. Simon is a skeptic. Remembering Simon's association with the University of Chicago, one is not surprised. The assumptions of the neoclassical economists may be well and good for constructing an abstract theory of behavior, says Simon.

But when it comes to the real world, in the words of a once popular song, "It ain't necessarily so."

Herbert Simon received the Nobel Prize in 1978 for his research into how real people make real decisions. Simon has been described as the economist "closest to Aristotle or a Renaissance Man"[14] in that his interests and capabilities range far beyond economics, to psychology, computer science, and public administration. He plays the piano and is an avid painter, often taking a sketch pad along with him on his travels. While a researcher at the RAND Corporation, he was frequently accused of monopolizing the computer to play chess.

In Simon's view of the world real people don't always behave rationally. Perfect rationality isn't possible in the real world, he says, which is much too complicated for people fully to understand or to make the calculations called for in neoclassical theory. Without full information, people cannot precisely compare the marginal benefits and marginal costs of all the alternatives facing them and cannot truly maximize net benefits. Even if people had all the requisite information for making rational decisions, Simon says, they would still face a fundamental scarcity: the scarcity of attention. The human brain simply cannot process every bit of information for choosing the optimal behavior. We cannot always choose the absolutely best health plan, the most dependable used car, the restaurant that most impresses a prospective client. To make the optimal choice would consume time and attention we could better spend elsewhere. Instead of always seeking the optimal, we get the best information we can for making the most practical choice, and then we stick with it.

And now we come to the most significant implication of Simon's work for the structure of human society. If the complexities of life make it impossible for ordinary men and women to make optimal choices, if no single individual has sufficient attention to consider all the positives and negatives of every decision, if an economic system cannot depend for efficiency on individuals' pursuit of self-interest—then how do we explain the real progress of human society? How do we explain our societies' evolution toward more productive, more knowledgeable, and generally more harmonious states?

Simon finds his answer in the very scarcity of information among independent men and women and the opportunities for enhanced information we enjoy when we join in groups.

Bounded Rationality and the Formation of Teams

Just as Adam Smith's name is associated with the "invisible hand," Herbert Simon's is associated with "bounded rationality." *Bounded rationality* describes the limits on information that make individual human beings disturbingly fallible. If rationality were unbounded, if people had all the information necessary for making decisions and the necessary attention to organize and interpret it, neoclassical optimization theory might explain how people really behave. Following neoclassical theory, decisions to promote individual self-interest would truly maximize social welfare. In a world of bounded rationality, however, we cannot assume, one, that individuals always behave in ways that promote their self-interest and, two, that the consequences for the larger society are beneficial. With bounded rationality we must accept the possibility that individuals acting on their own frequently make mistakes.

At some point in our evolutionary past primitive men and women recognized the limitations on their individual ability to make efficient choices, and they formed "teams" to share information and coordinate behavior toward more nearly optimal results. It's easy to imagine primitive hunters consorting together about the best ways to capture game, and gatherers about the best places to find fresh berries. To Simon, the interchange of information within such teams is an essential remedy for the scarcity of individual information.

Decision making by teams links individual rationality with social evolution. It creates the environment for altruism, a concept we have already encountered while studying the contributions of Gary Becker to economic thought. But Simon goes still further than Becker to put flesh on the concept of altruism, including its implications for genetic fitness and human evolution.[15] First Simon recognizes that altruism flourishes best in very special circumstances, generally involving kinship. He explains altruism toward persons not our own kin in terms of bounded rationality. With our bounded rationality, we need information from others if we are to survive as a species. In fact, rather than self-interest, our evolutionary survival depends on what Simon calls *docility*. Docility is one person's willingness to be influenced in his or her decisions by information provided by another. Since individual members of society are unable to make efficient decisions in isolation from other members, they accept informed suggestions from others. They are docile. And their docility leads to more efficient decisions and improved genetic fitness.

Bounded rationality and the formation of teams promotes acts of altruism. To the extent that altruistic acts increase the average fitness of society, says Simon, society will exert pressure on docile individuals to perform them. Docile individuals will comply, even if such decisions occasionally run counter to their personal self-interest. Throughout history, he concludes, as societies have grown more and more complex, people have required more and more information from other people. The effect has been to increase their docility and to increase their willingness to behave altruistically.

Altruism and Democracy

Our bounded rationality drives us to create teams, organizations, and institutions. We group ourselves into organizations within which we benefit from shared information. We are docile. In return for the benefits of shared information, we agree to suppress our self-interested inclinations; we willingly accept some reductions in our personal fitness for the sake of society's total fitness. We are altruistic. As conditions change and new information filters into our group, we adjust our behaviors to accommodate the new information. We learn from experience. Through the institutions we create, we achieve a certain balance between rational self-interest and social welfare, between chaos and order.

The verdict: Rational pursuit of self-interest is a useful concept for explaining human motivation but only if self-interest is interpreted broadly—beyond concern for material wealth but including all those qualities that satisfy individual preferences. Ironically, satisfying our selfish interests sometimes requires apparently selfless behavior—we give up our seat on a crowded bus, or we yield a concession in a legal contract. We do these things because we believe such behavior will be reciprocated, and it is that shared belief that holds society together. It's rather astonishing, therefore, that selfishness, a concept that seems so counter to social harmony, can actually be the basis for social cooperation.

PART 2
LIMITS TO RATIONALITY AND THE ROLE OF GOVERNMENT

Kenneth Arrow • *John Hicks* •
James Buchanan • *Ronald Coase* •
Amartya Sen

S uppose we accept the fact that human beings are selfish. And indeed, the neoclassical economists we discussed in Part 1 accept selfishness as the basis for a coherent system explaining human behavior. If selfish people act in ways calculated to maximize their personal welfare, they say, the result for society is efficiency in the use of its scarce resources.

Some neoclassical economists leaped from the conclusion that free markets maximize the personal welfare of individual buyers and sellers to the more extravagant conclusion that free markets also maximize the welfare of society as a whole. In this view, free markets driven by human beings' innate selfishness achieve maximum possible welfare for society, given available resource supplies and technology.

The economists you are about to meet question those optimistic conclusions. The economists in Part 2 explore the "adding-up question": the question whether combining individual preferences into collective decisions truly maximizes social welfare. And more fundamentally: the question whether achieving economic efficiency is also equitable—or fair—whether satisfying individuals' economic wants is consistent with satisfying society's moral values. To answer such questions requires exploration of the difficult issue of income distribution—to judge societies' systems for sharing income and the consequences both for economic efficiency and for social equity.

Chapter 5

INDIVIDUAL RATIONALITY
AND COLLECTIVE
IRRATIONALITY

I t isn't often that a doctoral student's dissertation sweeps through a profession and essentially transforms its thinking. The student whose dissertation transformed economists' thinking about social welfare is Kenneth Arrow. He and Sir John Hicks were awarded the Nobel Prize in 1972 for their explorations of the complex relationships among different phenomena in an economy and the implications of those relationships for economic outcomes.

Born to immigrants to the United States, Arrow grew up in a home that was generally poor in material wealth but rich in access to books. He read voraciously and developed a strong desire to organize information. During World War II he worked as a weather forecaster for the U.S. military forces, organizing statistical information about weather systems much as he would later organize statistical information about economics. In both cases, he tends to be skeptical about the predictive value of his statistics. He recalls an incident during the war when his fellow weather statisticians arrived at the judgment that their forecasts were no better than chance for predicting the weather. When they reported this judgment to their supervisors and suggested that the forecasting function be discontinued, they received this startling reply: "The Commanding General is well aware that the fore-

casts are no good. However, he needs them for planning purposes."
(And you thought Dilbert was a recent invention!)

Interestingly, Arrow extends his interest in organizing information to his preferences in art and music. In both pursuits, he looks to identify the patterns that form informational groups, whether of the artist's colors or the musician's chords. Especially with respect to art, Arrow says he prefers modern art to art that has expressive content because of the former's abstract patterns: the precise rectangles of a Mondrian rather than the plump figures of a Renoir. Arrow's contributions to economic thought reflect a similar ability to group information in patterns that permit meaningful assessments of human behavior.

Defining the Problem

Arrow saw a problem with the neoclassicists' optimistic conclusion that maximum personal welfare for individual members of society necessarily means maximum welfare for society as a whole. To understand the problem, it helps to distinguish between products received and benefits enjoyed: quantities of goods, housing, and health care, on the one hand, and, on the other, the personal satisfaction people enjoy from consuming such quantities. Measuring the first is simple; measuring the second may be impossible.

To guarantee that the existing distribution of products yields maximum welfare for society, society would have to be able to define and measure the satisfaction different people enjoy from their respective shares. Unfortunately, while a single individual may be able to estimate the net benefits she or he enjoys from a product, the thought processes that sort out one person's satisfaction cannot be extended to the satisfaction experienced by another. One person's crème brûlée may be another's egg custard. It is not possible simply to "add up" the welfare different individuals enjoy from their consumption and compute the welfare enjoyed by society as a whole. That would require verifiable quantities to add—definable, measurable, comparable quantities—and "welfare" just doesn't come in such quantities.

There is one characteristic of welfare that does seem to be common among all individuals. It is that gains in personal satisfaction tend to diminish as we acquire larger quantities of a particular product: the second unit (the time-honored example is slices of pizza) providing less satisfaction than the first, the third providing still less, and so forth. This characteristic was first identified by Daniel Bernoulli in the eighteenth century and is stated as the *principle of diminishing marginal utility*. Bernoulli observed that gamblers place a lower value on a potential gain from a coin toss than on an equal loss. In experiments even today, gamblers are generally unwilling to pay as much as $100 for a fifty-fifty chance to win $200, which suggests they enjoy more satisfaction from the $100 they already have than from a second $100 they might gain. From these sorts of observations, Bernoulli asserted the general principle that the personal satisfaction people associate with additional units of anything diminishes as larger quantities are acquired.

People differ in the satisfaction they enjoy from their possessions—which may be a really good thing. It's a good thing because our different preferences for possessions makes it possible for our society to enjoy maximum total welfare at the same time that our incomes are quite different. Consider the opposite possibility. If all members of society enjoy precisely the same satisfaction from every product they own and all experience the same (diminishing) satisfaction from further acquisitions, the only income distribution that maximizes society's welfare is perfect equality. With anything less than perfect equality, a society could increase its total welfare by transferring possessions from the well-to-do to the less well-to-do. The reason is Bernoulli's principle of diminishing marginal utility, which tells us that a unit of housing taken from a lavishly housed person reduces society's total welfare by less than a unit of housing transferred to a poorly housed member of society increases it.

For an unequal distribution of income to deliver maximum social welfare, it must be true that people enjoy different levels of satisfaction from the things they own, that a lavishly housed person's third unit of housing actually provides as much satisfaction as a poorly housed person's second unit. (The poorly housed person might not value housing as much as, say, the opportunity to attend concerts and sporting events.) If we enjoy different levels of satisfaction from the things we own, our society's income distribution can be unequal and still provide maximum social welfare.

How unequal? you ask. For an unequal distribution to yield maximum social welfare requires only that the satisfaction the fortunate few gain from their larger incomes is greater than the satisfaction lost by the unfortunate many. One person's ride in a limousine must provide more satisfaction than is lost when, say, fifty people have to travel by bus. Without a way to measure and verify personal satisfaction, the only way to ensure that an unequal distribution of income actually yields maximum social welfare is if everyone is happy with it. Only if an unequal distribution of income has unanimous support—from both the gainers and the losers—can we be absolutely certain that it balances the goal of economic efficiency with the goal of equity.

Considering Our Collective Values

The level of income inequality the society prefers is decided by the political process, and this is where Arrow's doctoral dissertation is so significant.

Arrow divides our decision making into two categories. In our private decisions, he says, we act as buyers and sellers, expressing our economic choices in markets. The preferences we express in markets are "tastes" and include our individual preferences for such products as wine or beer, books or music, mountain or beach vacations. Through our participation in markets, we "vote" for certain products because they maximize our personal welfare, however we subjectively define personal welfare. In our public decisions, Arrow continues, we act as citizens, expressing our social choices through the political process. The preferences we express through the political process are our "values." Through the political process, we vote for programs that, directly and indirectly, establish rules and procedures for distributing society's income.

Making Decisions Through the Political Process

So far, Arrow's thinking about social welfare is not inconsistent with the neoclassical economists' expectations regarding rational consumer choice. Where Arrow's dissertation departs from neoclassical theory is in its startling revelation that decisions made collectively (through the political process) may not be rational at all.

The reason is what Arrow called the *paradox of voting*.[1] The paradox makes it difficult for voters to arrive collectively at rational decisions, decisions that truly express our values. The paradox of voting was discovered by the eighteenth-century philosopher the Marquis de Condorcet and was explored further by a nineteenth-century mathematician Charles Dodgson, better known as Lewis Carroll, the author of *Alice in Wonderland*.

To understand the paradox of voting, suppose a nation must choose among three types of economic systems. Name the three types A, B, and C, and, to make the exercise more relevant, let A include economic institutions that ensure equality of income distribution, B, institutions that permit inequality in favor of manufacturing workers, and C, inequality in favor of knowledge workers. A society that prefers A to B and B to C, must for consistency prefer A to C. Decisions are rational in such a society if voters consistently choose institutions that promote A and reject C.

Arrow's doctoral dissertation showed how, with these choice options, majority voting may not accomplish consistent ordering of social preferences. Consider a population of three voters whose preference rankings are ordered as follows:

Voter 1 $A B C$

Voter 2 $B C A$

Voter 3 $C A B$

Notice that a majority of voters prefers A to B (voters 1 and 3), and a majority also prefers B to C (voters 1 and 2). Therefore, consistency in preferences between A and C would seem to dictate choice of A. However, if you look at the preferences again, you will note that a majority also prefers C to A (voters 2 and 3), making C the rational choice. Which choice is correct? In fact, according to Arrow, with as many as three options to choose among, it is impossible to guarantee a consistent social preference. In his words: "If consumers' values can be represented by a wide range of individual orderings, the doctrine of voters' sovereignty is incompatible with that of collective rationality."[2]

If we could measure the intensity of voters' preferences for A, B, and C, we could assign weights to their votes and correct the inconsistency in the results. Weights measuring the intensity of voters' preferences would reveal the one choice that satisfies the strongest preferences. In product markets we do weight the intensity of preferences—by our willingness to pay higher prices for more intensely preferred products. Prices are an objective measure that translates the intensity of buyers' subjective preferences into values that can be added and compared. We have no such measure for weighting voters' preferences, however, making it impossible to measure intensity of preferences.

This result is what Arrow called *the impossibility theorem* and is what gave his doctoral dissertation such significance. According to the impossibility theorem, whenever voters are presented with more than two alternatives, it is impossible to achieve consistent election results.

In fact, according to Arrow, there are only two ways to avoid the voting paradox: one, to appoint a dictator, whose preferences dominate the preferences of ordinary voters, or, two, to limit society's choices to two alternatives. Assuming that the former is unacceptable, the latter could be accomplished by pairing up choices and conducting two separate votes. In the first round voters would be asked to choose between two of the alternatives, and in the second, between the third alternative and the winner of the first round. Unfortunately, the final winner of such pairwise voting depends on the order in which the alternatives are considered, such that a particular interest group that controls the voting agenda could decide the outcome—whether or not that outcome reflects voters' true preferences.

Strategic Behavior Complicates the Political Process

There is another reason why pairwise voting yields inconsistent results: the tendency toward what economists call *strategic behavior.*

Not to be too blunt about it, strategic behavior means misrepresentation of one's preferences. For example, a first round of voting between only A and C in the example above would be won by C. But if voter 2 strongly prefers B over C, that voter might vote for A just to ensure that C does not make it into the second round. The resulting victory for A would satisfy the clear preferences of only one voter.

Probably the most obvious examples of strategic behavior occur in votes on new government programs. Voters who want a certain program and expect to gain from it may, nevertheless, vote against it, believing that revealing their preference for the program will obligate them to pay taxes to finance it. By misrepresenting their preferences, voters can defeat programs that increase society's welfare, while at the same time selecting other programs that diminish social welfare. This is the frequent result of another kind of strategic behavior, *coalition building*. As an extreme example of coalitions, consider a vote between two programs: one that divides income equally among three voters and another that divides income between two voters, with the third voter excluded from any income at all. Under these conditions, any two voters could form a majority coalition to select the second program, even though their choice may reduce both economic efficiency and society's sense of distributional equity.

Making Public Investments and Compensating Losers

Perhaps the most critical decisions voters make are those that decide public investments, investments that produce goods and services for the community as a whole and are financed by general tax revenues. Through tax-financed public investments, we reduce the quantities of goods and services to be purchased by private buyers and increase the quantities of goods and services to be enjoyed collectively. More public highways, for example, and fewer private autos to drive on them.

A public investment is efficient if at least one member of society is made better off and all others are at least made no worse off. With no one objecting, the public investment is also equitable, or fair. It is difficult to imagine a public investment that meets these conditions, since some of us are likely to suffer costs in even the best of circumstances.

To illustrate the difficulty, begin with production of a certain combination of products regarded as economically efficient, with consumers' marginal benefits equal to marginal costs in all private markets. Then consider a proposal to make a large social investment: a sports arena, medical research program, or stealth bomber, any one of which would use resources otherwise available for producing goods and services for private use. While providing benefits to some members of society, the proposed investment would impose costs on others. Whether the investment is efficient or not depends on its net benefits: the difference between the welfare gained by those who enjoy the benefits of the sports arena and the loss in welfare suffered by those who pay the taxes to finance it. A public investment is said to be efficient if it increases some individuals' personal welfare by enough to compensate fully any member of the society who suffers the added costs. In practical terms, if the sports arena adds enough to total production (either directly or indirectly) to raise the community's average living standards (or to permit a reduction in its tax rates), it is an efficient investment.

If a public investment encourages significantly greater private production, there may indeed be enough new goods and services to compensate all the cost-payers. And in fact, visitors to a sports arena typically pay a price for the privilege, which creates income for the facility's builders and operators, who then use their incomes to purchase homes, autos, clothing, and Florida vacations. The result is to encourage a burst of additional buying and selling that increases production of goods and services available for private distribution.

Modern Economies Must Deal With Spillover Effects

We rely on the political process to decide another broad category of resource allocation: situations where the welfare of one individual is affected by the optimizing choice of another—where, for example, a home owner receives positive benefits from a neighbor's purchase of a magnificent maple tree and negative benefits from his purchase of a noisy leaf blower. We call both kinds of effects externalities. *Externalities* are the (positive or negative) spillover effects we experience from an economic decision made by someone else. We experience the externalities without paying a price for the benefit or receiving compensation for the cost.

Without a price tag on externalities, it is difficult to consider their value and, therefore, their effect on society's total welfare. Indeed, this is how they are defined. When individual consumers choose lawn accessories, hobbies, and lifestyles solely on the basis of their own satisfaction, they ignore the benefits and costs their purchases impose on others. Their jet ski maximizes their personal satisfaction, which is their sole concern when deciding to buy.

The existence of externalities also complicates producers' decisions about the efficient quantities of products to produce. In free markets, business firms produce the quantities that maximize their net revenue: the difference between revenue received and costs paid. If markets perfectly reflect consumers' benefits and producers' costs, a firm's net revenue perfectly reflects its contribution to social welfare—the excess of benefits provided consumers over costs paid by producers. But where there are externalities, net revenue may not correctly measure a firm's contribution to social welfare. If a firm creates positive externalities that are not reflected in its sales revenue, for example, the firm's actual contribution to social welfare may exceed its measured contribution. The efforts it makes to improve worker skills or to clean up environmental pollution may not be counted at all. On the other hand, if the firm creates negative externalities that are not reflected in costs paid, the firm's actual contribution to social welfare may fall short of its measured contribution. Its noise, congestion, and general nuisance quotient don't show up when measuring its value to society. In fact, unless a firm's net revenue from production correctly reflects all its positive and negative contributions to social welfare, the firm receives incorrect incentives for making its production decisions. As a result, its positive contributions to social welfare will tend to be lower and its negative contributions higher than is economically efficient.

Markets have trouble measuring externalities. Ensuring maximum social welfare may require specialized institutions to monitor the positive and negative spillovers created in private markets. We already have some institutions that do this: in particular, zoning codes and protective covenants that define what we can do with our property, government agencies that limit air and water pollution, tax credits that reward energy conservation, a legal system that imposes liability on firms that supply unsafe products, and professional codes that proscribe unethical conduct. The constraints imposed by such institutions limit the free pursuit of individual self-interest and constitute another assault on the perfect system envisaged by the neo-classical economists.

Following Kenneth Arrow, the perfect temple of neoclassical theory recedes farther into the Grecian mist. Apparently, attaining such perfection among an array of less-than-perfect alternatives requires more consistency than human society can muster.

Chapter 6

THE TENSION BETWEEN INDIVIDUAL AND SOCIAL WELFARE

James Buchanan arrived on the scene when popular sentiment was turning sharply against a major role for government in the allocation of resources, a movement that culminated in the election in 1980 of that supreme enemy of big government, U.S. President Ronald Reagan. Buchanan was awarded the Nobel Prize in 1986 for his explorations into the political bases of economic decision making.

Buchanan is the only Nobel economist who speaks economics with a Southern drawl. Born into rural agricultural poverty, he attended Middle Tennessee State Teacher's College, where he said he received only a "mediocre" education. At the beginning of World War II, he was drafted into the U.S. Navy and served most of the war at fleet headquarters in the Pacific. After the war he enrolled in the University of Chicago and for the first time plunged into serious study. He had arrived at Chicago "not overtly political or ideological," he says, but basically a populist (a person who accepts significant government involvement in economic activity). There he came under the influence of Frank Knight and was "converted by the power of ideas, by an understanding of the model of the market."[3] Ultimately, Buchanan developed the *theory of public choice,* which explores the problems societies face when deciding how to allocate their collective resources.

Public Choice

Buchanan's public choice is a reaction against a tendency to turn over to government the authority to determine society's "general will" and to carry out programs to effect it. Belief in the general will and government's power to effect it was characteristic of Enlightenment thinking. Enlightenment philosophers believed humans to be rational and fully informed about the consequences of their decisions. Together, said Enlightenment philosophers, rational people can define the general will and authorize government to carry out programs consistent with that will.

Post-Enlightenment philosophers were skeptical about this. And, in fact, Western democracies lean toward a second way of deciding collective action, one that denies the existence of a general will and emphasizes instead the preferences of the individuals who make up the society.

An advantage of the individualistic view of collective decision making is that it does not require moral judgments. For a society to agree on a general will, it would have to declare wrong or immoral any actions contrary to that will—with all the tragic consequences that worried Friedrich von Hayek. Without a general will, society is not required to make moral judgments. In fact, says Buchanan, the only moral imperative underlying collective decisions should be the defense of individual preferences. Thus, Buchanan's individual-choice approach would not allow a particular individual (presumably one with superior knowledge) or a particular social group (one chosen by "history" to dominate decision making) to lay down the law that governs everybody else. Again, followers of Hayek can well appreciate the danger of the alternative.

For allocating society's collective resources, Buchanan rejects talk of maximizing social welfare, of summing net benefits, of reconciling individual tastes with collective values. He would replace economists' emphasis on efficiency in allocating collective resources with emphasis on the processes through which a society makes its resource decisions. Given Arrow's impossibility theorem, the correct process for ensuring efficient choices is through unanimous agreement on the rules under which such decisions will be made. Having unanimously agreed on rules through which our society makes its allocative decisions, we can accept subsequent decisions that enjoy less than unanimous support. (We can appreciate traffic laws, even if we are occasionally annoyed by red lights.)

The rules Western nations have established for making our collective decisions are embodied in all those institutions that support free markets and democratic governments. The two types of institutions are similar in that both aim at satisfying our personal tastes and at the same time reconciling our conflicting interests. Both recognize our human tendency to act so as to gain benefits for ourselves at the lowest possible cost. Thus, in markets we act as consumers, preferring "more" to "less" and seeking to acquire bundles of products containing as much as possible of preferred goods and services. We agree to exchange one bundle for another only if we gain more satisfaction from the bundle we receive than we lose from the bundle we give up: more kitchen appliances, for example, and less recreational equipment. In government we act similarly. Acting as voters we understand that we cannot have more of everything, and we agree to trade one bundle of government programs for a different bundle—but only if the net benefits of the programs we gain fully offset the net benefits of those we lose. This is the process we follow, for example, when we agree to pay higher taxes for the sake of improved public education.

But here the similarities end. In free markets our self-interested behavior increases social welfare. By our participation in markets, we help enlarge the economic pie. In government, on the other hand, our self-interested behavior serves only to divide the existing pie.

The Rules Behind the Process

Instead of authorizing government to make allocative decisions on our behalf, members of a free society must agree on a process for collectively making such decisions. The central element in a society's decision-making process is its constitution, its rules and institutions for deciding collective issues. And society's constitutional choice must be unanimous.

Unanimous agreement is required at the constitutional level because it ensures that all subsequent decisions are made fairly. Unanimity ensures checks and balances, protections for the rights of minorities, and procedures for amending the decision-making process. Parties to the constitutional choice are uncertain to which interest groups they will ultimately belong and how the rules they create will affect their own long-range interests. Therefore, they will agree only to rules that affect all groups fairly.

After the constitutional decision, subsequent decisions may not require unanimity. Unanimous support for subsequent decisions would require that every decision yield net benefits for every member of society, an extremely unlikely result and a requirement that is likely to prevent any collective action at all. Sad to say, anything less than unanimity raises the possibility that even one voter who votes no suffers a greater loss from the decision than all the benefits gained by the many voters who vote yes. Because it is impossible to measure objectively the losses and the gains, a society may establish voting rules that require particular levels of agreement that may be less than unanimous, depending on the nature of the issue.

The Costs of Collective Decisions

By late in the 1960s Buchanan was losing faith in government's ability to make efficient collective decisions. President Lyndon Johnson's "Great Society" had brought an explosion of government programs that appealed to particular interest groups but that Buchanan saw as divorced from the interests of ordinary citizens. At the start of the new century, the nation faces similar questions about affirmative action programs for deciding college admissions and awarding government contracts. Supporters of both sorts of programs defend them for bringing into productive work minority groups that have previously been denied access. Opponents criticize them for allocating resources on bases other than benefits and costs.

To judge the efficiency of such programs would require that we measure their long-term benefits and costs, including such positive and negative externalities as are difficult to measure. Without a laboratory for making controlled experiments, without a way to isolate societies with and without Great Society or affirmative action programs, it is impossible to come to a scientific resolution of either issue—which leaves them to be decided through the political process.

Buchanan sees political decisions as subject to two kinds of "interdependence costs."[4] The first is the cost of persuading voters to support the proposed program itself, including the costs of identifying the interests of particular voting groups, resolving conflicts, and trading off concessions among groups. We may think of *persuasion costs* as the alternative compensation that must be paid voters to bring their conflicting interests into harmony for taking any action collectively. (*Alternative compensation* is a positive term for what politicians describe more negatively as pork barrel—or most negatively of all, as bribery.) Persuasion costs are low when only a few voters are required for making the decision, because few voters must be compensated for their agreement.

Buchanan calls the second category of interdependence costs *external costs,* the costs some voters suffer when other voters approve programs that are harmful to the first voters' interests. Every government program yields benefits for some people and imposes costs on others. If only 1 percent of voters are required to approve a proposed program, those voters can create programs that yield benefits to themselves while requiring the other 99 percent of voters to suffer the costs. External costs are quite high. Even with a simple majority requirement, 51 percent of voters can impose external costs on the other 49 percent.

To minimize Buchanan's interdependence costs requires different voting rules for making different kinds of collective decisions. The required percentage for agreement could range from one extreme, in which a decision requires only one yes vote, to the other extreme requiring unanimous consent. The higher the percentage required for a yes decision, the higher the persuasion costs but the lower the external costs imposed on those who vote no.

Buchanan illustrates the behavior of interdependence costs with the diagram in Figure 1, in which the horizontal axis represents the percentage of yes voters required for a decision, ranging from zero at the origin and moving rightward toward 100 percent. The vertical axis represents interdependence costs associated with a particular government program, where interdependence costs are the sum of external costs and persuasion costs.

The bowl-like shape of the interdependence cost curve reflects the combined behavior of, first, external costs and, second, persuasion costs.

Looking first at the downward slope: A voter's agreement with this decision implies that he or she enjoys the benefits while others bear the costs. The cost is, therefore, external to this voter. If only a few voters are required for making this decision, the external costs

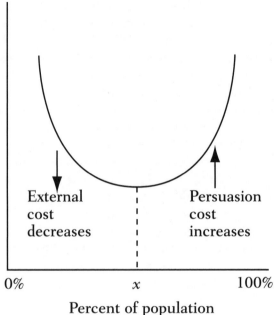

Figure 1

imposed on other voters are quite high, as reflected in the high initial level of external costs. As the percentage of voters that must agree with the decision increases, fewer voters experience external costs. This explains the downward slope of the interdependence cost curve (up to x percent of the population) as more voters agree to this particular government program.

Now looking at the upward slope: Persuading more voters to agree to a collective decision is costly, rising from a low cost when only a few voters most be persuaded, and approaching infinity when the required number of voters approaches 100 percent. Persuasion costs tend to be lower for homogeneous voting populations, whatever the required percentage of voters—people with similar tastes and living conditions generally agree more about particular government programs than heterogeneous populations.

Figure 1 identifies the efficient percentage of voters at 50 percent, implying that a simple majority is efficient for making this collective decision. A 50 percent agreement is not always most efficient, however. In fact, different types of collective decisions might have different configurations of interdependence costs and, therefore, different requirements for collective decisions. For programs involving property rights, for example, external costs probably begin higher on the vertical axis than is shown in the diagram. The implication is that allowing a few voters to decide issues involving property rights could result in confiscation, depriving many property owners of their rights and significantly increasing external costs. On the other hand, the persuasion costs of programs to protect property rights might be negligible. Most of us need little persuasion to agree to programs protecting property rights, since we either own or expect someday to own property. High external costs and low persuasion costs produce an interdependence cost curve that begins higher on the vertical axis and does not reach its low point until farther to the right along the horizontal axis than the 50 percent mark. This suggests that a supermajority (indeed, almost unanimous agreement) might be required for making collective decisions involving property rights.[5]

A contrary example involves government programs improving public education, fire and police protection, and so forth. Providing these services to larger numbers of people brings economies of scale in production, and economies of scale reduce external costs even when relatively few people benefit directly from the service. The result is relatively low external costs, so the sum of external and persuasion costs could reach a low point with fewer than 50 percent of the voters.

The Issue of Privatization

Regardless of the efficient fraction of voters required for agreement, efficiency requires that services provided by government yield benefits at least as great as their total interdependence costs.

One way to estimate the benefits enjoyed from a government program is to estimate what people would pay for the service if it were provided by a private firm. Without a collective decision to provide public education and police protection, for example, we would all have to purchase our preferred quantities from private firms, balancing off the personal satisfaction we enjoy with the cost paid.

Buchanan illustrates the public-private choice by making a simple change, as shown in Figure 2. Along with the bowl-shaped inter-

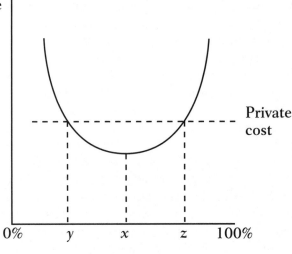

Figure 2

dependence cost curve, he adds a cost line for providing the service privately. Because private cost is not affected by the fraction of voters required for a collective decision, we draw the cost line horizontally at the appropriate value on the cost axis. If the private cost line lies above the interdependence cost line for any portion of its length, the cost of collective action to provide the service is less than the cost of private production.

In Figure 2 interdependence costs are indeed lower than private costs for between y and z percent of voters, so that this service might be provided collectively at lower cost than privately. National defense is a service whose private cost line lies above the interdependence cost line, and the opposite may be true of health care.

Dealing With Decision-Making Problems

Whatever voting rule a society establishes for making its collective decisions, voters have ways of undermining the rule. Considering that voters generally behave selfishly, this is not a surprise.

Before taking a position on a proposed government program, each voter requires information about his or her personal benefits and costs. Acquiring such information is time-consuming and, therefore, costly. Whatever information costs are experienced by a single voter are multiplied many times over when many voters must take the time to seek out information regarding a program's likely benefits and costs.

Information costs are further increased by some voters' tendency to conceal information, with the aim of influencing the decision in such a way as to further their own interests. We call such behavior *strategic*, and we find it also in voters' tendency to form coalitions for sharing information and voting as a bloc. Coalitions enable individual voters to transfer their voting rights to a group of voters who share common interests; but coalitions undermine whatever voting rules a society establishes. Consider a population of 49 voters and a voting rule that requires a simple majority: 25 votes. Now suppose the 49 voters are grouped into 7 coalitions of 7 voters each, with each coalition voting as a bloc based on its particular special interest. To achieve a majority requires the support of 4 of the 7 coalitions, yielding 28 votes. But each coalition's position on the issue is determined by voting within the bloc, such that only 4 of the voters in each coalition are required for that bloc's vote: a total of 16 votes. If only 4 voters in 4 coalitions are required to approve a government program, the voting rule is effectively changed from a simple majority to a minority: from $25/49 = 50$ percent to $16/49 = 32$ percent.

Coalitions reduce significantly the percentage of the voting population required for taking collective action, whatever the voting rule. Remember that the smaller the percentage of voters that is allowed to approve a government program, the greater the external cost suffered by voters who oppose it. And the more likely it is that programs are approved even though the cost of collective action is greater than the cost of providing the service privately.

Achieving a winning coalition of voters is made simpler by logrolling. Logrolling can be described as "You scratch my back and I'll scratch yours." You vote for my government program and I'll vote for yours. Logrolling simplifies the process of securing agreement from the 4 voting blocs required in the example above. In fact, with logrolling a minority with strongly held preferences can out-vote a majority whose preferences are less strongly held. With logrolling the percentage of voters that actually benefits from a government program may be substantially less than the percentage that votes for it.

Essentially, logrolling is vote-trading. It helps voters express the intensity of their preference for a particular collective action, where the intensity of preference depends on the magnitude of their benefits and costs. In product market decisions, we express the intensity of our preferences by our willingness to pay higher or lower prices. With logrolling, a voter with intense preference for a certain program has a similar privilege: to ensure support for an intensely preferred program while at the same time agreeing to support another program in which the voter has less interest.

Not all logrolling takes the form of explicit vote-trading. Some vote-trading is implicit in that it only assumes reciprocal support for alternative programs, the most common example of implicit vote-trading being the formation of political parties. Political parties bring together voters with generally consistent preferences but with strong or weak preferences for particular programs. A political party helps reconcile all these different preferences, encouraging voters with strong preferences for one program to agree to other programs for which they have weaker preferences.

Coalitions and logrolling drive a society toward greater allocations of resources to collective actions. When coalitions and logrolling are combined with general taxation, the tendency toward excessive allocation is even greater. Logrolling enables minority coalitions to enjoy the benefits of government programs, while general taxation requires all voters to pay the costs. With strategic behavior, there is no way to ensure that government programs are more efficient than alternative employments of resources, including production by private firms.

Well, perhaps there is one way. One way to reduce the distortions caused by strategic behavior and to increase the efficiency of public-private resource allocation is through side-payments. *Side-payments* are compensations paid by the gainers from government programs to the cost-payers. Done correctly, side-payments reduce the advantage to gainers and cause decisions to be based solely on the net benefits provided to the society as a whole. Only if a government program truly increases society's net benefits can voters who benefit directly from the program compensate the cost-payers.

Indeed, according to Buchanan, a requirement to make side-payments limits public investments to only those programs with positive net benefits. Side-payments squeeze out inefficient programs and leave in place only government programs whose gains can be compensated by transfers of real income. Side-payments have another advantage over vote-trading. Unlike vote-trading, side-payments do not require that resources be allocated to inefficient programs simply as a quid pro quo to secure voters' approval of efficient programs.

Although side-payments are more efficient than vote-trading, they are not as common in democratic societies. Because side-payments render the gainers from government programs no better off than the cost-payers, they leave unchanged the initial distribution of net benefits. Given that many government programs are intended to change the distribution of net benefits in some way, side-payments would defeat that objective.

Considering Urban Sprawl

If you live in a modern city, you understand all too well the likely consequences of allowing organized groups of voters to decide the allocation of public resources. As more and more city dwellers leave our cities for new homes in the suburbs, they require new roads, water and sewage systems, and perhaps even mass transit. Since such services must be provided for entire areas rather than in a straight line, their costs increase with the square of the distance from the central city. The rising costs of urban "sprawl" must be paid by area taxpayers, whether or not they have ever enjoyed the comforts of suburbia.

Suburban dwellers pay rising costs, too, in longer and more congested commutes. In fact, commuters in Atlanta, Georgia, are estimated to drive an average of 35 miles per day, thus spending 80 minutes daily in their automobiles. This is time that might otherwise be spent designing or marketing a product, maintaining or enhancing personal property values, or otherwise improving living standards. Suburban dwellers also need places to shop, which are generally concentrated in shopping malls. Building a mall strips an area of trees and green plants and substitutes concrete, in both cases irreparably changing the environment. The fact that malls are accessible only by automobiles leads to traffic congestion and air pollution, the effects of which can be damaging to life and health.

Local politicians have the authority to control urban sprawl by limiting building permits for homes and retail establishments. Most hesitate to exercise their authority, however, given the power of suburban coalitions to vote them out of office. Furthermore, new buildings represent taxable value for local government budgets, a significant incentive to permit development. In fact, while we regret the costs of sprawl, we have few tools to combat it. Respect for property rights limits our ability to dictate proper land use. On the other hand, efficient use of land requires consideration of the negative externalities entire areas suffer because of haphazard development.

Some land developers are hoping to redirect land use by building self-contained communities, with offices and retail establishments within walking distance of homes—somewhat the way cities first developed centuries ago. Whether families and businesses will accept this new-old way to live may determine the efficiency of land use for decades to come.

And Lately?

Following the period when Buchanan did most of his work, distrust of government's ability to make collective resource decisions has deepened. During the 1960s and 1970s bitter conflicts over civil rights and the Vietnam War reversed the positive view of government most U.S. citizens had held during World War II. Today, even more people express disillusionment: with government's apparent inability to serve the needs of the nation, with political parties' apparent dominance by special-interest groups, and with individual voters' apparent ineffectiveness for expressing their own interests.

In part, the reason for today's widespread disillusionment is our vast communications media for disseminating information (mostly bad) about government programs. For political parties and candidates, the availability of the media and the cost of using it force an almost slavish commitment to large moneyed interests: labor unions, professional associations, industry and trade groups, even representatives of foreign governments. Pressure from organized interests diminishes government's ability to act in the public interest, to serve ordinary men and women who are less able or less inclined to form organizations and exert pressure for the sake of personal interests. As far back as 1961, President Eisenhower warned the nation to beware of the dominance of the "military-industrial complex" for making collective resource decisions, and today Japan worries about its "Iron Triangle" of politicians, bureaucrats, and big businesses.

In part as a result of their disillusionment with government, citizens of democratic governments around the world are voting less, and political parties are becoming less effective for deciding policy. This is regrettable. We need political parties to aggregate the interests of diverse groups, to inform government of popular concerns, and to promote consensus for remedial policies.

Interestingly, voters' current disillusionment with government does not generally mean they support radical cuts in government's size and scope. Rather, voters want a government they can trust to care about the needs of ordinary people, to protect the worthy interests of minority groups, to provide desired services efficiently, and, insofar as is consistent with these objectives, to leave individuals pretty much alone.

Chapter 7
A BETTER WAY TO HANDLE EXTERNALITIES

C an markets be rational? Can rational individuals, participating in markets, make the decisions that allocate resources efficiently for the society as a whole? Can they do all this without significant government involvement? In short, is there life in neoclassical theory after the issues raised by Arrow and Buchanan?

Probably the most creative answers to these questions were offered by British-born economist Ronald Coase. Coase was awarded the Nobel Prize in 1991 for his explanation of that most basic of all economic institutions, the business firm, and how collecting many functions into a single firm can satisfy society's needs, independent of government. Coase's exploration of business firms doubtless led to his second major accomplishment, the formation of a brand-new branch of economics: law and economics.

In perhaps the most frequently cited article in all of economics literature, Coase tackles the issue of positive and negative externalities: the positive and negative consequences of market decisions that are not included in the optimizing calculations that guide buyers and sellers. Because externalities are not easily measured, they are generally omitted from buyers' calculations of benefits and costs. But decisions that yield externalities have become more and more critical as our economies have developed beyond such face-to-face contacts between buyers and sellers as are typical of primitive economies. Primitive peoples exchanging fish for pigs do not have to worry about the depletion of fish populations or the aromatic clouds that form over pig pens. As economies have grown, however, handling these sorts of externalities has become a major responsibility of government.

Tackling Externalities

A modern economy generates lots of externalities, and negative externalities tend to get the most attention. Air and water pollution. Noise and congestion. Trash and spoiled landscapes. Such are the almost inevitable by-products of modern production techniques. They are inevitable only to the extent that they occur outside market calculations that would attach a cost, a true cost of production that requires compensation. The problem is that, as economies decentralize, diversify, and employ greater division of labor, production processes become so widely separated that locating the source of negative externalities and exacting their costs from the responsible party have become more and more difficult.

Some economists have long regarded externalities as a source of "market failure" and, therefore, a reason for government involvement in economic decision making.[6] In the case of negative externalities, these economists want government to identify and measure the costs a firm imposes on the community—costs for which it ordinarily does not pay compensation—and make sure that it pays. Firms that reduce negative externalities might be rewarded with subsidies, which might also be paid to firms that create positive externalities. Through pollution taxes, fines, and subsidies, firms would experience benefits and costs that truly reflect their positive and negative contributions to social welfare.

To the extent that a market "fails," it appears logical to call on government to correct the failure. Coase worried that one admission of failure would invite others, however, so that too soon markets would be dangerously hobbled by constraints that interfere with their efficient operation.

And this is where Coase introduced an entirely new way of thinking about negative externalities.

A Classic Example

Consider a rancher who pastures cattle adjacent to a farmer's grain fields. Cattle occasionally wander off the pasture and trample nearby stands of grain. The grain farmer loses a part of the crop, or, reverting to economic jargon, suffers a negative externality.

The pre-Coase solution to this problem would be to authorize government to outlaw activities that create a negative externality for the farmer—or, alternatively, to evaluate the damage caused by the externality and collect a tax or fine from the rancher, with the revenue paid as compensation to the farmer. Is this the most efficient solution? Absolutely not, replies Coase. To paraphrase his rather outrageous conclusion: Without government restraints on the rancher, the farmer may produce too little grain, but with such restraints the farmer may produce too much grain! What defines too much grain? you ask. There is too much grain, replies Coase, if actions taken to protect the farmer's crop reduce production of cattle by more than society gains from the larger quantity of grain.

Here is Coase's fundamental point: that both the rancher and the farmer have rights, the rancher to raise cattle and the farmer to produce grain. Both rancher and farmer are responding to the demands of consumers. Both contribute net benefits to society, and both should be encouraged to continue doing so. Maximizing society's welfare requires that both activities be carried to the point at which gains in society's welfare are just equal to the costs. This rule is the same as would be applied to any activity; the only difference here is in making sure that costs include the costs of negative externalities. Unless both parties account for the costs their behavior imposes on the other party, both will attempt to produce more than the efficient quantity of their product.

Now consider the consequences of government involvement to favor the rights of one or the other. If government were to compel the rancher to reduce his herd for the sake of preserving the farmer's crop, the cost to society would be the smaller quantity of beef available in markets, reflected in higher beef prices. In this solution to the problem, the society would have exchanged the negative externality imposed on the farmer for a negative externality imposed on the rancher. And it is not clear that society is better off for the choice!

For government to arrive at the efficient solution to this issue, it would have to identify the efficient quantities of both products, which would require much more information than is generally available to government but is freely available at the level of the interested parties. That is the level at which decisions regarding the allocation of resources should remain. Indeed, in the absence of government involvement, the rancher and the farmer can negotiate a settlement that maximizes the net benefits from both types of production, taken together.

The Shape of the Agreement

Our next question might ask what form that settlement might take. Whose interests in the issue should prevail, and who should be held responsible for compensating the other? Before Coase, the typical answer to this question referred to the initial distribution of property rights. If the farmer acquired the land before the rancher, it was said, the farmer's interests should prevail, and the rancher should compensate for any damage to the grain crop. If the rancher preceded the farmer, the rancher was due compensation.

Coase gives a surprising answer to the question regarding initial property rights. In fact, he says, it doesn't matter which party owns the initial property rights. For the efficient solution to this issue, it doesn't matter how the initial property rights were distributed, and it doesn't matter who is held legally responsible for compensation to whom. If the parties are left alone to negotiate the matter, whatever arrangement they decide will maximize society's net benefits. (A small, but potentially large, condition was inserted here, which is discussed later in the chapter.)

Suppose grain is so highly valued in the market that the damage from the lost crop reduces the farmer's sales revenue by more than the rancher gains from the associated cattle sales. To avoid experiencing such a significant loss in revenue, the farmer would be willing to pay any amount up to his potential loss to persuade the rancher to, say, reduce his herd to a level that can be fed on more secure pastures. The farmer gains from such an agreement because his payment to the rancher is less than the value of the grain he would otherwise lose from wandering cattle. The rancher also gains, because he receives more from the farmer than he would have collected from cattle sales.

Now consider the opposite possibility, that beef is more highly valued in the market. Following similar reasoning: If beef is more highly valued in the market, reducing the rancher's herd would reduce his revenue by more than the farmer gains from associated grain sales. This time, the rancher would be willing to pay any amount up to his potential loss from reducing the herd to persuade the farmer not to cultivate the strip of land adjacent to the pasture. The rancher gains from such an agreement because his payment to the farmer is less than the revenue he gains from marketing the added cattle. But the farmer also gains from a higher payment from the rancher than he would have collected from his own sales of grain.

Certainly both parties to this issue would prefer to operate without consideration of the other. But because both parties create value for society, society's interest is that the parties conduct their operations efficiently, with the greatest surplus of benefits over cost. If reducing the rancher's herd involves a greater loss to society than the larger grain crop, the rancher should pay the farmer and produce more beef. If reducing the farmer's grain crop involves a greater loss than reducing the rancher's herd, the farmer should pay the rancher. The determining factor in either case is the market value of the product: the market value of beef producible on the land relative to the market value of grain. Both these values are determined by the freely expressed preferences of consumers. Thus, the information provided by buyers of beef and grain is key to the efficient resolution of this issue. Through information provided in markets, society maximizes the net benefits it enjoys from the use of its available land.

And all this without any government involvement at all.

Coase arrived at his rather unorthodox conclusion as a result of his experience with the British government's allocations of the radio frequency spectrum. Broadcasting rights must be allocated along the spectrum so as to avoid signal interference, and the government was concerned that its decisions should preserve the initial distribution of property rights. At first Coase agreed. But then he realized that whatever the initial distribution of broadcast rights, that distribution would be modified by independent transfers among the broadcasters, with each transfer adding benefits to one broadcaster in excess of the costs experienced by the other. Through their independent negotiations, broadcasters would ultimately arrive at the welfare-maximizing distribution of rights along the spectrum.

You might have noticed a significant characteristic of Coase's solution, one that involves the ultimate responsibility for compensation. Whether the rancher compensates the farmer for the lost grain or the farmer compensates the rancher for the lost beef, the ultimate source of the compensation is the consumer—or more broadly, the society as a whole, which must pay prices for beef and grain that include compensation for alternative uses of the land. The prices society pays to remedy negative externalities aim not to eliminate externalities but to achieve the efficient level. (Are you reminded of Gary Becker's efficient level of crime?)

Coase described many examples of negative externalities, including noise from a manufacturing plant that disturbs a scholar, fumes from chemical processes that damage children's lungs, traffic congestion from urban living that slows commerce. In general, society tolerates negative externalities that yield benefits at least equal to their cost: manufactured output of value at least equal to the scholar's output, chemical products of value at least equal to the health damage, urban amenities at least equal to the cost of slower commerce. Our societies make these kinds of comparisons every day and decide production accordingly.

An ancient case involving candle-making in France summarized society's choice this way, and one does not need command of the French language to understand the point: *Le utility de la chose excusera le noisomeness de la stink.*

On Lighthouses and Beehives

Coase's wandering cattle are examples of negative externalities, but Coase also showed how positive externalities can be handled efficiently by free markets. Positive externalities are benefits enjoyed by people who do not pay the full costs of production. Economists' concern is that unless the producers of positive externalities are fully compensated, they will cut back their production, and society will suffer a reduction in net benefits. To avoid the loss of positive externalities, it is said, government must undertake activities that yield positive externalities.

Not so, argues Ronald Coase, and for the same reason that he would leave government out of most decisions regarding negative externalities.

Economists who favor government production of positive externalities have used particular examples to support their position: the lighthouse, which provides guidance to ships whether or not shippers have paid to produce the light; and the beekeeper, whose bees pollinate apple blossoms whether or not apple growers have paid the beekeeper. Supporters of government involvement call on government to provide (or subsidize the producers of) these services. Without government involvement, they argue, producers of positive externalities would not have sufficient incentive to provide the efficient quantity. The economy would not have enough lighthouses, beehives, and similar necessities.

The argument seems persuasive until one looks at the facts. The facts are, as summarized by Coase, that throughout history lighthouse associations and beekeepers have negotiated agreements with users of their services, and they have received compensation sufficient to yield proper production incentives. Ocean shippers have subscribed to lighthouse services, he says, or they have paid fees upon entering ports made safer by lighthouses. Apple growers have paid beekeepers to locate their hives near apple orchards. In negotiations similar to those dealing with negative externalities, producers and consumers of positive externalities have been able, without government involvement, to agree on compensation that appropriately values the positive externality.

Coase's ideas about how free markets can handle externalities—without government involvement—were so counter to prevailing views that he was called upon to defend them before other economists. The story is that he argued far into the night with a group of disbelievers from the University of Chicago (including two future Nobelists, Milton Friedman and George Stigler), who entered the meeting ridiculing his ideas but left as staunch supporters. Apparently, his logic was overwhelming, even for his most discriminating colleagues.

Tackling the Efficient Organization of Business Firms

Coase's contribution to the economic theory of externalities was spectacular. But his most fundamental contribution to economics was made years earlier, when he was only 21 years old, a time of his life, he says, when the "sun never ceased to shine."

Coase was reared by parents who lacked formal education past age 12 and who pursued fairly menial occupations. In childhood, he was afflicted with a disability that required him to wear leg irons, and he was sent to a school for physical defectives. An only child, he was frequently left alone to spend much of his time in academic pursuits and was recognized early as academically gifted. Later, he was awarded academic scholarships, and by happenstance (he says he was not qualified for history and disliked mathematics) he chose to specialize in business. In that subject he found a vast new world of exciting puzzles to solve. One puzzle was particularly challenging. It was the apparent contradiction in economic theory between two acknowledged truths: the first, the expectation that free markets efficiently coordinate a nation's resource allocation without central control, and the second, the recognition that individual business firms do require central control to bring about that coordination.

Why, he asked, is central control necessary at the level of the individual firm but not at the level of the entire nation? It was this puzzle that led Coase to the concept of *transactions costs,* a totally new concept in economic theory.

Transactions costs are not a problem in Coase's example of the rancher and the farmer, since two people can meet fairly easily to resolve their differences. With as few as two parties and one fairly straightforward issue, negotiations can be simply pursued to the efficient solution, with costs limited to the externalities themselves. But the rancher-farmer example was extremely simplified, allowing for perfect information on the part of both parties and omitting many of the complexities that might occur in actual negotiations about such matters. In the real world negative externalities comprise a wide range of consequences and involve thousands, even millions, of people and are much too complicated to be solved by two-party negotiations. When more than a single rancher and farmer are parties to an issue, the costs of making the necessary transactions increase significantly.[7] As more people become involved (perhaps even some that are yet unborn) and as the range of consequences increases, the costs of arriving at an agreement must be added to the costs of the agreement itself.

Transactions costs tend to increase as populations increase and as economic institutions grow and become more complex. With increased division of labor, decentralization of industry, and diversification of production, for example, the parties to a transaction are separated by longer distances, greater divergences of interests and information, perhaps even differences in methods of problem solving. All these things make transacting agreements more and more costly. A society can afford to pay rising transactions costs only if further division of labor, decentralization, and diversification increase production by more than the increased distances, divergences of interest and information, and differences in methods of problem solving increase the costs of making transactions.

The study of transactions costs is what led Coase to his most fundamental contribution to economic theory. Stated simply, if growth in business firms brings on increased production, and if growth also brings rising transactions costs, firms may reach some size at which gains in production from further growth fall below the associated increases in transactions costs. In other words, given the typical behavior of benefits and costs from larger size, there may be an efficient size beyond which firms should not grow.

A typical firm is a collection of activities ranging from product conception and design, through various stages of production, to advertising and delivery to final consumers. All such activities could be carried on by independent firms, buying from and selling to other firms until the finished product is ready for sale. Many products even now are produced through such a process, by independent firms spread across nations and even continents. (The nostalgic among us were disheartened recently to learn that the Sara Lee Corporation will henceforth produce none of its own cakes but purchase them from other suppliers.)

The problem with allocating responsibilities among many firms is that, with so many transactions at so many points along the chain of production, the costs of making transactions increase significantly. With the proliferation of firms, contract negotiations become

more complicated, delivery times less dependable, and even the survival of certain firms in the chain more uncertain. If all the transactions could be carried on within a single firm, it might be easier to
coordinate processes and reduce transactions costs—and this is
what has given rise to multifunction firms. A multifunction firm can
convert external transactions costs to internal administrative costs
and may operate more efficiently than could many independent
firms carrying on their interrelated functions.

The Problem of Principals and Agents

However, even with improved information technology, increasing the
number of functions ultimately leads to increases in the cost of
transactions. One cost increase arises out of the separation of managers from production workers: the separation of the control of production from its actual performance. Economists describe the separation of control from performance as a "principal-agent" problem,
where the principal is the manager or controller and the agent is the
person who carries out the instructions of the manager. As firms
grow in size and in variety of functions, the separation of agent from
principal widens, and that separation makes more difficult the job of
coordinating the performance of the agent with the instructions of
the principal, in the worst case even diminishing overall production.

When the principal-agent problem reduces a firm's ability to generate net benefits, growth in internal functions should stop. Limiting
a firm's functions inevitably limits its capacity for division of labor,
decentralization, and diversification and may limit its potential for
increasing productivity. To avoid limits to productivity growth, many
firms undertake measures to reduce the principal-agent problem:
improving information and coordination between managers and production workers, reducing conflicts of interest and, it is hoped,
increasing incentives to increase the firm's ability to carry out its
many functions.

A popular remedy for the principal-agent problem is quality cir-
cles, in which workers share among themselves and with managers
their firsthand knowledge of production processes. Another is team
production, in which teams of workers perform a number of func-

tions, with all the workers contributing toward a completed product. Another is worker representation on boards of directors or even worker ownership of company stock. Still another is the payment of bonuses or profit shares to workers for superior performance. All such measures are intended to give production workers a stake in the growth and profitability of the firm—and, therefore, incentives to contribute to that growth and profitability. To the extent that such methods succeed, they reduce internal conflicts, reduce transactions costs, and increase net benefits from firm growth.

Chapter 8

IS THERE ROOM IN ECONOMICS FOR ETHICS?

When it announced Amartya Sen as the 1998 recipient of the Nobel Prize in Economic Sciences, the Swedish selection committee described him this way: "By combining tools from economics and philosophy, he has restored an ethical dimension to the discussion of vital economic problems." Some commentators found less merit in this accomplishment than did the selection committee, one even describing his work as not "serious economics." To those dissenters, ethics is outside the domain of a discipline whose goal is to become more "scientific."

Indeed, some of Sen's professional colleagues would strip their subject entirely of ethical values and emphasize self-interest as the only proper goal of human behavior. Others would agree that self-interest is a powerful motivation, one that explains much of behavior—but not all. Rather early in life, both in our personal lives and in the life of human society, we discover that advancing our own self-interest depends to a large extent on permitting others to advance theirs. Indeed, we organize our individual lives and the life of our society to achieve a kind of balance among all our competing self-interests.

We take turns. We respect our neighbors' rights as we expect our neighbors to respect ours.

Preoccupation with self-interest has not always been true of economics. From economics' earliest beginning until the development of neoclassical economics, there was no sharp boundary between economics and politics. In fact, the study of economics began as a body of thought known as *political economy*, the modifier implying concern for the social consequences of private behavior. Over time, as economics developed into a recognized discipline, it reduced its emphasis on its "political" aspect—how to distribute what the economy produces—and increased its emphasis on "economy"—producing more things to distribute. From this more growth-oriented perspective, the fundamental question asked by economics became: How can society achieve the rising standards of living that growing populations demand?

The need for practical solutions to pressing problems guided economists toward what Amartya Sen calls an engineering approach to the subject that seeks the best means for achieving what are society's presumed goals.

Positive and Normative Economics

Economics' new objective to produce more goods and services shifted economists' attention from "normative economics" (what should be) to "positive economics" (what is). Positive economics makes no judgment about what goals might be proper for society but presumes the goals include maximizing income or wealth or something indicative of material well-being. The split in economic thought stressed economic logic over social morality, practical means over proper ends, and ultimately, engineering solutions to economic problems over the ethical considerations that underlie economic decisions. In recent years, the connections between these separate ways of thinking have loosened further and become more asymmetrical: that is, economic logic has been allowed to influence the ethical content of economics, but ethical concerns have been excluded from economic logic. Sen finds this regrettable because if ethical considerations do affect our behavior, then they cannot be ignored when attempting to describe, explain, and predict economic events.

Amartya Sen invites us to return our attention to the questions: "What should be?" and "How should we live?" Indeed, Amartya Sen asserts that attention to what should be will actually improve our standards of what is. He believes that a focus on ethical considerations will improve our ability to realize our self-interested goals.

Moreover, he asserts that increased attention to normative economics can restore economics to its prominent position in the world's history of intellectual thought. Sen quotes with dismay a jingle written about John Stuart Mill, a noted nineteenth-century economist:

> John Stuart Mill
> By a mighty effort of will
> Overcame his natural bonhomie
> And wrote "Principles of Political Economy."[8]

Sen laments the suggestion that the intellectual pursuit of economics required Mill to sacrifice his good-natured friendliness. Is economics necessarily distinct from "bonhomie"? he asks. Is it not more appropriate that economics rejoin its segmented halves for more comprehensive contributions to intellectual thought?

Seeking Support From Adam Smith

Today's strictest rationalists harken back to Adam Smith. To many of his followers, the venerable Scot appeared to glorify individual self-interest, seeing in self-interested behavior the source of maximum welfare for the society as a whole. Jingles are so rare in our sober subject that I feel compelled to ask the reader's indulgence in one more, this one involving John Stuart Mill's illustrious predecessor and the founder of modern economic thought:

> Adam, Adam, Adam Smith
> Listen what I charge you with!
> Didn't you say
> In the class one day
> That selfishness was bound to pay?
> Of all doctrines that was the Pith,
> Wasn't it, wasn't it, wasn't it, Smith?[9]

And this is, of course, the popular impression of Smith's philosophy. Actually, such accounts of Adam Smith's beliefs are unfair and incomplete. The first modern economist actually emphasized the consistency between the rational pursuit of self-interest and what he called self-command, which he defined to include "fellow feeling" toward others and restraint in the individual pursuit of self-interest. Smith even suggested that the interest of the "great community" might occasionally require that our "own little interest should be sacrificed."

To the extent that economics has neglected ethics, it has failed to assume its rightful place in intellectual history. Economic tools, which are so powerful for explaining the pursuit of self-interest, are just as powerful for dealing with ethical issues.

The Consequentialists and the Deontologists

One way to evaluate our economic choices is to acknowledge two ways to distinguish good behavior from bad: the consequential way and the deontological way. The consequential way looks at the consequences of behavior and determines its rightness or wrongness by the rightness or wrongness of the consequences. Imagine yourself at the wheel of a speeding cable car careening down one of San Francisco's hilly byways. Suddenly, standing directly in the path of your cable car are five people, powerless to get out of the way of certain death. Well, perhaps not certain, because there is a turnoff into which you could steer the car where—as (bad) luck would have it— only one person stands in the direct path of your car. What should you do? The consequentialist would turn the car. The consequentialist would approve of an active decision to cause one death if that decision avoids the even more negative consequence of five deaths.

Sen finds the consequentialist way of thinking akin to neoclassical economics, which judges decisions on the basis of their consequences for society's total welfare. In fact, this is the source of much criticism of neoclassical theory—what the critics see as its extreme focus on the consequences. The problem is that an extreme focus on maximizing social welfare detracts attention from the process through which that goal is achieved. Processes are the focus of the deontologists. The deontologist way of thinking considers the process through which maximum social welfare is achieved and would avoid behavior that lacks ethical support (and, therefore, would not turn the cable car).

Process Rules

Concerns about the processes that underlie decisions lead a society to establish a set of rules, in effect, a moral code that specifies the processes through which the society achieves maximum welfare. Compliance with society's moral code brings rewards, both in the form of benefits we gain from our own behavior and in the form of benefits we gain from the compliance of others. Both types of gains, in turn, create incentives to obey society's rules.

Perhaps society's most fundamental process rules are those that involve property rights. The expectation that others will comply with property rules creates incentives to build and acquire property. From process rules, property owners gain some assurance that the sacrifices required to obtain property are not wasted. Other fundamental process rules are those that involve borrowing and lending. Without some assurance that borrowers will comply with the terms of loans, few lenders would have incentives to make them. Thus is our moral code intertwined with our economic life, applying rational analysis toward maximum social welfare, in both aspects.

Amartya Sen and the Economics of Hunger

Born in India, Amartya Sen was a child in Bengal at the time of the great famine of 1943, an experience that profoundly affected his life and career. He recalls vividly the starving peasants that came to his grandfather's door to plead for pitiful handouts of rice. The famine killed an estimated three million people, even though overall food production in India was quite adequate to sustain them. Sen resolved to understand a system that so massively failed to serve its people.

Sen's investigations into the Bengalese famine led him to the following realizations. People establish their command over food either directly, through what he calls an "exchange with nature," or indirectly, through exchanges with other members of society. It is the failure of the second method that yields the most widespread hunger. Such failure can have either of two causes, the more obvious cause being general economic slumps, and the less obvious, general economic booms. It is easy to understand how diminished supply in slumps can cause hunger in the population as a whole. But it is also true that unequal expansion in booms can bring hunger to large segments of the rural laboring class.

The Bengalese famine was a result of the second cause, unequal expansion in economic boom. Heavy spending during World War II had pushed up incomes and prices in India's cities. While food prices soared, rural incomes did not rise. The rural-to-urban shift in income distribution brought radical hunger.

Democratic societies refuse to tolerate wide income inequalities, says Sen, and the extreme poverty that results. But India was under colonial rule, and the colonial leaders were immune to democratic pressures. Feeling no obligation to correct the tragic consequences of income inequality, they stood aside and allowed millions of India's poor to starve.

Policies to alleviate hunger include both food relief and cash relief. Sen sees the first approach as a mere palliative, with only short-term effects, and recommends instead the latter. By increasing the effective demand for food, he says, cash relief to poor people prompts food suppliers to make the sorts of long-term investments that permanently reduce the incidence of hunger. Cash relief also leaves to private businesses the responsibility for developing food transportation and distribution systems and for building the infrastructure that is so essential to further industrial development. Cash relief counteracts the frequent tendency among food suppliers to transfer food from famine-stricken regions into regions that offer greater returns. And cash relief requires less interference with the recipients' normal economic activities, thus yielding other economic and social benefits. Doubtless, these are some of the reasons that recent solicitations for aid to earthquake victims in Turkey have stressed cash relief.

Cash relief has many critics. Without an immediate increase in food supplies, increased spending for food might increase inflation. Sen suggests that food price inflation is not necessarily a bad thing, since the effect of inflation is to transfer food from heavy consumers to famine victims.

Amartya Sen continues to be a controversial figure in economics, regarded by his opponents as a shallow thinker and by his supporters as one of the deeper thinkers in the profession. Sen expresses his own view of his role as attempting to juggle many balls, and preferring to juggle many balls badly than to demonstrate virtuosity with one ball. He is married to the well-known economic historian Emma Rothschild, who reports on his interest in wine, conversation, and laughter—preferences to which even noneconomists can relate. An aside: Amartya's name means "one who deserves immortality."

PART 3
MEASURING TO UNDERSTAND

Ragnar Frisch • *Jan Tinbergen* •
Tjalling Koopmans •
Leonid Kantorovich • *Trygve Haavelmo*

E conomics is a social science—a science of human behavior. Some people regard the term *social science* as a self-contradiction, an oxymoron, like "jumbo shrimp." How can there be a "science" of social behavior, they say, when social behavior changes with every conceivable change in human conditions? Is it ever possible to understand—or, even more problematic, to predict—how the many sources of human behavior interact to produce a particular outcome? If none of these things is possible, is there any point to economics at all, other than as historical descriptions of human events as they occur?

It's difficult to imagine questions more demeaning to a profession dedicated to scientific inquiry. Needless to say, economists resist the implied conclusions with every fiber of their being. Economists admit that their science can never be as precise in its laws or principles as a physical science, one with laboratories for making controlled experiments and arriving at repeatable results. Still, even without laboratories, social scientists retain two valuable sources of understanding about their subject: first, their capacity for analytical thought and, second, empirical data describing real-world events. In much the same way as laboratory observations serve the chemist or physicist, analytical thought helps the economist organize information from past experience, note its regularities and relationships, and suggest theories, or hypotheses, to explain human behavior.

Chapter 9
BUSINESS CYCLES
AND DYNAMIC ANALYSIS

In the 1930s, depression gripped the industrialized world. Factories idle in a world of want. Workers unemployed in a world of technological opportunity. Banks failing in an economy desperate for bank loans. Governments apparently helpless to relieve economic distress. All these conditions required explanation. The economists you are about to meet believe that improved analytical techniques can help us understand the kinds of behavior that create such economic woes and, through that understanding, find ways to avoid them in the future.

Business cycles were nothing new to the world economy. Indeed, from the start of the industrial era, industrialized nations often experienced wide swings in economic activity, with rising prosperity followed by "panic" and then depression. (What student of American history has not sweated over exam questions about the panic of 1837 or 1857 or 1873 or—pick a year?) In its time, each economic crisis appeared to be unique, each bringing its own wrenching disruptions and hardships, and each resulting from a unique precipitating event: a bad harvest, a war or revolution, a setback in a major technology. It was only around the turn of the century that economists shifted their attention from describing particular economic crises to exploring the common attributes of these recurring phenomena.

Because agriculture then constituted a significant share of national output, the earliest studies of business cycles focused on fluctuations in the farm economy. Economists collected data on farm prices and incomes and used statistical tools to identify year-to-year regularities and relationships. Some economists noticed that changes in the farm economy coincided with changes in the behavior of heavenly bodies: for some, the regular appearance of sunspots; for others, the regular movement of the planet Venus relative to the sun. From these observations, some economists (no longer credible, to be sure) concluded that business cycles on earth are a result of causes outside the earth's economy, perhaps as far distant as celestial bodies.

To attribute economic behavior to causes outside the economy (not necessarily in outer space!) is to identify the causes as exogenous. An exogenous cause is an external shock and differs from an endogenous cause, which is generated within the system itself: an earthquake as opposed to an earth-moving project. Both have economic consequences, but the exogenous shock is less easily explained, predicted, and controlled.

After farm income, business-cycle analysts turned to production of pig iron, like food a commodity essential to an industrializing economy. And like food production, pig iron production had been known to fluctuate, the result of such causes as a long-term upward trend, arising out of year-to-year growth in demand for tools and equipment made from pig iron; seasonal changes in demand, arising out of variations in construction activity during a single year; random shocks to demand, arising from such events as wars or interruptions in trade; and, of particular interest to business cycle economists, cyclical changes in demand associated with recurring cycles in business activity. All these tendencies are at work all the time, of course, overlapping each other and making a confusing mix of up-and-down movements, each one offsetting or reinforcing another.

Time-series analysts use statistical tools to sort out all these tendencies, to isolate the effects of trend, season, and random shocks, the better to focus on the effect of business cycles alone. The first step in time-series analysis is to remove the long-term trend. To do this, the analyst first plots on a graph points representing quantities of pig iron produced in each of a series of months. Then the analyst draws a straight line through the cluster of points, the line beginning and ending at points representing months with similar economic conditions. The analyst calculates the rate of change from start to finish along the straight line and defines as long-term trend the average change per month; perhaps 0.25 percent per month or 3.0 percent per year. Subtracting the trend effect from each data point leaves only those effects on production that are explainable by seasonal, random, and cyclical causes.

The second step in time-series analysis is to remove the seasonal effect. By first calculating the average quantity produced during the same month in every year, the time-series analyst determines the typical quantity produced in each month. Subtracting the typical monthly quantity from each month's trend-adjusted quantity leaves the portion of each month's pig iron production that is not explainable by trend or seasonal causes and, therefore, is evidence of cyclical behavior or random shocks. Finally, by using moving averages, the analyst smoothes out the random shocks in the data and isolates the portion of pig iron production that is attributable to business cycles.

Business cycle data behaved much as time-series analysts expected, rising and falling in a fairly regular pattern with only slight differences in the duration and amplitude of particular cycles. One analyst likened the fluctuations to those of a pendulum struck intermittently by peas. Business cycles are like swings of a pendulum, he said, repeating themselves in a fairly regular pattern. Projectiles crashing into a pendulum upset its rhythm, but it quickly returns to its regular motion until struck by another pea.

The pendulum and the peas raise two questions about business cycles: the question of "impulse" and the question of "propagation." The impulse question refers to the initial change in business conditions that precipitates the cycle, the event that starts the pendulum swinging. The propagation question refers to the tendency for cycles to recur, the force that keeps the pendulum swinging even if no more peas are flung at it.

The Development of Econometrics

In their investigations of such questions, the earliest students of business cycles followed the analytical process familiar to the physical scientists, shifting back and forth between theory and data and ultimately using statistical techniques to test their theories. The end result of their effort was econometrics: a body of statistical techniques for scientifically analyzing observed economic behavior. As its name implies, econometrics combines mathematical and statistical tools toward the testing of economic hypotheses. Its objective is economic theory that more accurately explains behavior in the real world.

You will not be surprised that the Nobel econometricians began their careers as mathematicians. You may be surprised that many began also as physicists. As physicists, they became accustomed to precise laws defining constant relationships between cause and effect: the predictable effect of temperature on gases and the predictable effect of the earth's rotation on the ocean's tides. It is understandable that economists trained initially as physicists would seek the same sorts of laws to explain social behavior: the predictable effect of an investment tax credit on new capital formation and the predictable effect of lower interest rates on employment.

There is another characteristic of the Nobel econometricians you may find even more surprising: their fundamental concern for human welfare. This is not to suggest that such concern is uncommon among economists, of course. But people do not always associate concern for human welfare with mathematicians and physicists—perhaps because we believe mathematicians and physicists to be caught up in matters above and beyond the mundane concerns of everyday life. Nevertheless, in their personal characteristics and in their work as econometricians, the econometricians blend a capacity for scientific inquiry with a deep concern for human welfare.

Econometrics links the mathematical way of thinking, the physics of cause-effect relationships, and a personal concern for human welfare with active programs to affect economic activity.

Econometric Models

The first task of these econometricians was to build models of economic behavior. A model is a simplified view of reality, including essential features of the real world but omitting unessential details. Much as a cellophane and pasteboard model serves as a sort of midpoint between an architect's abstract idea and a real office building, an econometric model serves as a midpoint between economic theory and real economic activity. Some models are descriptive only, useful for comparing economic conditions across regions or across time. Or a descriptive model may be used to answer what-if questions, asking the likely consequences of certain changes in economic conditions. Using a descriptive model to project the consequences of change is a form of simulation, which is the equivalent in economics of an experiment in a chemistry laboratory. What happens if I mix this with that? Unlike chemistry experiments, which may have explosive consequences, the consequences of economic simulation are observable only in the behavior of numbers, a real advantage over laboratory experiments when the welfare of real people is at stake.

Policy-oriented econometric models go beyond mere description to include a *preference function,* defined as a mathematical equation to be maximized through specific changes in government policies. The process is similar to optimization, the process we consumers use to maximize personal welfare from our consumer choices. For making economic policy, the goal to be maximized is generally total output, employment, export growth, or some broad index of economic activity.

The Search for Regularities

The first economist to be described as an econometrician was the Norwegian economist Ragnar Frisch. In fact, Frisch coined the name of the method he believed would "at long last establish economics as a science."[1] Along with Jan Tinbergen, Frisch was awarded the first Nobel Prize in Economic Sciences in 1969 for bringing to economics the mathematical tools essential for scientific analysis of economic behavior.

Frisch built on the earlier ideas of such scientists as Evariste Galois, who lived in the early nineteenth century. In Galois' short life (he was killed in a duel over a woman at age 21) he introduced the idea of *transformations:* mathematical expressions describing how particular values of certain factors are "transformed" into particular values of another. Galois believed that through his transformations, scientists could discover the general causes and underlying principles of things—in effect, the "laws" of nature.

Discovering the laws of nature appealed to Ragnar Frisch. Frisch characterizes himself as a lover of wisdom, and he sees econometrics as a way to gain wisdom.[2] Even more apocalyptic, Frisch sees econometrics as a means toward human survival. Our chances of survival are greater, he says, the more "regularities" we can discover in our "outer world." Clearly, creatures that understand the regularities of the sun, the earth, and their own bodies, can better adapt to and make use of such regularities. Frisch believes that history's long evolutionary struggle eliminates species that are unable to identify regularities in their environment—one pathetic example being certain friendly whales that are unable to distinguish the regular visits of commercial whalers from those of harmless whale-watchers.

Uncovering the regularities of life is the essence of understanding and, ultimately, species survival. Unconsciously, we learn about the regularities of life through our sense organs. We see, smell, feel, and hear events from which we make our generalizations about the world. Consciously, we learn about life's regularities through experiments. Indeed, experimental techniques are a way to extend the information-gathering function of our sense organs. According to Frisch, the importance of econometrics is "to push forward by leaps and bounds the line of demarcation from where we have to rely on our intuition and sense of smell."[3]

Not all regularities are evidence of cause-effect relationships. In fact, Frisch warns against concluding that just because two things occur together, it must be true that one causes the other. Econometric conclusions that misstate cause-effect relationships are examples of what he terms *spurious correlation*. To illustrate spurious correlation, Frisch points to data associating the numbers of tourists visiting the Norwegian coast with the number of flies also documented in those areas. To wrongly attribute an area's attractiveness to tourists to the number of flies might lead policymakers toward policy decisions that increase the number of flies.

For another example of spurious correlation, researchers have discovered that families with cappuccino machines tend to have healthier babies. But what is the true cause-effect relationship here?

Explaining Demand

Frisch's first cause-effect relationship was that most basic relationship in all of economics: the one between buyers' demand for a product and its price. Understanding the factors that determine product demand enables economists to estimate price elasticity of demand: the responsiveness of buyers to changes in a product's price. Information about buyer responsiveness to price change helps supplying firms set prices. A supplier of cell phones that believes buyers respond significantly to price changes, for example, is more likely to reduce than to raise price. A lower price will attract proportionally more cell phone users, so that the firm's total revenue increases. On the other hand, a metropolitan transit authority that believes riders respond very little to price changes is more likely to raise price. Commuters who depend on public transportation have no choice but to pay, so that the transit authority's revenue increases.

The earliest attempt to model consumer demand probably occurred half a millennium ago in Britain. Britain's Tudor and Stuart monarchs had provided food relief to their poorer subjects, but their royal successors abandoned such programs. Without sufficient nourishment, hard work in Britain's harsh climate brought widespread hunger and, ultimately, food riots. Gregory King was the first in recorded history to propose something like a demand curve to explain the relationship between the price of grain and the quantities purchased by the poor. Then, by combining demand for grain with the available supply, he was able to predict the magnitude of future grain shortfalls.

Although Britain's agriculture was probably more productive than agriculture on the European continent, her more unequal distribution of income brought widespread malnutrition, chronic illness, and diminished work capacity. Over time, improvements in agricultural production and increases in caloric intake increased the work capacity of British workers, bringing more lower-tier workers into the labor force and eventually contributing as much as one-third to Britain's industrial growth.[4]

Building Frisch's model of demand required, first, data on quantities demanded at various prices and, then, *least-squares regression* to estimate the relationship between price and quantity demanded. Least-squares regression was developed in the late nineteenth century and first used to analyze genetic data. In fact, Frisch himself used least-squares to improve the genetic quality of his own beehives. Least-squares regression creates the algebraic equation that best describes the cause-effect relationships between variables. It does this by minimizing the sum of the squares[5] of differences between actual data points and points determined by the regression equation—hence, "least-squares."

Econometricians' first attempts to estimate demand equations were not very successful. Pairs of price-quantity data collected at the same time clustered about one price but revealed no information about the entire demand curve. In fact, instead of revealing a complete demand equation, data collected at the same time defined merely the intersection between the current demand curve and current supply. Price-quantity data collected at different times might provide more useful information. But using data from different times introduces the likelihood that factors other than price might have changed as well, so that differences in quantity demanded cannot be attributed to differences in price alone.

To remedy this problem, econometricians use indexes or ratios to adjust data taken at different times for changes in other factors. For example, a general increase in all prices would distort the quantity data associated with every price. In this case, the econometrician would use a price index to express price relative to other prices—the process economists use to assure us that, even though our phone bills have gone up, the relative price of telephone communications has actually gone down. Another example would be a population increase, which would bring an increase in quantity demanded for most products whatever their price. In this case, the econometrician might express quantity in per capita terms, by dividing quantity data by population. Using indexes or ratios to standardize data preserves as nearly as possible the ceteris paribus (constant) conditions required to reveal the true relationship between quantity demanded and price only.

Even with all these adjustments, the early econometricians could not be sure that the data they collected truly reflected the cause-effect relationship of interest. In fact, their earliest estimated demand curves actually sloped upward, contrary to all their assumptions regarding buyer behavior. An upward-sloping demand curve implies that buyers purchase larger quantities when price rises, which would (if true) require a major overhaul of all economic theory—not a welcome prospect at all.

Ragnar Frisch helped to provide an explanation. The problem with econometricians' early demand equations resulted from incorrectly identifying the effect of the causal variable as quantity demanded. The true effect of the price change was quantity supplied.

Frisch dubbed the confusion over demand curves the *identification problem*. The problem arises from changes in factors other than price that cause shifts in the entire demand curve. If consumer tastes change for example, or if more families move into the market area or rising incomes enable consumers to spend more for all the things they buy, price-quantity data cannot be associated with a single demand curve. Price-quantity data collected after any such change in market conditions actually reveal points on different demand curves where each intersects with a conventional upward-sloping supply curve. To understand this point, visualize a conventional downward-sloping demand curve that intersects an upward-sloping supply curve that is relatively fixed. Then, over time, imagine that changes occur in conditions other than price that affect consumer behavior but are not adjusted for in the data. With changing market conditions, we would expect the demand curve to shift, revealing a new quantity at whatever price is shown on the fixed supply curve. These are the data, says Frisch, that the early econometricians mistakenly believed constituted demand. Whatever equations they estimated using these data describe not a downward-sloping demand curve but an upward-sloping supply curve.

To distinguish demand equations from supply equations, the econometrician must first determine whether demand or supply is more likely to be shifting or relatively fixed over the period covered by the data. If supply is relatively fixed, the econometrician concludes that price-quantity data indicate shifts in demand, so that the resulting least-squares equation traces out a supply curve. This result is likely to hold for certain types of manufacturing, where frequent changes in consumer tastes cause changes in quantities demanded but where quantities supplied are relatively fixed by manufacturers' relatively fixed productive capacity. Agricultural production may behave differently, with consumer demand for farm products relatively fixed for long periods and supply unstable because of changes in growing conditions. Over time, as supply curves for farm products shift about, price-quantity data describe purchases occurring on a fixed demand curve.

Eventually, econometricians included other causal variables along with price in their demand equations: all the many other factors that influence demand, such as consumers' preferences or tastes, consumers' incomes, numbers of consumers, or prices of other products. A demand equation for wine, for example, might include along with price the percentage of the population that emigrated from Europe, an indication of consumers' preference for wine over other beverages. A demand equation for DVD players might include along with the price of DVD players the price of DVDs. Estimating equations with more than one causal variable requires multiple regression, which is a bit more complicated than least-squares regression but may produce a more valid cause-effect explanation of demand.

Even multiple regression does not eliminate entirely the possibility that factors that affect demand are missing from the regression equation. Frisch acknowledges that every estimated equation includes errors resulting from omitted variables. So he includes in his basic demand equations an error term to represent all those factors that affect demand but are unknown (or unknowable) to the examiner. If it were possible to know and correctly record all the factors affecting buyer and seller behavior, Frisch asserts that it would also be possible to determine the exact cause-effect relationships between the variables of interest: the exact effect of a half-percent increase in mortgage rates on demand for new homes, the exact effect on employment of a million unit drop in demand for new homes, the exact effect of a percent increase in unemployment on the nation's total income, and on and on and on.

On and on, that is, until a business cycle looms.

It is this sort of connectedness across markets and across time that Frisch sees as the originator of business cycles.

Explaining Impulse and Propagation

A comprehensive business cycle theory would have to resolve the old mystery surrounding cycles, the mystery underlying impulse and propagation. In short, a correct explanation of business cycles would have to explain, first, the factors that initiate a cycle and, then, the factors that cause cycles to recur with some regularity.

To explain impulse and propagation requires distinctions as to the location of initiating conditions, whether inside the economic system (endogenous) or outside (exogenous). Frisch identifies exogenous shocks as providing the initial impulse. Then, he says, since buyer and seller responses to an exogenous shock tend to lag behind the initial impulse (by larger or smaller amounts), their responses cumulate into endogenous changes in spending, thus creating the cycle.

It is as if a rocking horse were occasionally struck by random blows. The horse's natural stability is disturbed following the blow, more or less so depending on the strength of the blow. But the magnitude of the disturbance is limited by the fixed structure of the horse. Although exogenous shocks occur randomly and with varying levels of force, a rocking horse continues to rock in roughly the same pattern. It can rock somewhat faster or more vigorously following an exogenous shock, but it does not rock so hard as to break apart or fly into the air.

The rocking horse analogy helps Frisch reconcile theory with actual data. The economic system is essentially mechanical, he says. Its endogenous structure creates a natural tendency toward regular fluctuations. But the fluctuations vary in intensity from rather mild to explosive, depending on the strength of exogenous shocks.

Frisch goes beyond his explanations of business cycles to recommend policies to correct them. Using econometrics, policymakers should combine the nation's preference function with data defining its resource base and in that way identify the economy's optimal future direction. Then, by implementing appropriate programs, government policymakers can help move the nation toward the goal of maximum social welfare.

Chapter 10
BALANCING REALISM WITH SIMPLICITY

The Dutch economist Jan Tinbergen shared the first Nobel Prize in Economic Sciences with Ragnar Frisch in 1969. Tinbergen also shares Frisch's concern for the world's "little" people, as well as his hope that improved understanding of business cycles can lead to policies that will improve economic efficiency.

Tinbergen is another of those economists who received an early education in mathematics and physics. As a student at Princeton he became acquainted with the world's preeminent physicist Albert Einstein. Eventually, Tinbergen changed from physics to economics, where he believed he could do more good for society. Tinbergen describes true happiness as understanding "all of a sudden" something you did not understand before. Perhaps he has trouble understanding sports and automobiles—for which he expresses a profound dislike. He enjoys music, however, and his rather unusual hobby is street cars (whether riding or collecting, I have been unable to discover).

Tinbergen builds on Frisch's investigations of demand to construct econometric models of supply. But, he cautions, it is impossible to understand either demand or supply without including in the regression equation other causal variables along with price: in the case of demand, income; and in the case of supply, costs of production.

One of Tinbergen's early regressions deals with the supply of beef and includes as a causal variable the price of livestock fodder. Tinbergen expected to find that an increase in the price of fodder in one period would increase the cost of raising cattle and bring on an increase in the price of beef in the next. He was surprised to find just the opposite: that a higher price for fodder actually brought a lower price for beef. How can this be? he must have thought—until he realized what must be happening in the market for beef. A high price for livestock fodder makes raising cattle so costly for many ranchers that they slaughter their stock prematurely and send larger quantities to market. The increased supply pushes price down. Hence, higher production costs, lower product prices.[6]

Reduced-Form Equations

All of which illustrates the challenges and opportunities we encounter when we attempt to translate the complex conditions found in the real world into simple mathematical equations. Unfortunately, the more realistic we make our models, the more complicated they become.

Tinbergen helped resolve the trade-off between realism and simplicity in econometric models by combining groups of mutually dependent equations into what he called a single *reduced-form equation*. A reduced-form equation shows how a causal variable in one equation can affect variables in other equations, in a long causal sequence: mortgage interest rates affect demand for housing, which in turn affects demand for workers, which affects wage rates, which affect income. Tinbergen's reduced-form equations compress much such information into a single equation—to the enormous relief of the econometrician who otherwise would have to solve many separate equations simultaneously.

For econometric models to truly describe the real world, Tinbergen argues, they must be made "dynamic." Although to noneconomists, *dynamic* means exciting, progressive, and infused with energy, this is not quite the way econometricians use the term. To an econometrician, dynamic refers to the fact that tomorrow's economic activity may be a response to events that occurred yesterday. Consider producers' demand for new equipment. We might expect producers' demand for equipment in year 0 to depend directly on the profits they expect in year 1. But expected future profits themselves depend on profits in previous years. Therefore, it is appropriate also to consider profits in year −1 as an indirect cause of producers' demand for equipment in year 0. Fortunately, there are statistical techniques that easily calculate the cumulative effects in one year of lagged causes in previous years.

Groups of equations that include backward-and-forward feedback across time are called *recursive systems*. In somewhat the same way that an echo reverberates back and forth across a canyon, recursive systems reveal immediate causes and their previous causes—and the previous causes of previous causes ad infinitum.

Explaining Aggregate Demand and Supply

From explaining demand and supply in a single market, it was a natural step to explaining *aggregate demand* and *aggregate supply*, demand and supply in the economy as a whole. Studies of aggregate demand and supply belong in the category of *macroeconomics* as opposed to *microeconomics*, which involves demand and supply in particular markets. Compare these functions to viewing the economy first through a microscope and then through a telescope. Solving an economywide econometric model yields an estimate of the output of all the goods and services produced in the economy as a whole, the value familiarly known as gross domestic product, or GDP.

Building an economywide econometric model requires three steps.

- Step one is to define the demand and supply variables that cumulate to determine GDP—consumer demand for new autos, interest rates on new home mortgages, international demand for farm exports, and so forth—and to state a theory about their cause-effect relationships.
- Step two is to construct the mathematical equations that describe the variables' cause-effect relationships. Most likely, the equations will include some lagged relationships and some relationships having backward and forward feedbacks.

Defining the variables and constructing the cause-effect relationships among them requires successive iterations—from step one to step two and back again to one until the equations duplicate as nearly as possible real economic behavior. Ultimate completion of step two yields a hypothesis, a theory that explains how variables within the model interact to determine the nation's GDP. To complete the model and test the hypothesis requires step three.

- Step three in building an economywide econometric model is to gather historical data and estimate through multiple regression the effect on GDP of each of the causal variables.[7] Then, to verify her estimated equations, the econometrician substitutes data from different countries and different time periods in her regression equations, and compares the estimated effects on GDP with actual GDP.

Admittedly, no system of equations truly describes the infinite complications that constitute a real economy. And solving any set of estimated equations yields estimated values that differ from actual values. The differences between actual values and values produced by an econometric model constitute the model's error. If in successive applications of the model the errors appear to be correlated in some way, this implies the existence of an important causal variable that is not included in the model. The econometrician may have to return to steps one and two and identify the omitted variable. If errors are not correlated, this implies that they are the effects of random, unknowable causes drawn at random from a normally distributed universe of unknowable causes. Errors resulting from random causes do not by themselves contradict the theoretical assumptions embodied in the model.

Tinbergen goes on to reduce his set of dynamic cause-effect equations to a single reduced-form equation. Through his reduced-form equation, he shows how changes in certain factors affect economic activity as a whole and how even small changes are carried along in time by a chain of related factors, with the result that a single change continues to be felt through numerous future periods, like an echo.

An Example

To consider just one part of Tinbergen's macroeconomic model, take his reduced-form equation for corporate profits in the current year

(year 0). The equation includes two sets of causal variables, the first set describing the effect on current profits of events in the current year, including the availability of credit, demand for new homes, farm income, and random events. The second set of causal variables describes the effect on current profits of events occurring in four previous years: years -1, -2, -3, and -4. Events occurring in the current year affect current profits through the first set of variables, and their effects are carried along in the second set of variables to affect profits in subsequent years. Thus, the second set of variables describes the endogenous consequences of the exogenous events that occur in the first set.

Indeed, Tinbergen's profit equation weaves together the two elements of business cycles: the basic economic mechanism (the pendulum, as reflected in the behavior of four previous years' profit) and the outside influences (the peas, as reflected in random events of the current year). Disturbances caused by random events and the cumulative effects of such disturbances make each business cycle different. Still, one mechanism links all these causal factors together to produce the current value of GDP.

Perhaps the most useful application of models like Tinbergen's is to forecast significant turning points in economic activity: the points when economic expansion changes to decline, when rising employment changes to rising unemployment, when slowing inflation changes to rising inflation. Conceivably, having identified turning points, governments could be ready with appropriate policies for affecting future economic activity. Unfortunately, Tinbergen shows that government cannot achieve a set of targets for specific economic variables (such as full employment, a stable price level, and balance in international payments) unless it employs an equal number of policy instruments (such as the level of government spending, tax rates, and the growth rate of the money supply). A single policy tool—perhaps increased government spending—might be effective for reducing unemployment, he says. But a simultaneous reduction in inflation would require an additional tool—say, reductions in the money supply.

The effect of this generalization is the "Tinbergen rule," which states that for every policy goal there must be a complementary, independent, enabling policy instrument.

Chapter 11

ACKNOWLEDGING
AND INCORPORATING
ERRORS

Until Tjalling Koopmans, also from the Netherlands, the standard econometric model was believed to be both causal and exact—in the language of econometricians, *deterministic*. Deterministic models are believed to produce a true regression equation which, when the true values of the causal variables are inserted, yield the correct value of the variable of interest.

Tjalling Koopmans doubts that many econometric models are truly deterministic. His contribution to economic thought has been to explore the errors that creep into all attempts to translate complex human behavior into simple mathematical relationships. (He might agree with the cynic who said, "Statistics means never having to say you're certain.")

Several sources of errors in econometric models are obvious: errors in measuring the causal variables, omission of certain causal variables (including some variables that might be unmeasurable), or incorrect specification of the cause-effect relationships among variables. Koopmans adds another source of error: the error the econometrician commits when selecting sample data from a large population.

Estimating equations and testing theoretical relationships normally does not require (and generally cannot accommodate) the use of every single piece of data. Instead of using every observation, econometricians work with samples drawn from a much larger body of data. The problem with using sample data is that certain characteristics of the population might not be contained one-for-one in the chosen sample, such that a cause-effect relationship estimated from sample data might veer off from the true relationship.

When the information used in a problem is uncertain, the usual remedy is to attach probabilities to the solution. The earliest econometricians were uncomfortable with the use of probability, however. The laws of probability are intended to apply only to repeatable experiments or controlled variations, and economic conditions are not repeatable or controllable. Economic data are not drawn randomly from a large population distribution either. (They are not drawn independently from the conventional urn containing black and white marbles.) Rather, data used in econometric analysis are associated with particular time periods. They behave cyclically, and they are affected by random shocks.

Koopmans admits all this but insists that the laws of probability are still applicable to econometric studies. He suggests that an entire sample of data, including many observations, should be treated as a single drawing from a large number of possible samples. (Each marble in the urn represents not one piece of data but an entire sample, one of the almost infinite number of samples that could be drawn from a single large body of data.) Whether the sample drawn has the same characteristics as the larger population depends on the size of the sample. In fact, with samples amounting to at least five percent of the population, there is a strong probability that the sample truly mirrors the data from which it is drawn. Depending on the size of the sample, econometricians can state a probability of, say, 95 percent that their estimated equation truly reflects the cause-effect relationship being investigated.

Tjalling Koopmans received the Nobel Prize in 1975 along with Leonid Kantorovich for their applications of econometrics toward policy for efficiently allocating scarce resources.

Projecting Optimal Energy Policies

A good way to learn econometrics is to have a job routing ships among ports for loading and unloading. Koopmans' early career experience with British merchant shipping stimulated his interest in using transport resources efficiently, identifying the costs associated with different routes, and choosing the least-cost way to move freight from here to there. From scheduling ships, Koopmans moved to policies involving the efficient use of the world's energy resources.[8] Making energy policy requires much information and involves relationships that overlap many disciplines. Such complicated interactions among so many variables offer many possibilities for error.

For deciding energy policy, Koopmans recommends the same optimization process the neoclassical economists use for maximizing personal welfare: that is, estimating the benefits and costs from successive units of a particular energy source and maximizing net benefits. To estimate benefits, he uses energy demand curves as reflections of the personal satisfaction consumers expect to receive from energy, now and in the future. (The prices consumers are willing to pay for energy are the best indicators we have of the personal satisfaction they expect to receive.) To estimate costs, he extrapolates the future historical trends in the cost of producing energy. He looks for a positive difference between consumer demand curves (benefits received) and firms' production costs (costs paid). Then he identifies any positive difference as net benefits, the benefits consumers enjoy from all present and future uses of energy over and above the costs paid. The optimal level for consuming a particular type of energy is the level at which consumption of one more unit adds more to costs than to benefits, thus yielding zero net benefits.

Koopmans extended his model of efficient energy use to forecast the likely effect on the nation's GDP of sizable reductions in energy supplies, and he was pleased to discover relatively small effects. In fact, his model projects the national economy adapting rather well to energy shortages—by improving equipment used for extracting natural fuels, for converting fuels to energy, and for transporting and using energy.

The ease with which consumers adjust to energy shortages implies a high price elasticity of demand, which means that gradually rising prices of energy will cause greater proportional reductions in quantities demanded. To the extent that individual nations can improve their efficiency for using energy, they increase price elasticity and reduce their dependence on the world's limited energy supplies.

Policy Planning

Koopmans argues that, with enough information and using econometric models, government policymakers can simulate actual markets and decide optimal policy toward other types of resource use, as well as energy. Hence he disagrees with the neoclassical economists' belief that only markets can allocate resources efficiently. The neoclassical economists believe that central resource allocation is not likely to yield efficient outcomes. Koopmans believes that central planners can respond to the price system just as efficiently as markets do.

Koopmans developed a technique for guiding policymakers toward efficient resource allocation, a technique that was also developed independently by his co-prize-winner Leonid V. Kantorovich. Kantorovich grew up in Russia's St. Petersburg at the time of the Russian Revolution. He began work in the plywood industry, where he was assigned the problem of cutting large pieces of plywood into smaller pieces that would minimize waste while maximizing the products' total value. He saw this problem as not very different from the problem central planners face when allocating a nation's limited resources for producing various products. For his advice to Soviet central planners, Kantorovich was awarded the Lenin Prize.

The Koopmans-Kantorovich technique for efficient resource allocation is called *linear programming*. While initially intended to guide central planners, linear programming also helps individual business firms plan the most efficient use of their available resources. Imagine a firm that can produce three products, X, Y, and Z, that yield unit profits of $.50, $.75, and $.90, respectively. The firm's objective is to produce the quantities of the three products that yield maximum profits. The obvious course of action would be to produce as much as possible of product Z, except for an unpleasant fact. The fact is that the firm has only limited supplies of certain resource inputs, A, B, and C, required in various amounts for producing all its products. X requires, say, 1 unit of A, 2 units of B, and 3 units of C, while Y requires 3 units of A, 2 units of B—you get the point. The problem is to allocate the given quantities of resources, A, B, and C, among the to-be-determined quantities of products, X, Y, and Z, so as to maximize profits (rather like cutting a single sheet of plywood into its most valuable pieces).

Linear programming begins by creating a set of inequalities: algebraic expressions that allow the use of resource inputs to fall short of the available quantity but not to exceed it. Using simple algebra, linear programming enables the firm to explore all the combinations of products that are possible within given resource limitations, rank the combinations according to profit, and ultimately narrow the decision down to the one combination that yields maximum profit.

Linear programming problems are typically solved by a computer, using a program similar to the one that enabled IBM's "Big Blue" to defeat world chess champion Garry Kasparov. Before each move, IBM's computer would evaluate all the possible moves, including all the opponent's possible responses to each move, and zero in on the one move that would move "Big Blue" closer to a win—a horrendous number of calculations for a mere mathematician but simple for a giant computer.

To move beyond production planning for a firm to planning for an entire nation, planners would first state the available quantities of particular resources in the economy as a whole, second, the quantities of those resources required for producing each product, and, finally, the price (hence, benefits to consumers) of each product. With this information linear programming can calculate the optimal combination of products within the production capabilities of the economy. Thus, with complete information about prices and quantities, linear programming can enable government planners to accomplish the objectives sought by the neoclassical economists: to allocate scarce resources in such a way as most nearly to satisfy the wants of the people—in other words, to maximize social welfare.

Chapter 12
PROBABILITY IN ECONOMETRIC MODELS

Truly understanding and correctly modeling economic behavior would be simple if people behaved like machines and were governed by known cause-effect relationships—as a rotary engine is governed by pistons and volatile gases. Unfortunately, understanding people is less like understanding machines and more like understanding weather. Certain factors are known to affect weather, of course: ocean currents, high-altitude wind directions, geographical features, and the like. But constancy in all these factors does not guarantee constancy in weather conditions. In fact, weather has such a wide range of causes that we can only state with some probability what will be the likely effect of known factors (contributing to our frustration when a 10 percent chance of rain turns out to be a record-setting deluge). Applying probabilities to econometric modeling is the contribution to economic thought of Trygve Haavelmo, winner of the Nobel Prize in 1989.

Contrary to first impressions, the effect of associating probabilities with econometric models is actually to strengthen them. Without probability, an econometric model might be expected to provide the "correct" solution to a cause-effect question. But however accurate the model's data and however precise its statistical analysis, its solution is easily undermined by the infinite variability of the real world. Indeed, no projections derived from econometric modeling can ever be precisely correct, given the complex circumstances the models attempt to replicate. Probabilities strengthen econometric models by bridging the gap between the econometrician's theory about how the world works and how the world really works.

The Philosopher-King

According to some students of econometrics, Trygve Haavelmo is the economist who comes closest in the modern era to Plato's philosopher-king. Perhaps Haavelmo's characterization as philosopher-king grew out of his broad vision of life on earth. In Plato's ideal society a wise and benevolent ruler decides the necessary policies for making society operate efficiently. Nothing could be farther than this from the neoclassical vision of a society governed entirely by ordinary men and women making decisions in their own self-interest.

The earth is home to five billion people, Haavelmo explains.[10] Cut off from organized human society, most of Earth's people could not survive more than a few weeks. To support the means toward human survival, organized society establishes rules of behavior. Changes in objective conditions require changes in society's rules, with appropriate changes in behavior.

Haavelmo visited the United States as a student in 1939 and, he says, for reasons beyond his control remained for seven years. (World War II was raging in Europe and discouraged a return to his native Norway.)

Under the tutelage of a world famous statistician, Haavelmo built an econometric model of the Great Depression. His model explains food consumption as dependent on prices and per capita income and concludes that in 1935, in the depths of the Great Depression, average food consumption was less than 94 percent of average food consumption a decade earlier. Similarly, real capital investment per capita was only 28 percent of its level before the Depression. In general, prices were only 70 percent of their previous highs and prices received by farmers only 67 percent, indicative of the severe stresses on income suffered by farmers and production workers.

Ultimately, Haavelmo also introduced econometricians to statistical *multicollinearity*, which refers to the possibility that some of the causal variables in a relationship are actually coordinated in some way, so that they rise and fall together. When variables are coordinated, their combined effect on the variable of interest may be easy to see, but it may be difficult to distinguish their individual effects. The more complicated are the relationships under examination, the more likely are the econometric results to be distorted by multicollinearity.

Somewhat prophetically, Haavelmo warns economists to be skeptical about their theories, for "whatever be the 'explanations' [of economic phenomena] we prefer, it is not to be forgotten that they are all our own artificial inventions in a search for an understanding of real life; they are not hidden truths to be 'discovered.'"[11]

Chapter 13

ARTIFICIAL INTELLIGENCE, EXPERT SYSTEMS, AND POLICY WONKS

Econometric methods are now being used in many aspects of economic life unforeseen by the first econometricians. Perhaps the most ambitious use is *artificial intelligence,* a term that brings to mind a giant computer that solves complex problems much as a human brain would solve them. A more down-to-earth use of artificial intelligence is *expert systems,* econometric models that duplicate the analytical thinking of experts in a particular field and simplify the process of choosing among alternatives. Even in government, variations of econometric models now help policy "wonks" design programs that ensure the most efficient uses of government funds.

Probably the most widely used examples of expert systems for routine decision making are the credit-risk models used by banks and other lending institutions to assess loan applications. Whatever information might influence a living, breathing loan officer to grant or refuse a loan are built into an econometric model for evaluating a loan applicant's creditworthiness. For example, information about potential borrowers' present employment, time at current address, marital status, and outstanding obligations affect their ability to live up to their loan agreement. By quantifying the typical effects of all these factors, the bank's credit-risk model can automatically decide whether to make the loan.

Expert systems are also useful for managing a bank's own credit risks. A bank's risk-management model includes information on such things as potential defaults on the bank's outstanding loans, credit ratings on bonds held by the bank, and current interest rates and trends in business profits. With a valid risk-management model, a bank is better able to decide the proper amount of capital to hold in reserve against an adverse change in business conditions.

In both these instances, instead of requiring living, breathing experts to evaluate every situation independently, lending institutions distill the experience of many such experts into a reusable guide to future decisions. Changes in any of the factors experts typically consider when making their decisions can easily be included in expert systems, automatically affecting the ultimate recommendation on whether to extend a loan to a new borrower or whether to add to the bank's capital reserves.

At the level of the national economy, econometric models can guide policymakers to the most efficient solution to broad policy problems. One especially pertinent example: education and the most efficient way to bring the nation's public education system up to a level consistent with the needs of tomorrow's workers. To do this requires an econometric model that links the costs of educational inputs with the value of educational output. Deciding the output to be maximized may be problematic in the case of education, since there is disagreement over the most appropriate measure of educational output. Improved test scores are a possible measure, if one believes that test scores are a true indication of the value of education. Improved earning capacity is another, if one believes that a person's ability to succeed in a job is indicative of educational value. Neither measure is perfect, of course.

However educational output is defined, the next steps are to identify significant causal variables and to use multiple regression to estimate the effects of each variable on educational output. With such estimates, the econometrician can project the consequences for educational output of, say, increasing teachers' salaries, reducing class size, or lengthening the school day or year.

Models that measure educational output by test scores typically use *cross-sectional data:* data from across a range of educational systems during the same brief time period. An obvious causal variable would be different school districts' per-student expenditures on education. Others are local students' family income and socioeconomic status, along with their parents' education and commitment to education. Unfortunately, all these causal variables are so inextricably linked as to make distinguishing their individual effects extremely difficult. One study that attempts to sort out the effects on test scores of per-student expenditures has found a consistently positive relationship.[12] In fact, a $2000 increase in spending per student has been found to increase test scores by more than one-tenth of a standard deviation, or roughly 5 percentile ranks. (Instead of ranking in, say, the 85th percentile of students nationwide, students rank in the 90th.) Another model that substitutes the student-teacher ratio for per-student spending has found a consistently inverse relationship, suggesting that reducing the student-teacher ratio by eight students increases average test scores by almost one-fifth of a standard deviation. This is equivalent to an average increase of 7 percentile ranks.

A problem with studies of this kind is the possibility of feedback from the effect of interest to the causal variables (from test scores to per-student spending or pupil-teacher ratios). Consider the possibility that low-scoring school districts might attempt to improve test scores by spending more on schools or by reducing the student-teacher ratio. In this case, the direction of causality would run the "wrong way," with lower test scores apparently causing increased spending or lower student-teacher ratios.

While test-score studies use data taken from a brief period of time, studies assessing students' income-earning potential require longitudinal data, continuous data that describe particular students during the 20 or so years following their high school graduation. Fortunately, almost 40,000 pieces of data are available for this purpose, describing more than 9000 students from almost 900 high schools across the United States. Econometricians use these data to estimate the effect of education on lifetime earnings, with special attention to the large gap between the earnings of high school graduates and workers with postsecondary education.[13] For studies involving income, causal variables include, along with years of schooling, all those other factors that contribute to earning potential—such things as students' family background and ability that may affect both years of schooling and potential earnings. The problem of reverse causality complicates this analysis, too, since persons who expect to earn high incomes are more likely to make greater investments in post-secondary education. The econometrician must adjust for such factors to avoid mistakenly giving additional years of schooling credit for increases in earnings that would have occurred anyway.

When multiple regression is performed on these data, the results show an 8 percent increase in annual earnings for each additional year of postsecondary education. When the results are adjusted to remove the effects of family background and ability, the increase in earnings drops to 6.5 percent, still an impressive rate of return on investments in education. The return on vocational education is smaller at 1.5 percent but consistently positive.

Some econometricians have used these same techniques to estimate the total return to the nation as a whole of the federal government's assistance to local education.[14] Their studies conclude that federal assistance amounting to $6 million over 12 school years that reduces a student-teacher ratio of 30 to 1 to 25 to 1 yields almost $30 million in added lifetime earnings. With an income tax rate of roughly 25 percent, the projected tax yield to the federal government is almost $7.5 million—suggesting that investment in education truly pays off.

PART 4
WHEN CYCLES BECOME DEPRESSIONS

Paul Samuelson • *Milton Friedman* •
James Tobin • *John Hicks* •
Robert Lucas • *Franco Modigliani*

For the econometricians to show that a market economy might tend inexorably toward business cycles was bad enough. To admit that an economy might collapse into continuing *depression* was even worse! Seemingly inexorable, unyielding, and unmerciful depression was the problem of the 1930s. Still, out of worldwide depression and economic distress emerged a revolution in thinking that changed the course of economic theory and policy for decades to come—indeed, perhaps forever.

Nineteenth-century economists didn't worry much about business cycles, focusing instead on economic growth: long trends in economic activity to which they believed economies would eventually return following short-term fluctuations around trend. They identified particular cycles by subtracting from contemporary economic data the effects of long-term trend, seasonal fluctuations around trend, and random events. Still, they were never able to construct a coherent theory of cycles or—more important—to prescribe appropriate policy remedies. Twentieth-century economists were compelled to study business cycles. In the 1930s the British economist John M. Keynes proposed a new theory to explain business cycles, one that drew upon the econometric model developed by Jan Tinbergen. Tinbergen's model explained how spending in one year is a response to events occurring in previous years: years -1, -2, -3, etc. Keynes extended Tinbergen's explanation to show how different types of spending interact to cause business cycles.

The Nobel economists in Part 4 took on the task of interpreting, applying, and critiquing Keynesian economic theory explaining business cycles, along with the policy recommendations that emerge from it.

Chapter 14

BUSINESS CYCLES AND THE UNEMPLOYMENT-INFLATION TRADE-OFF

Economics is full of paradoxes, situations that seem to defy logic: A banner crop year can actually make farmers worse off. An increase in unemployment may actually be good for the stock market.

The prolonged depression of the 1930s introduced another paradox that cried out for explanation: extreme want at the same time that resources capable of satisfying those wants stood willing and able to work. Padlocked factories, failing businesses, and idle workers were not at all the logical consequence of neoclassical economic theory. Neoclassical theory promises that free markets will "clear," equalizing demand for and supply of finished products and the labor required to produce them. This benign result seemed not to be happening in the 1930s, as inventories piled up unsold and workers languished in unemployment.

To bring relief to distressed workers and failing businesses required new explanations of economic behavior and, perhaps, new government policies to remedy the suffering brought on by economic crisis. World War II temporarily replaced concerns about depression with concerns about national defense. But after the war economists focused again on the problem of unemployment of the nation's and—even more ominous—the world's productive resources.

Government's first policy remedies were confused and cautious, especially so since the war had been fought to rein in too powerful governments. Although the fascist government of Nazi Germany had succeeded in reducing unemployment, it had also inflicted incalculable costs on its own and neighboring peoples, most notably in terms of the loss of personal freedom. Meantime, the communist government of the Soviet Union had promised both economic efficiency and political freedom but failed to deliver either. Even in the United States, the oppressive tactics of Congress during the McCarthy era brought home to Americans the possibility that a powerful government might threaten the freedoms of its people.

Thus a dilemma: While economic reformers warned of revolution unless governments were given more power to relieve economic distress, followers of Friedrich von Hayek condemned those same reformers for inviting tyranny.

Supporters and opponents of government policy toward business cycles have a fundamental disagreement: whether there is a trade-off between unemployment and inflation. Believers in the supposed trade-off see economies as fluctuating between high levels of production, with nearly full employment and rising prices, and low levels of production, with unemployment and falling (or roughly stable) prices. They illustrate the unemployment-inflation trade-off with a Phillips curve, first drawn by A. W. Phillips in 1954. Phillips plotted a century's worth of data linking Britain's unemployment with wage inflation and discovered an inverse relationship: low unemployment in a particular year typically associated with increasing wage inflation, and vice versa. Opposing values of the two variables gave Phillips' graph a downward slope, as shown in Figure 3.

The apparent link between unemployment and wage inflation suggests a link between unemployment and general price inflation, low unemployment generating high wage costs and prompting increases in the prices of finished goods. And vice versa, of course. Thus, some economists substitute price inflation for wage inflation on the graph's vertical axis and use the Phillips curve to confirm the supposed unemployment-inflation trade-off. If Phillips' inverse relationship between unemployment and inflation is valid, they argue, then an excessive level of either might be corrected by government policy.

Believers in the Phillips curve acknowledge that the cost of reducing one problem is most likely an increase in the other. Policy

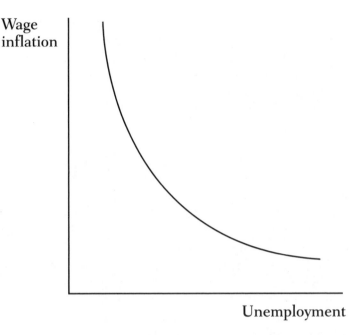

Figure 3

to reduce unemployment, to offer more workers more job opportunities, worsens tendencies toward wage-price inflation, while policy to reduce inflation so reduces the nation's total spending as to throw more workers out of work. If there truly is a Phillips curve, however, valid for all times and places, government might target a particular combination of unemployment and inflation that minimizes the pain associated with the two maladies taken together.

On the other side of the argument are the doubters, who question whether there really is an unemployment-inflation trade-off. Instead, say the doubters, there is a certain rate of unemployment that will prevail, almost regardless of government policy. The doubters tend to see the Phillips curve as not downward-sloping at all but vertical at a certain normal, or natural, rate of unemployment (generally between about 5 and 6 percent). They worry that the chief consequence of government policy to push unemployment below its natural rate is to push up inflation.

As confirmation of this view, the doubters point to governments' efforts to reduce unemployment in the late 1970s. In many of the world's industrialized countries, government policies to reduce unemployment pushed inflation into double, even triple and quadruple, digits, all without significant gains in employment.[1] Continuing inflation as high as 15 percent slashes our money's value by half in less than five years; continuing inflation of 1000 percent, in only six hours! The doubters' conclusion: For government to meddle in economic affairs is just too risky and should be discouraged.

Paul Samuelson Believes in the Phillips Curve

No economist is more exuberant in the practice of economics than Paul Samuelson. Samuelson describes economic analysis as play, not work, an "enchanted forest" that continues to delight with ever new challenges and opportunities. He facetiously dates his birth as the day he arrived at the University of Chicago to study economics.

Samuelson was awarded the Nobel Prize in 1970 and is perhaps best known as the world's foremost interpreter of Keynesian business-cycle theory and policy. He has had a long and productive career, having produced the textbook that introduced generations of post–World War II college students to economics. Let others write the nation's laws, he says, if I can write the textbooks. And indeed his introductory text has had wide political impact having been produced in 14 editions and having outsold every other economics book in history (4 million copies). It is used in more than a dozen translations all over the world. Through another major work *Foundations of Economic Analysis*, Samuelson brought the strength of mathematical logic to economics and in that way helped develop economics as science. Mathematics does not lie, he seems to say. He is a prodigious writer, producing an average of five scholarly articles a year.

Samuelson grew up during the Great Depression near the steel mills of Gary, Indiana. Steel production collapsed during the Depression, and Gary's steel workers joined the one-third of U.S. workers who couldn't find full-time jobs. Too many workers' families were starving, while farmers' crops were rotting in the fields. Samuelson was uncomfortable with contemporary explanations that blamed job losses on "uppity" workers, and he hoped that Keynesian theory and the policies derived from it would help restore the U.S. economy to full employment.

Keynesian theory begins by breaking down a nation's income into flows of spending from all its various spenders. Total spending from all the nation's spenders becomes sales revenue to business firms, whereupon business firms distribute their revenue as income to suppliers of resources used in production. The largest part of business revenue goes to workers in the form of wages; then interest payments go to suppliers of financial capital, rent to suppliers of land, and profit to the entrepreneurs who initiate production. Once income is paid to workers, entrepreneurs, and suppliers of land and capital, that income is available for new spending, forming a never-ending flow of, first, spending, then income, and, again, new spending and income ad infinitum.

The United States is a nation of high-spenders. Total spending in the United States passed the $1 trillion mark as recently as 1970 and climbed above $8 trillion in 1998. The increase in spending pushed median family income in the United States from about $10,000 in 1970 to almost $40,000 in 1998. Much of the apparently stupendous increase reflects only inflation, however, which reduced the dollar's value to less than a third of its earlier value. Family incomes actually increased only about a quarter between 1970 and 1998, in spite of the fact that more wives had taken paying jobs outside the home.

The largest component of total spending is consumer spending—about two-thirds going for autos and appliances, food and clothing, dental care, entertainment, and whatever else consumers deem appropriate for our modern lifestyles. As consumers, we decide how much of our incomes to spend for consumer products and how much to set aside in savings.[2] Our consumer spending goes first to businesses and eventually comes back to us as income, available for respending. Our saving is made available to business firms for investment spending for new capital goods, such as inventories, raw materials, machines, and component parts. One firm's investment spending becomes another's sales revenue, which also returns to us eventually as income.

For the nation's total income, employment, and prices to remain stable, everything we receive as income must continue to circulate as spending. Spending for new cars, videos, etc., must provide wages, interest, rent, and profit, which must be spent again—for more videos, air travel, whatever—if there are to be jobs and incomes for the nation's workers.

If we decide not to spend some of our incomes, ergo, to save, whatever portion of income we fail to spend for consumer products must be spent by businesses for investment goods. This is a rather startling pronouncement. It implies that our independent decisions to save must necessarily coincide with businesses' independent decisions to invest if income, employment, and prices are to continue at the same level. With investment precisely equal to saving, none of the nation's income flows unspent out of the spending stream, prompting job losses and unemployment. Likewise, with investment just equal to saving, no excess spending flows into the spending stream, creating inflationary pressures in labor and product markets. With investment precisely equal to saving, the nation's total spending and income continue relatively stable, avoiding—one hopes—either of A. W. Phillips' extremes.

Economists like to illustrate relationships metaphorically, and a plumbing metaphor is popular for illustrating the relationship between saving and investment. Start with an ordinary bathtub. Consider the level of water in the tub as total spending (and, hence, income). Saving is water flowing out of the tub, and business investment spending is water flowing in. Only if the flows are equal is the level of water in the tub stable. An excess of one or the other changes the level of water, and the changes are analogous to rising or falling income—with up or down movements in inflation and unemployment along the Phillips curve.

One reason for the neoclassical economists' indifference to business cycles is their confidence that investment will, in fact, be equal to saving. Investment and saving tend to be equal, they say, because of businesses' automatic responses to the interest rates charged for borrowed funds. If saving were temporarily to increase beyond investment, the supply of funds available for investment would exceed business plans for investment spending. But the effect of an excess supply of funds is for interest rates to fall, which reduces the cost of borrowing and encourages businesses to increase their investment spending until the two flows are equal. The reverse occurs if investment were temporarily to increase beyond saving, so that interest rates rise. In neoclassical theory, changes in interest rates and the responsiveness of businesses to those changes are part of the self-regulating process of the market system, adjusting businesses' investment spending to the available supply of saving so that income, employment, and prices remain stable.

The prolonged depression of the 1930s appeared to contradict this benign assumption. As savings flowed unspent out of the spending stream, incomes fell. Formerly prosperous workers peddled apples on street corners, and business owners sought relief from economic distress in suicide. Confidence in the self-regulating properties of a market system plummeted, and economists struggled toward a better explanation of national income. Here enters John M. Keynes. Keynes explained the relationship between saving and investment differently from the neoclassical economists, and his explanation constitutes the central core of Keynesian economic theory.

It doesn't make sense to suppose that high saving encourages high investment spending, declared Keynes, since high saving must mean that consumers are not spending very much and that new investments will not be very profitable. In fact, when saving rises above investment, it is more likely that business investment spending will fall further. When falling investment spending is combined with falling consumer spending, the effect is to aggravate the initial decline in spending and the ultimate decline in income.

Differences between saving and investment arise out of the quite different motivations of savers and investors, said Keynes—savers seeking future security, and investors seeking future profits. Different motivations call for different saving and investing plans. In Keynesian theory, the equality of saving and investment (a stable level of water in the tub) comes about not because of adjustments in business investment spending but because of changes in income and, hence, adjustments in households' ability to save. If saving falls relative to investment, for instance, high consumer spending causes incomes to rise until higher incomes permit saving to rise as well. More workers producing more products for more prosperous consumers can afford to save more. On the other hand, if saving increases relative to investment, lower consumer spending causes incomes to fall until at some lower level of income people are too poor to save. At that lower level of income, the lower level of saving is finally equal to the lower level of investment, so that income stabilizes. Not a very attractive prospect, but one that Keynes believed came to pass in the Great Depression.

The practical consequence of differences in saving and investment plans is unwanted changes in business inventories: high saving leading to unsold goods, gathering dust in storerooms and adding nothing to business revenue; low saving leading to stock outages and dissatisfied customers. Both circumstances prompt changes in business plans: the first, cutbacks in production, layoffs, and cancelled orders to suppliers; the second, the reverse. Both responses affect the nation's total income and its position on the Phillips curve—whatever you believe about its slope.

A casual review of inventory changes in the years immediately following World War II does suggest a correlation between large increases or decreases in business inventories and changes in the nation's income, employment, and prices. The correlation has weakened in recent decades, however, as new information technology has helped businesses manage inventories more efficiently. Indeed, the Japanese Kanban system enables manufacturers to order materials just-in-time, while bar codes enable retailers to keep inventories continuously in line with current sales. The effect is an almost immediate response to changes in consumer spending that probably helps smooth out tendencies toward business cycles.

The Cumulative Effects of Changes in Spending

Paul Samuelson's most important contribution to economic thought was to refine and express mathematically all Keynes' fundamental ideas and, most especially, Keynes' policy recommendations for correcting the instability brought on by differences between saving and investment. He begins with an assumption regarding consumer spending, the fairly reasonable assumption that the chief determinant of consumer spending is consumers' incomes. When incomes rise or fall, consumer spending rises or falls, too—not by as much as the change in income but by some fraction of the change, the remaining fraction added to or taken from accumulated savings. By spending just a fraction of changes in income, we try to maintain a fairly constant level of spending relative to our total incomes. And in fact, consumer spending in the United States has averaged about nine-tenths of take-home pay for the past half century, a rate of spending that is fairly consistent with our shop-till-you-drop lifestyles.

The fraction of a change in income that consumers spend is important in Keynesian theory because, while describing our individual responsiveness to changes in income, it also describes the tendency of changes in individual consumers' spending to cumulate into larger changes in all the nation's spending. Start with an autonomous increase in business investment spending—perhaps a decision among many firms to install new telecommunications equipment. Some firms' new investment spending becomes sales revenue for other firms' and is distributed to households as income. As their incomes increase, consumers increase their spending by the customary fraction of the change in income. Perhaps they upgrade the living room furniture and eat more of their meals out. The magnitude of the new consumer spending determines whether the initial increase in investment spending causes a major or a minor increase in production of new consumer goods. The magnitude of added consumer spending is especially critical when you reverse our example and consider an autonomous reduction in investment spending—this time, a perception among firms that they are overstocked with equipment relative to current sales. In this case, as fewer investment dollars flow into other firms and ultimately to households, fewer dollars are available for new consumer spending. Consumers postpone replacing the faltering refrigerator or getting Junior's teeth straightened. Again the magnitude of the reduction in total spending depends on consumers' tendency to change their spending with changes in income.

Our individual tendencies to respend part of changes in income determine the magnitude of business cycles. The reason is that one consumer's spending becomes another consumer's income, which that consumer also spends. Thus, a first round of consumer spending contributes to another consumer's income and a second round of spending, which contributes to another consumer's income and a third round of spending, and so on. The point is that an autonomous change in spending from any source can generate a series of changes in consumers' incomes followed by changes in consumer spending, with cumulating effects on the nation's total production, income, and employment.

The same effects occur in reverse, of course. If investment spending slows or stops, our incomes fall, forcing us to cut spending. This cut in spending reverberates negatively along a chain of many households. Following an autonomous change in spending and many rounds of spending changes, the final change in the nation's total income is the result of what Keynes called the *multiplier effect,* where the multiplier is determined by our individual tendencies to spend a certain fraction of an increase in income (or to reduce spending when income falls).

The higher our overall respending rate, the higher the Keynesian multiplier. With a rather high respending rate, increases in income prompt consumers to rush out and purchase improved home appliances, enjoy new entertainments, and flaunt new fashions, so that the nation's total income increases significantly. Or, when income falls, the reverse. Autonomous changes in investment spending (or in any of the basic components of spending) can produce explosive reactions (up or down) in consumer spending and incomes, a lesson U.S. policymakers learned in the Great Depression, when investment plummeted. From total investment spending of $16.7 billion in 1929, investment sank to $1.6 billion in 1933. In the meantime, consumer spending plunged by 40 percent, and national income to one-half its previous value!

Here we come to the moral of this story. It is that even small fluctuations in investment spending can cause wider fluctuations in incomes, with potentially disruptive consequences for business profits, job opportunities, and, in turn, the living standards of ordinary people. The disruptive consequences can be either too much spending and production or too little—"too much" and "too little" being defined in terms of the nation's available resources and technology. Whatever a nation's wealth of resources and level of technology, there are always limits to its capacity to produce more goods and services. If spending for new goods and services exceeds that limit, the usual result is upward pressure, first on wages and then on prices. Price inflation affects different groups differently, distorting the value of our incomes and adding uncertainty to all our consuming and investing decisions. Both effects diminish the ability of free markets to deliver the products we want. On the other hand, if spending for new goods and services falls short of a nation's capacity to produce output, the usual result is reduced job security, lower incomes, and poorer standards of living—not a characteristic of efficient markets either.

Government's Role in Offsetting Changes in Private Spending

If Keynes' interpretation of business cycles is correct, if cycles are caused by a gap between private saving and investment, then government can help remedy the problem, which is the ultimate objective of the Keynesian economists. By reducing disruptive fluctuations in income, employment, and prices, Keynesian economists believe government can help make the economy more efficient.

Allowing for government participation in the economy calls for two changes in Samuelson's model of national income: the first, to add government spending to total spending, and the second, to subtract tax payments from consumers' incomes. When we speak of government spending, we are referring to purchases of such things as military aircraft, highways, school buildings, police and fire protection. We are not including government payments to welfare recipients, unemployed workers, and recipients of farm subsidies. These payments are not regarded as spending until the recipients actually spend them; they are officially designated as *transfer payments*. Transfer payments are sometimes more quaintly described as "negative taxes," which is how they are described later in this chapter.

Not surprisingly, changes in government spending and taxes have consequences for total spending, income, and employment. When government purchases new military aircraft, incomes in the aircraft industry rise by the amount of the added government spending. Then, as workers in that industry spend the customary fraction of their higher incomes, the nation's total income grows by a multiple of the added government spending—whether more or less depending on our average respending rate. Subtracting tax revenues from income has less pleasant results, reducing consumer spending and reducing national income, again by a multiple of the tax paid.

Fiscal Policy

The use of government spending and taxes to smooth out the highs and lows of business cycles is called fiscal policy. Folklore tells us that *fisc* was the name applied to the basket the early Roman tax collectors carried about the empire on their tax-collecting rounds. All of which suggests the rather dreary conclusion: The more things change, the more they stay the same.

We describe fiscal policy as expansionary or contractionary. The first, increasing government spending or decreasing taxes to offset such unwanted reductions in private spending as could lead to multiple reductions in total income. The second, decreasing government spending or increasing taxes to offset unwanted increases in private spending that could lead to the reverse. In short, expansionary fiscal policy changes total income by increasing government spending and/or decreasing taxes, while contractionary fiscal policy decreases government spending and/or increases taxes.

Some fiscal policy is discretionary: determined at the discretion of the current Congress and the President. Decisions to change tax or spending laws are made by congressional tax and appropriations committees, with presidential consent. Deciding discretionary fiscal policy is generally a long and contentious process, best accomplished when elections are nowhere in sight and voters are preoccupied with other matters.

Other aspects of fiscal policy are automatic: occurring according to laws already on the books. Because automatic fiscal policy requires no new legislation, it can be accomplished more quickly and less contentiously than discretionary policy. Automatic fiscal policy occurs mainly through the structure of income tax rates, the main feature of which is a progressive tax rate schedule. A progressive rate schedule applies higher tax rates to successive increments in taxable income:[3] for the first $30,000 a tax rate of, say, 14 percent; for the second $30,000 a rate of 28 percent; for the third $30,000, 39 percent; and so on. (At one time the U.S. income tax schedule included 14 tax rates, the highest, 90 percent! Don't feel too sorry for the taxpayers who paid the highest rate, however, since it applied only to wages and salaries in excess of about $2 million, calculated in today's dollars.)

With a progressive tax structure, low-income taxpayers are subject to only the lowest tax rate, and middle-income taxpayers the lowest and middle rates. High-income taxpayers pay all indicated rates on the indicated amounts of income, with the result that they pay a higher fraction of their total incomes in federal income taxes than do low- and middle-income taxpayers. In fact, in 1998, the top fifth of income earners in the United States paid about 29 percent of their income in federal income taxes, the middle fifth about 19 percent, and the lowest, 5 percent. The top 5 percent of income earners, persons with incomes in excess of $100,000, received one-third of all the nation's income but paid one-half of all federal income taxes.

A qualification: Automatic fiscal policy is accomplished mainly through the progressive federal income tax schedule. But only about half of federal tax revenues comes from personal income taxes. Most of the remaining half comes from FICA, or Social Security contributions, paid mostly by low- and middle-income taxpayers. In fact, when the employers' portion of FICA is included along with the workers' contribution,[4] most taxpayers in these classifications pay more FICA tax than federal income tax. The effect is to make their total tax liability a larger fraction of income than is suggested by their income taxes and to make the federal tax system as a whole less progressive.

A rate schedule that taxes higher incomes at higher rates helps prevent wide swings in spending: by increasing taxes in greater proportion than the increase in income when incomes are rising and by reducing taxes in greater proportion than the reduction in income when incomes are falling. In both cases, the result is smaller changes in consumers' disposable income than in total income and, hence, smaller changes in consumer spending. By moderating tendencies toward wide swings in consumer spending, a progressive tax schedule helps moderate the cyclical behavior of income, employment, and prices.

A second component of automatic fiscal policy is what I described earlier as negative taxes: government payments that, in effect, transfer purchasing power from taxpayers in general to persons in particular categories. Negative taxes are officially known as transfer payments, the most familiar of which are welfare and Social Security benefits, unemployment compensation, and subsidies paid to some farmers. Like progressive income taxes, negative taxes have automatic consequences for disposable income, automatically increasing recipients' disposable incomes when the nation is on the downside of a business cycle and automatically reducing disposable incomes when the nation starts the upside. The reason for the difference is that more people retire, apply for unemployment compensation, or receive welfare benefits when business is bad than when business is good. Automatic changes in transfer payments help their recipients offset cyclical changes in income and, therefore, help moderate tendencies toward business cycles.

Here we find the core of Keynesian business cycle policy, as explained by Paul Samuelson. Keynesian fiscal policy calls for changes in government spending and taxes to offset autonomous changes in private spending. When private saving falls below investment, so that the nation's total spending increases faster than its capacity to produce goods and services, government spending should be cut and tax rates increased. (Or tax revenues should be allowed to increase automatically as progressive tax rates are applied to workers' rising incomes.) When private saving rises above investment, so that total spending is below the nation's productive capacity, government spending should be increased and tax rates reduced. (Or tax revenues should be allowed to fall automatically, as consumers' falling incomes are subject to lower tax rates.)

If one more allusion to bathtubs is tolerable, whenever too much water drains from the tub, government should pour more in, and vice versa. Sounds simple, doesn't it?

Of course, it's never quite as simple as it sounds, since both expansionary and contractionary fiscal policies have consequences for the government's budget: in the first case, yielding a budget deficit and in the second, a budget surplus. Ideally, according to Keynes, budget surpluses and deficits would alternate during the upswings and downswings of private spending, and there would be no long-term accumulation of government debt. If this does not happen, so be it. In fact, according to Keynes, changes in government debt are not as damaging to the economy as are wide swings in income, employment, and prices.

So Much for Theory—Now for the Facts

Which, of course, you have already figured out. You have already figured out, one, that budget deficits are easier to accomplish politically than surpluses, whatever the behavior of private saving and investment. And, two, that budget deficits build up year after year to an enormous government debt. Government borrowing in one year is repaid by borrowing again in a subsequent year, so that the federal debt of the United States has grown from less than $300 billion at the end of World War II to almost $6 trillion today. The commonly expressed outrage asserts that government debt currently amounts to more than $20,000 for every man, woman, and child in the country! The stupendous increase of the federal debt is mitigated by the even more stupendous increase of the nation's total income, however, so that the total debt, while 17 percent greater than the nation's annual output (GDP) at mid-twentieth century, is at the start of the twenty-first century 35 percent less.

About one-third of the federal debt is owed to trust funds of the federal government—chiefly the Social Security and highway trust funds—which collect taxes earmarked for particular purposes and purchase interest-earning government securities until the funds are needed. The remaining privately held debt is mostly (80 percent) owned by savers in the United States, so that interest and principal payments on the debt stay within the nation. (The average man, woman, and child in the country, therefore, also owns almost $15,000 of the debt.) The only out-of-pocket cost of U.S. government borrowing, then, is interest paid to foreign holders.

So, is government debt good or bad? The answer is—as is so often the case in economics—"it depends." It depends on whether government deficits enable the nation to become more productive and, therefore, better able to service debt. Or whether borrowed funds are used for trivial, short-term, expedient purposes, not contributing to increased productivity. It depends also on whether elected representatives have the fortitude to run budget deficits only under conditions indicated in Keynesian theory: that is, when private spending is low relative to the level required for full employment. Lacking that fortitude, elected representatives (pressured, to be sure, by the voters who elect them) tend to run deficits even in periods when private spending alone is sufficient to ensure full employment. The likely consequence of deficits at full employment is not to increase the nation's production of new goods and services but rather to increase their prices. History is littered with the remains of governments that succumbed to political pressures to cut taxes and increase spending, with insufficient attention to the consequences for inflation.

Keynesian Theory Comes to Japan

Like children who are urged to save more of their allowances, Americans are often urged to save more—to be more like the Japanese, whose saving rate is prodigious.[5] Perhaps because of their longer history, the Japanese are more accustomed than Americans to thinking about long years in the future and ensuring long-range security for themselves and their descendants. Japan's traditionally high saving rate means less spending for consumer goods and services and, therefore, less incentive for businesses to borrow for making investments, in spite of interest rates as low as 1 percent. A similar drive to save on the part of the Japanese government moves it to balance its budget—or, better yet, to accumulate a surplus—so that government spending is too low to offset low spending in the private sector.

With Japan's low domestic spending, maintaining a stable level of income and employment has come to depend on export sales: sales to foreigners of cameras, cell phones, video and sound equipment, and all sorts of gadgets prosperous consumers around the world want to buy. In sum, Japan's economic stability has come to depend on sales to consumers abroad rather than on sales to Japanese consumers. But reliance on export sales subjects Japanese firms to increasing competition from producers in emerging market economies: in particular, the newly industrializing Asian nations that have embraced modern technologies with a vengeance.

Meeting the competition from low-cost producers in emerging economies requires that Japanese currency be cheap enough to make Japanese exports attractive. And in fact, the Japanese yen has recently been falling in value, in part because Japanese savers have been selling their yen for dollars to invest in the United States. Who wouldn't, when U.S. businesses offer substantially higher returns than the 1 percent available on yen investments? Unfortunately, the cheap yen has made it more difficult for Japanese consumers to buy foreign goods, further worsening domestic living standards and reducing the ability of foreign producers to sell their products in Japanese markets.

Critics of Japan's domestic policy worry about that nation's tendency to oversave, which creates a persistent gap between saving and investment. Even with interest rates at rock-bottom levels, there is little incentive to borrow for domestic investment, so that the gap between saving and investment has been corrected by falling incomes. Over a recent year, real production in Japan dropped by almost 4 percent, with devastating consequences for Japanese workers and businesses. Worsening recession has reduced Japan's purchases from other Asian nations, as well as from the United States. When other nations are unable to sell their exports to Japan, their economies slow too, all of which threatens a widening of the recession that has paralyzed the Japanese economy.

To prevent the spread of Japan's recession, the U.S. government has urged the Japanese government, in general, to reduce domestic saving and, in particular, to increase government spending and reduce taxes. Shifting to expansionary fiscal policy would convert

Japan's government from a saver to a spender and offset the private sector's prodigious saving rate. While producing a multiple effect on national income, government spending for infrastructure, along with higher disposable incomes for Japanese consumers, would also improve the quality of Japanese life. Higher total spending would increase the expected profitability of domestic investment and encourage businesses to expand Japan's productive capacity.

But the Japanese government has steadfastly resisted U.S. recommendations. Why? Probably because of its entrenched belief in a vertical Phillips curve. If policy to increase spending in Japan sets off inflation, Japan's cell phones, cameras, and electronic devices would become less attractive to foreign buyers. With reduced demand for Japan's exports, more Japanese workers would face unemployment. The Japanese yen would lose further value, making it even harder for Japanese consumers to buy foreign products and for Japanese savers to buy foreign investments. Till now, earnings from investments abroad have been a major source of income in the face of the declining profitability of domestic investments.

How Business Cycles Can Perpetuate Themselves

Before leaving our discussion of business cycles, we might return to the question of impulse and propagation, first encountered by those econometric observers of pendulums and rocking horses. Along with 1972 Nobel economist Sir John Hicks, Samuelson extends Keynes' business-cycle theory to show how business cycles can be generated automatically in an otherwise stable economy. Whereas Keynes showed how a change in investment spending can begin a cumulating up- or down-swing in income, Samuelson and Hicks show how a one-time change in any of the various kinds of spending can generate a continuing series of cycles over an indefinite future period.

The Samuelson-Hicks explanation of impulse and propagation depends on businesses' normal responses to changes in sales: in particular, business investments in the new capital resources necessary for satisfying an increase in demand for finished products. To take the simplest example, consider an industry that on average requires for production materials and machines worth four times monthly sales. In a beginning month, industry sales are $250 million, and producers' stock of materials and machines is valued at $1 billion. Now assume a one-month increase in spending (consumer, business, or government spending—it doesn't matter) of $10 million. To satisfy the demand for finished products requires an increase in businesses' capital resources amounting to four times $10 million or $40 million. When firms in this industry add $40 million in new investment spending to the initial increase in spending, the effect is to increase total spending further, giving a boost to the next month's income. Let's suppose consumers respond to their higher incomes by spending a certain percentage of the increase.[6] Remembering the multiplier effect, respending a certain percentage of increases in incomes implies a third increase in total income. The multiple increase in consumer spending calls for another proportional increase in capital investment. Total income rises yet again.

The upward swing in income continues as long as monthly increases in sales of finished products are sufficient to require increased business spending for materials and machines. At some point, however, production and sales reach the economy's absolute limit, and investment spending falls. The effect of falling investment spending is: first, to halt the rise in income and rein in consumers' ability to spend; then, to bring on multiple reductions in income; and ultimately, to reduce even further firms' requirements for new materials and machines.

The downswing in income continues until firms' existing capital resources decline to a level sufficient to serve the lower level of sales. When businesses are finally forced to purchase new capital resources, the result is a multiple increase in income, with increasing consumer spending as well, so that the process we have just described repeats itself.

Perhaps it isn't too much of a stretch to compare cycles of capital resources with the cycles ecologists observe occurring in a particular animal habitat. Picture what happens when a new species of fish is introduced into a pond. At first the population grows lustily, until it reaches the limit of the pond's carrying capacity. At that point, enough of the fish must die without replacement, until the population shrinks to a level easily supported by the environment. Only then can the fish population begin to expand again, so that the whole process repeats itself, rather like a business cycle.

We call the tendency of a one-time change in spending to generate continuing business cycles the *accelerator effect*. Thus, the accelerator explains the up and down swings in investment spending brought about by changes in current sales. As the accelerator (which magnifies investment spending) interacts with the multiplier (which magnifies consumer spending), an economy can experience wide swings in production, income, and employment. The higher the value of the spending multiplier and the greater the capital stock required to satisfy demand for finished products, the sharper are departures from stable growth.

Samuelson's inevitable conclusion: A market economy exhibits natural tendencies toward instability. A system that tends toward wide swings in spending, income, and employment requires automatic and discretionary fiscal policy to smooth out the economic highs and lows.

Paul Samuelson has described himself as the economic profession's last generalist. And it's undeniable that his contributions to economics extend widely beyond the business cycle—into mathematical economics, economic growth, international trade, public investments, and consumer spending habits. Even so, Samuelson describes his career in economics as one in which he was "overpaid and underworked." He admits to a tendency to avoid unpleasant tasks, saying that he always "washes the forks last" since, if nuclear war breaks out, he may not have to wash them at all.

Samuelson acknowledges his accomplishments modestly, comparing himself to the old farmer who said, while spitting in the pond, "Every little drop helps." The economics profession is not as modest when describing his contributions to modern economic thought.

Chapter 15

WHEN GOVERNMENT INVOLVEMENT INTERFERES WITH ECONOMIC EFFICIENCY

Keynesian business-cycle theory and the implied fiscal remedies were too radical for U.S. policymakers during the depressed 1930s. Rather than expansionary fiscal policy, it was government spending for ships, tanks, and planes during World War II that finally routed the Great Depression and restored full production and employment in the industrialized world. At the height of World War II the U.S. government ran a budget deficit amounting to almost a third of the nation's annual income, and total federal debt more than doubled. Fears of a return to depression after government spending returned to normal led Congress to pass new legislation requiring government to use its power to maintain the maximum practical level of employment.

Congress' new legislation was dubbed the Employment Act of 1946, and it was not without opposition. Opposition came primarily from groups convinced that a market economy would, if left alone, automatically correct tendencies toward business cycles. Government involvement in the economy, through discretionary fiscal policy, could damage a free economy's natural tendency toward efficient, stable employment and prices. The chief opposition to government involvement in the economy is led by economist Milton Friedman, who was awarded the Nobel prize in 1976.

Friedman is another colorful economist who is excited and challenged by the study of economics. "What makes [economics] most fascinating," he says, "is that its fundamental principles are so simple that they can be written on one page, that anybody can understand them, and yet that very few do."[7]

Friedman was born to immigrant parents from a part of eastern Europe that later became part of the Soviet Union. His family, he said, never enjoyed an income sufficient to raise them above the poverty level. His father died when Milton was a child, and he financed his schooling from scholarships and from jobs as waiter and clerk. He says he was fortunate to be exposed to an education that combined strong emphasis on theory with practical emphasis on empirical analysis and real-world institutions. During World War II he worked for the U.S. Treasury, where he played a role in establishing the system of income tax withholding, an accomplishment that later caused him some embarrassment, since income tax withholding strengthens a government's power to tax.

Friedman had another humbling experience in another wartime assignment, when he was called upon to analyze the durability of certain metal alloys used in jet engines. The alloys had to withstand extreme temperature variations, and Friedman used multiple regression to estimate the suitability of various alloys for this function. Having performed rather sophisticated econometrics and identified the most suitable alloy, he arranged actual temperature tests to verify his results. To Friedman's chagrin, his recommended alloy failed within about two hours, a result that forever diminished his confidence in multiple regression for correctly projecting cause-effect relationships.

A Hands-Off Policy Is Best

To understand Friedman's opposition to discretionary fiscal policy, it is helpful to look at his position on government relief for flood victims—and, by extension, government assistance for victims of other types of natural disasters. Flood damage, he says, is generally the result of improper land use: locating homes and businesses on land subject to flooding. Low prices for low-lying land encourage buyers to locate there. But low prices for their land should also leave buyers with sufficient funds to purchase flood insurance or otherwise protect their property against flood damage. If government provides financial assistance to flood victims, owners of low-lying land will lack the incentive to take such action. The effect is, first, to encourage the location of homes and businesses on land subject to flood damage and, second, to increase the involvement of government in location decisions. Government involvement reduces the ability of free markets to allocate land resources efficiently. In effect, Friedman argues, government involvement encourages flood damage!

What is true of government programs to assist flood victims is even more true of government programs to affect income, employment, and prices. All such programs discourage the sorts of behavior that would automatically correct the problems the programs intend to solve.

Believers in the self-regulatory powers of free markets expect businesses to respond to changes in consumer spending by changing prices. When consumer spending falls and inventories pile up unsold, businesses can avoid cuts in production and employment by cutting their prices. Lower prices increase sales, eliminate surplus inventory, and encourage suppliers to resume production. The same automatic responses are true in markets for labor, since a surplus of workers (unemployment) causes workers to reduce their wage demands and encourages businesses to hire more workers. So says neoclassical theory, and so says Milton Friedman. In free markets, falling prices and wages offset declines in spending, without any need for government to get involved in the nation's spending decisions.

Of course, the reverse is true when consumer spending increases beyond the capacity of the economy to produce goods and services. Thus, in neoclassical theory, temporary adjustments in wages and prices offset unwanted changes in spending, so that real production and employment remain fairly stable—and all this without any government involvement at all. In fact, government's only responsibility should be to provide the proper supply of money for carrying on economic activity.

The Important Role of Money for Stabilizing Spending and Income

We define a nation's money supply to include ready spending power: primarily cash and checking accounts, which in the United States amounted to about $1 trillion in 1998. In general, a nation's money supply turns over at a fairly constant rate during any fixed period of time, currently about eight times a year in the United States. We know this because total spending in 1998 was roughly $8 trillion, so cash and checking accounts totaling $1 trillion must have been spent, on average, about eight times.

With a given amount of money and a roughly constant rate of money turnover, there is an upper limit to the amount a nation's consumers and businesses can spend. If there are increases in spending in some markets, along with shortages and price increases, there must be proportional decreases in spending and price reductions in others. Firms in the former markets will flourish, expanding production and employment, while firms in the latter markets will contract, releasing workers for other employments. Since price increases in expanding markets are offset by price reductions in declining markets, there is no general inflation.

When the economy is left alone to regulate itself, total spending will tend toward the level that yields maximum economic efficiency. The only role for government in such a system is to maintain a money supply proportional to the nation's productive capacity. As productive capacity grows, the supply of money should grow as well. But only so much as to permit spending to increase in line with fairly steady increases in the nation's capacity to produce goods and services. No more, no less.

Friedman's political objections to discretionary fiscal policy are even more compelling than his economic objections. Decisions about changes in government spending take time to effect, he says, and consumers' responses are delayed as well. Time lags between the decision to implement a particular government program and the program's intended effects make evaluating effects difficult. Was it last year's agricultural assistance program that boosted farm income or abundant rainfall during this year's growing season? Without an answer to questions like this, it may be difficult to resist political pressure for more such programs. Friedman agrees that tax policy can be implemented more quickly than other government programs—thanks to the withholding tax!—but tax policy is even more subject to political pressure than is spending policy. His main worry is that political pressure will come to play a greater role in economic policy-making than the goal of economic efficiency.

Early in his career, Friedman had occasion to present his opposition to discretionary fiscal policy to John M. Keynes himself. Keynes was editor of the *Economic Journal,* an influential publisher of economic research. Friedman submitted two articles to the *Journal,* and both were rejected for publication, a rather humiliating experience for someone of such acknowledged capabilities. Some years later, when the value of Friedman's scholarship came to be more widely recognized, Keynes atoned for his early rejections by granting Friedman a lifetime subscription to the *Journal,* which Friedman has continued to receive for more than 60 years—at a saving of about $50 a year.

The Federal Reserve Regulates the Money Supply

Changes in the money supply are effected by the Federal Reserve Banks, working through financial institutions to change the level of new lending.[8] New lending creates new checking accounts and, therefore, new money. For the first decade or so after it was established in 1913, the Fed was cautious in using its money-creating powers, and during the 1920s fairly steady money growth probably helped achieve overall economic stability. The Fed faced its first real challenge in the 1930s when, according to Friedman, it failed miserably. As consumer spending slowed and prices fell, business investment spending fell, too. The supply of money available for lending came to exceed businesses' desire for loans, this in spite of the fact that interest rates were plummeting. In neoclassical theory, an excess supply of funds to lend and lower interest rates for loans should have encouraged businesses to borrow for new investment. Regrettably, business conditions were so depressed as to stifle profit expectations and squelch incentives to invest. Lacking borrowers for available funds, banks reduced their lending, so that checking accounts (and, therefore, the money supply) fell by one-third. National income fell by half and prices by a third.

According to Friedman, avoiding the impending economic crisis required that the Fed continue creating money at the 1920's rate. Unfortunately, efforts to create money are successful only if businesses expect borrowing for new investments to be profitable—and a deteriorating business climate does not produce such expectations. Economists have a saying for a situation when attempts to create new money are thwarted by poor business expectations: "You can't push on a string." It is possible to reduce the money supply by reducing the lending powers of banks and other lending institutions—in effect, by pulling money out of the economy. But it is not possible to push money into the economy if no one wants to borrow.

Of course, the nation did eventually emerge from the Great Depression. Considered only in terms of economics, World War II substituted for expansionary fiscal policy, with massive U.S. government spending and massive deficits financed by borrowing. During the war and for some years after, the Federal Reserve Banks assisted the government in its borrowing by increasing the money supply faster than normal and keeping interest costs from rising. In a sense, the Fed surrendered to the U.S. Treasury its authority over monetary policy, an arrangement that was definitely not healthy for the long term. By the mid-1950s, the Fed recognized the danger of turning control of monetary policy over to a government so susceptible to political pressure, and it resolved to regain control. Since then the U.S. government can no longer depend on faster money growth to finance its spending programs. Indeed, a resolute Fed, determined to maintain tight control over money growth even in recession, probably helped defeat Presidents Carter (1980) and Bush (1992) for reelection.

Friedman's Concerns About Monetary Policy

Milton Friedman looks to money as the primary way to regulate economic activity, but he objects to what he calls a "naive" approach to monetary policy. In a period of recession, he says, the naive approach calls for "expansionary monetary policy," speeding up money growth to push interest rates down and encourage businesses to borrow, thus increasing investment and employment. In a period of inflation, the naive approach calls for "contractionary monetary policy," slowing money growth and allowing interest rates to rise, discouraging spending and restraining price inflation. Thus, the naive approach calls for frequent changes in money growth to offset unwanted changes in private spending.

Friedman argues that expansionary and contractionary monetary policy will not stabilize employment and prices but will in fact worsen tendencies toward wild up and down swings.

First, he says, expansionary monetary policy cannot reduce interest rates except for very brief periods. The reason is that lenders include in their lending rate a premium for expected inflation. Lenders want a certain "real" interest return, a return that more than compensates for inflation over the life of the loan. Therefore, lenders add enough points to their desired real return so that the "nominal" interest rate they receive includes expected inflation. If expansionary monetary policy increases expectations of inflation, lenders will add a higher inflation premium to the interest rates they charge on loans. The effect of a higher inflation premium is to eliminate whatever advantage to borrowers was intended in the faster money growth.

Neither is employment helped by expansionary monetary policy, declares Friedman. More critical than monetary policy for determining employment are the nation's technological progress, the rate of business investment, and the real cost of hiring workers. These are the things that affect levels of output and consumer spending, ultimately dictating the quantity of labor required for satisfying consumer demand. Indeed, the nation's employment is the result of millions of independent decisions affecting millions of private markets and requiring what Friedman calls a certain "natural rate" of employment. Expansionary monetary policy might temporarily push employment above the natural rate, he says, but the increase will quickly be reversed. When increased demand for workers pushes wage rates up, employers will find ways to conserve high-cost labor, so that ultimately employment will return to its natural rate.

If there is, in fact, a natural rate of employment as Friedman maintains, there can be no permanent trade-off between unemployment and inflation—in other words, no downward-sloping Phillips curve. If the Phillips curve is actually vertical, expansionary monetary policy cannot reduce unemployment but can cause such a surge in wage inflation that no more workers will be hired. Contractionary monetary policy cannot reduce employment either, but can cause wage inflation to fall while businesses continue to employ the same

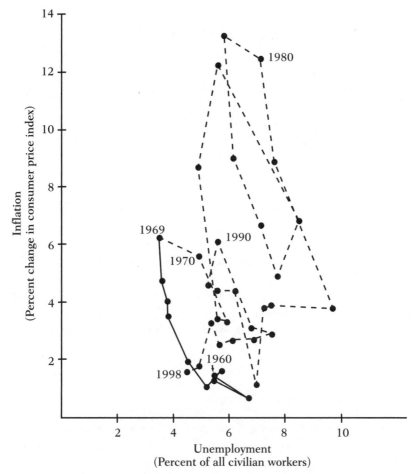

Figure 4   SOURCE: Economic Report of the President, 1999.

numbers of workers. Employment will hover around the natural rate, whatever the direction of monetary policy, a conclusion that is consistent with the neoclassical economists' assumptions regarding the other self-regulatory capabilities of a free market economy.

So many factors affect employment and inflation that it is difficult to make a clear judgment about the true Phillips curve. A graph drawn from U.S. employment-inflation data in the 1960s looks pretty much like the one A. W. Phillips drew. But in the 1970s and 1980s the U.S. curve traced a path more like that of the proverbial drunken sailor. In the mid-1990s the curve seemed to settle down, and by the end of the decade was looking rather vertical, a compliment to Friedman's expectations. (See Figure 4.)

To avoid unsettling the Phillips curve, Friedman recommends what he calls the *monetarist approach* to monetary growth. The monetarist approach avoids both expansionary and contractionary monetary policy but rather calls for steady money growth. Perhaps in an ideal world, says Friedman, expansionary or contractionary monetary policy might be effective for offsetting changes in market conditions. But since the real world does not provide enough information for adjusting policy correctly and efficiently, it is best to avoid changes in money growth.

Friedman goes so far as to suggest that regular, steady growth in the nation's money supply could be accomplished without Federal Reserve Banks—with only a giant computer program that automatically increases the money-creating power[9] of the nation's banks and other lending institutions as our nation's productive capacity increases. Supposedly, a mechanical process for increasing the money supply would be immune from the political pressures that might otherwise distort the decisions of the Federal Reserve.

Chile's Economic Miracle

Milton Friedman is among those rare economists who have enjoyed the opportunity to see their ideas about economic policy actually implemented in the real world. A military coup in Chile in 1973 put in power General Augusto Pinochet at a time when Chile's economy was in shambles, with both widespread unemployment and rampant inflation. Pinochet's military government called upon members of the "Chicago school" of economists, Friedman in particular, for advice about curing the nation's economic ills. Friedman's first advice was what he called *shock therapy,* significant cuts in government programs and the money growth that had been required to finance them. Such drastic changes were intended to reduce the role of government and restore the dominance of free markets for making economic decisions.

While successfully cutting inflation in half, reductions in government spending and money growth also brought severe recession and a 13 percent drop in Chile's national income. After five years of stagnation, however, Chile's economy surged ahead in what observers

called an "economic miracle," and Friedman's shock therapy was proclaimed a success. It was deemed so successful that Chile's monetary
authorities decided to peg the Chilean currency to the U.S. dollar:
that is, to limit money growth to the quantity of dollars Chile could
earn through its exports. Limiting the supply of Chile's currency
caused its value to increase, as desired, but the currency's increased
value also made Chile's exports more costly to foreign buyers, as not
desired. The resulting loss of export sales brought on a new recession
and, ultimately, the overthrow of Pinochet's military government.
Nevertheless, Chile's economy today remains one of the healthier
economies of Latin America.

The Debate Between Fiscal and Monetary Policy

The debate between Paul Samuelson and Milton Friedman boils
down to a debate over the relative effectiveness of fiscal policy and
monetary policy. The effectiveness of fiscal policy depends on the
Keynesian multiplier, which converts changes in government spending and taxes to changes in national income. For fiscal policy to
achieve its objectives, the spending multiplier must be measurable
and stable. A measurable, stable multiplier provides the information
policymakers need to determine the precise change in government
spending or taxes that is needed to yield the desired change in
national income.

According to Milton Friedman, the Keynesian spending multiplier
is not stable, so that fiscal policy can never be precisely correct. First,
he says, consumer spending depends not so much on current income
as on our expected permanent income—the lifestyle we expect to
enjoy during an entire lifetime of work. Temporary changes in income
do not affect permanent income and, therefore, do not affect consumer spending. In fact, the principal effect of temporary changes in
income is not on spending but on saving, a short-term increase in
incomes bringing on an increase in current saving, and a decrease
bringing on a decrease. If temporary changes in income affect only
saving, the effect is to change the nation's average respending rate in
the opposite direction from the change in fiscal policy, diminishing or
eliminating entirely its effectiveness.

The effectiveness of monetary policy, on the other hand, depends
on the rate at which the available money supply is spent: the rate of

money turnover. To achieve regular, steady increases in total spending, an increase in the money supply must not be offset by a decrease in money turnover. Happily, according to Milton Friedman, money turnover tends to be more stable than consumers' respending rate and the multiplier derived from it.

Consider this explanation. Money turnover depends on two kinds of payments: consumers' payments for consumer purchases and businesses' payments to workers and suppliers. Both types of payments change with changes in economic conditions and institutions, but the change is likely to be slow and predictable. An economy dominated by agriculture, for example, makes payments fewer times during the course of a year than an economy with debit cards and electronic funds transfer. It is natural that money turnover should increase during the transition from the former to the latter. But such a transition does not occur overnight, so that for purposes of current monetary policy, money turnover is virtually constant. Or so says Milton Friedman.

With a fairly constant rate of money turnover, changes in the money supply can be calibrated correctly to achieve fairly steady increases in total spending and income. Under such conditions, says Friedman, monetary policy becomes a more dependable means than Keynesian fiscal policy to achieve stable employment and prices.

Friedman's money-supply rule would allow the money supply to grow only in line with increases in productive capacity. With resource supplies in the United States growing at about 1.5 percent annually and with technological progress increasing resource productivity by about 2 percent, total production in the United States can grow about 3.5 percent a year. Increasing the nation's money supply between 3 and 4 percent annually would provide just enough spending power to purchase all of the nation's newly produced goods and services, thus avoiding either unemployment or inflation.

Bring on the giant, money-creating computer!

Communications Technology and Money Turnover

All this depends on stable (or at least predictable) money turnover, however. In 1998 money turnover was about eight times during the year. Why? What determined our decisions to turn over our money holdings at that rate, and what made decisions in 1998 different from or the same as decisions in prior years? Arbitrary changes in money turnover disturb the link between steady money growth and the full-employment, noninflationary level of total spending.

In fact, annual money turnover almost doubled during the 1960s and 1970s, rising from less than four in 1960 to reach seven at the beginning of the 1980s. (Calculating money turnover is simple. Just divide the year's total spending, or GDP, by the year's average money supply, and the answer is the average number of times each dollar was spent.) The rapid increase in annual money turnover in the 1970s is generally attributed, first, to that period's unusually high inflation and, second, to the steps ordinary men and women take to protect themselves against inflation.

Holding onto money is foolish in inflation, since the value is constantly eroding. Rational people turn money over fairly quickly in inflation, as the German people did in the 1920s when inflation eroded the value of the deutsch mark to 1/400,000,000,000,000, 000,000,000 of its former value. Rampant inflation drove German workers to insist on being paid before noon of every workday so that they could use their lunch breaks to spend their deutsch marks before they lost further value. Instead of holding idle money in inflation, people want to buy something whose value increases by enough to offset the decrease in the value of money. For at least one German this meant pianos, and he accumulated dozens. For most Americans in the 1970s this meant financial assets, which are easier to store than pianos! Today we protect against inflation by shifting our money out of non-income-earning cash and checking accounts and into financial instruments that earn interest or dividends. Then the sellers of these financial instruments use our (otherwise idle) money to operate their businesses—all in all, adjustments that increase money turnover.

During the 1970s, the public's demand for protection against inflation encouraged financial institutions to create alternatives to cash holdings. Mutual fund shares, options and futures, and shares in securitized mortgage pools are the most familiar new financial instruments, appealing to small savers, professional traders, and institutional investors, respectively.[10] Improved communications technology has made it possible to exchange financial instruments quickly and easily, enabling Americans in the 1970s continuously to adjust their money holdings to suit their current requirements. By creating such attractive alternatives to cash and checking accounts, financial innovations contributed mightily to the exceptional increase in money turnover in the decade leading up to the 1980s.

And this is where we meet the Nobel economist most associated with money turnover, James Tobin.

Chapter 16

HOLDING MONEY IS THE REVERSE OF MONEY TURNOVER

If economists were certain Friedman's steady-money-growth rule would guarantee economic stability, they could put their feet up and declare their economic theorizing done. Don't expect this to happen. In fact, for Friedman's rule to successfully stabilize total spending, the rate of money turnover must not change (or must change so predictably that money growth can be changed in the opposite direction to accommodate it). When we consider the changeability and unpredictability of human behavior, we are not surprised to hear Friedman's steady-money-growth rule challenged.

Examining people's decisions regarding money turnover absorbed the attention of economist James Tobin, Nobel laureate of 1981.

Tobin describes economics as a fascinating intellectual challenge, somewhat like mathematics or chess, he says, but even more exciting because it has the potential for affecting political decisions. He recalls as a Harvard undergraduate being "drawn into economics when [Keynesian] Theory was an exciting revelation for students hungry for explanation and remedy of the Great Depression." Keynesianism was not accepted readily at Harvard, however; Tobin's professors actually dividing nine to two in opposition.

Following the U.S. entry into World War II Tobin enlisted in the U.S. Navy, and in Naval ROTC he became friends with the novelist-to-be Herman Wouk. In Wouk's popular novel *The Caine Mutiny*, Tobin appears as the midshipman Tobit, who was said to have a "mind like a sponge," a phrase that describes the actual Tobin yet today.

Tobin is a quiet, gentle man, with an "Irish twinkle" in his eyes. He says he enjoys fishing, dancing and jazz, skiing, and boating. In his rumpled tweed jackets and calm professorial demeanor, he exudes a strong sense of virtue and civic duty. At Yale, Tobin is credited with building the leading center for economics in North America.

Money and Other Financial Assets

Our decisions regarding money turnover—to spend it—are the reverse of our decisions to hold it. The rate of money turnover, is, therefore, the reverse of our desire to hold cash and checking accounts. If our desire to hold cash and checking accounts is constant—a rather large "if"—then the rate of money turnover is also constant. If money turnover is constant, then fairly steady growth of the nation's money supply, along with fairly steady growth in productive capacity, will yield stable employment and prices. This is the necessary assumption underlying Friedman's steady-money-growth rule.

To hold more (or less) money does not mean that we are more (or less) wealthy. It means that we have decided to hold more (or less) of our total wealth in the form of cash and checking accounts, with less (or more) in the form of other types of assets. The cost of holding money is the opportunity we give up by not using the money to purchase an income-earning asset. By buying a corporate bond, for instance, we transfer our cash or checking account to a corporation that can use it productively. The corporation pays us a return for the use of our money that is commensurate with the productivity the corporation gains through its use. Other financial assets pay other forms of income: short- and long-term government securities pay interest, and stocks pay dividends or capital gains from price appreciation. The returns on income-earning assets constitute the "opportunity cost" of holding wealth in the form of idle cash and checking accounts, rather than using our money to purchase stocks, bonds, and government securities.

(Apparently Tobin himself is indifferent to wealth and its trappings. When informed of the Nobel Prize and its substantial financial award, Tobin's wife indicated an expectation that they would probably use the money to buy him a new bicycle and rent a television set to watch the World Series.)

There is a downside to holding income-earning assets, of course. Although we enjoy the income, we also give up a certain amount of convenience that comes from holding money. The convenience of holding money for making transactions is called *liquidity*. Thus, our decision to hold cash and checking accounts depends on a comparison between, on the one hand, the income we give up when we hold our wealth in a non-income-earning form and, on the other hand, the liquidity we give up when we hold stocks and bonds. The greater the earnings we stand to gain, the more willing we are to give up liquidity. And vice versa, of course.

Tobin began his career working for the U.S. government during World War II, making statistical forecasts of civilian demand for commodities needed in defense production. His investigations into the civilian demand for steel naturally led him into investigations of demand for other things and, ultimately, the allocation of household income between spending and saving. By combining cross-sectional data from family budget surveys with time-series data on total spending, he was able to show the effects on consumer spending of long-run changes in income, wealth, and other variables. From these early investigations, it was a logical move to investigate the effectiveness of various policies to affect spending: specifically, the effectiveness of Keynesian fiscal policy versus Friedman's monetary policy for correcting business cycles.

The Market for Money

We might think of Tobin's monetary theory as focusing on money demand—the public's desire for liquidity—while Friedman's focuses on money supply—the current quantity of money and its rate of growth. Tobin's theory explains people's demand for money similarly to explanations of demand for other things. Both kinds of demand depend on costs, and the cost of holding money is the income we give up when we hold a non-income-earning asset. If the return on income-earning assets is low, the cost of holding idle money is low and we want to hold more of it than if the return on income-earning assets is high.

Suppose the Federal Reserve accepts Friedman's steady-money-growth rule, increasing the money supply by, say, 3.5 percent a year. Some of each year's added money will go into our desired holdings of cash and checking accounts. Typically, we need more money every year to pay for ordinary consumer purchases, which increase fairly steadily with our fairly steadily rising incomes. Beyond the amount we need for making ordinary payments, we use the increased supply of money to purchase income-earning assets issued by businesses. Businesses use our money for paying workers and suppliers and for making productive investments. If all these money holdings increase at a steady rate, well and good. We continue to hold the same portion of income in the form of money and, consequently, money turnover doesn't change.

A business cycle can change these placid relationships of course, but not so much as to worry Milton Friedman. If spending should speed up or slow down, he says, automatic adjustments will go to work to change money turnover and stabilize total spending. Consider first a booming economy, with too much spending and threats of inflation. Our increased payment needs increase our desired money holdings and reduce the amount available for purchasing income-earning assets. With less money available for buying corporate stocks and bonds, the required rate of return on business investments increases and discourages business investment spending. Money turnover falls, total spending returns to normal, and the inflation threat subsides. The opposite adjustments occur in recession. In both cases, steady money growth and automatic changes in money turnover correct tendencies toward business cycles—all without any active government involvement to change money growth.

Not to be too argumentative about it (which is not his style) Tobin sees a problem with Friedman's benign conclusion. The problem results from Friedman's expectation that in recession we will use more of our money to purchase income-earning assets. Imagine the thought processes that would accompany this decision. Total spending is lower than required for full employment. Incomes are falling. Layoffs are imminent. Are you going to be in a rush to shift your wealth into corporate stocks and bonds? Especially if stocks and bonds are paying lower returns? Aren't you more likely to reduce your risks by holding onto your cash and checking accounts? If you behave as Tobin expects, you will hold more of your money idle, so that money turnover does not increase to correct the cyclical decline in spending. Perversely, money turnover may even fall. (Money turnover did fall in the recession of 1991.) If money turnover falls in recession, steady growth in the money supply cannot work to stabilize spending and prevent unemployment.

Tobin worries that there might be a certain low rate of return on income-earning assets at which people will no longer part with liquidity, in view of the risk associated with holding stocks and bonds. Whatever additions to the money supply policymakers achieve in recession will not go for purchasing other financial assets at lower rates of return but will be added to idle cash and checking accounts. Idle cash and checking accounts provide no stimulus to business investment—and make no contribution toward the Fed's objective of increased total spending.

We call the responsiveness of people's money holdings to changes in the rate of return on income-earning assets the *interest elasticity of money demand.* More generally, it is the percentage increase in cash and checking accounts associated with each percentage decrease in the rate of return on income-earning assets. James Tobin's fundamental contribution to monetary theory and policy was to investigate the interest elasticity of money demand as a means toward understanding the potential effectiveness of Friedman's steady-money-growth rule. If the demand for money is relatively interest elastic, he says, money holders respond to reductions in the rate of return on interest-earning assets by holding more idle cash and checking accounts. In recession, it would be most helpful for people to shift their idle money into income-earning assets, to put downward pressure on interest rates and encourage businesses to borrow and spend. But if people's demand for money is relatively interest elastic, any decrease in interest rates will cause them to increase their holdings of idle cash and checking accounts. With more idle money holdings, the rate of money turnover falls, and total spending remains at recessionary levels.

Tobin described a relatively high interest elasticity of demand for money as a "liquidity trap," an infinite increase in people's desire to hold readily spendable cash and checking accounts, versus holding other more risky and less liquid financial assets. People's preference for holding cash and checking accounts is likely to increase with declining business conditions, he says, particularly with rising unemployment, increasing job losses, falling business profitability, and growing business failures. These are the very conditions that the Fed attempts to correct with a steady-money-growth rule.

In general, economists have found little evidence to confirm the existence of a liquidity trap. Actually, people's desire to hold idle money has shrunk over recent years, mostly in response to new opportunities for earning a return on other financial assets: including, for example, more widespread stock ownership, pension fund shares, insurance savings programs, and participation in mutual funds. Until the 1980s, Federal Reserve regulations prohibited banks from offering such opportunities to their depositors. When banking regulations were relaxed in 1980, bank depositors demanded more income-earning opportunities for their money. The result has been a dramatic drop in cash and checking accounts (relative to total income) and a marked increase in annual money turnover—climbing almost to eight by 1998, as we have noted.

While increasing the rate of return on our money, new types of financial assets have made more difficult the Fed's job of projecting money turnover and planning the efficient growth rate for the money supply.

Synthesizing and Simplifying a Raft of Macroeconomic Theory

At this point in our discussion, having explored the rather complex theories underlying business cycles and policy, we may feel the need for simplification and synthesis. British economist John Hicks is a synthesizer. His chief contribution to economic theory has been to assemble the various explanations of business cycles and business cycle policy and combine them into a coherent whole.

Hicks's synthesis suggests that both Keynes and Friedman have made important contributions to our understanding of business cycles. Both theories are correct in their fundamental requirements. For income to remain stable, saving must equal investment (Keynes); at the same time the money supply must satisfy money demand (Friedman). Otherwise, buyers and sellers, lenders and borrowers will change their behavior to correct the imbalance, changing income and interest rates in the process. The effect can be either too much spending and inflation or too little spending and unemployment—either of which might call for remedial government policy.

Hicks himself is rather tolerant of government involvement in the economy. For an economy to enforce a no-government rule, he says, it would have to have perfect markets, with perfect competition, perfect information, perfect resource and product mobility—conditions that never were and never will be. "It is useless," he continues, "to close one's eyes to the defects of competition because one is so much in love with an ideal competitive system, set up in heaven."[11]

A noninflationary, full-employment economy is not the inevitable result of automatic adjustments in free markets, declares Hicks. In fact, whether an economy reaches high or low employment depends on millions of individual decisions in millions of independent product and money markets. In product markets, buyers and sellers are constantly interacting, equating demand and supply for many thousands of products and arriving at market-clearing prices. The effect of product-market behavior is a particular level of total spending and a level of income that equates saving with investment. Whatever the ultimate level of spending, it may not be the level that ensures full employment without inflation. Likewise, in money markets, millions of borrowers and lenders are constantly interacting to equate demand for money with the money supply and arriving at a market-clearing price, the interest rate. It may not be the interest rate that encourages businesses to invest precisely the amount that ensures full employment without inflation.

Chapter 17

THE PERVERSE EFFECTS OF EXPECTATIONS

E conomists propose theories for explaining economic activity, and they derive policies for modifying it. Even dedicating the finest minds toward explaining economic activity, however, cannot guarantee a definitive prescription for curing society's economic ills. Again, and not to belabor the point, because their subject is society, economists cannot make use of the kinds of laboratories that in the physical sciences permit controlled experiments proving (or, more correctly, failing to disprove) the conclusions that emerge from their theories.

Without laboratories, one way to test economists' theories is to invite competition among theories. Just as we rely on competition in product markets to encourage innovative technologies, we rely on competition among economic theories to encourage innovative thinking and enrich understanding. Such a fundamental revolution as the Keynesian revolution was bound to encourage much innovative thinking. While the Keynesian revolution supported an active role for government in economic affairs, competing theories arose to undermine confidence in government's ability to improve economic performance.

One body of opposition has attacked the fundamental method of Keynesian economics: its focus on aggregate behavior. These critics charge that the Keynesian focus on total consumption, investment, employment, and inflation ignores behavior in individual markets. For more accurate information on aggregate behavior, they argue, one must look first at behavior in individual product markets, labor markets, and money markets. In the jargon of economics: To understand macroeconomic behavior, it is necessary first to understand its microeconomic foundations.

The standard bearer of this movement is economist Robert E. Lucas, Jr. Lucas received the Nobel Prize in 1995 for pointing out the implications of people's expectations for the success or failure of government's economic policy.

Lucas grew up in a political family and perhaps learned early in life the value of logical argument for understanding social phenomena. He is unstinting in his contempt for Keynesian economics, deploring "the obstinate resistance to evident fact described by Keynes, and repeated as 'history' by two or three generations of Keynesians."[12] In effect, Lucas advocates a return to the business cycle investigations of some of Keynes' predecessors, those nineteenth-century economists who described business cycles in terms of society's attitudes and institutions. We need to identify the institutional sources of business cycles, Lucas says, and make whatever changes in society's institutions are essential for economic stability. By promising temporary gains in employment, he goes on, Keynesian policies divert attention from policies that would more effectively guarantee stability in the long run.

The better way to stabilize economic activity, he says, is to allow wages and prices to rise or fall, whichever is required to balance demand with supply. Unless wages are allowed to fall in recession, demand for labor can fall short of supply, with the result that workers can't find jobs. Likewise, unless prices are allowed to fall, the demand for new products can fall short of supply, with the result that inventories pile up and businesses have to cut production. The reason wages and prices do not often fall is society's institutions: its labor unions, business associations, and—worst of all—government programs. By preventing wages and prices from falling, such institutions perpetuate imbalance in labor and product markets and worsen tendencies toward business cycles.

Lucas disagrees as well with the Keynesian conclusion that the unemployment and inventory accumulation that result from market disequilibria are involuntary. If workers are without jobs and inventories are piling up, he argues, the reason is the voluntary decisions of participants in those markets. He explains his reasoning using a concept introduced by John Muth in 1961 and described as *rational expectations*. People's rational expectations affect their labor- and product-market behavior, he says, and explain tendencies toward unemployment and inventory accumulation.

Lucas's theory of rational expectations hit the economics profession like a thunderbolt, obliterating economists' confidence and generating, in Paul Samuelson's rich vernacular, "creeping humility" with respect to policymakers' ability to stabilize economic activity.

According to the rational expectationists, businesses and workers decide their current behavior according to their expected benefits and costs using the best information currently available. In product markets, businesses' expectations concern prices and the benefits to be gained from selling products for higher prices. In labor markets, workers' expectations concern wages and the benefits to be gained from taking jobs at higher wages. Different markets experience different prices, the result of differences in consumer demand and differences in production technologies. Higher-than-normal prices in some markets alert businesses to higher-than-normal demand for their products. Businesses respond by increasing production in those markets and reducing production in markets with lower-than-normal demand and, hence, lower-than-normal prices. Differences in wages affect labor markets in much the same way, attracting workers into markets with higher-than-normal wages and away from markets with lower-than-normal wages.

Decisions to increase production and employment in particular markets are efficient if price increases have occurred only in those markets. They may not be efficient if all prices have increased. Increases in all prices are generally the result of too rapid growth in the money supply. When businesses and workers suspect that too rapid money growth is causing all prices and wages to increase, they are less likely to interpret higher-than-normal prices as indicators of higher-than-normal demand—more likely as merely a reflection of general price inflation. They will not take steps to increase production and employment, and economic activity will stall, in spite of generally higher wages and prices.

Rational expectations also affect behavior across time. People perceive current wage-price inflation as either temporary or permanent. If businesses and workers believe wage-price inflation is only temporary, they increase current production and employment to take advantage of currently high prices. They expect to return to normal rates of operation when wage-price inflation has returned to normal.

All these behavioral changes occur only with respect to temporary wage-price inflation, however. If businesses and workers expect wage-price inflation to be permanent, there is no incentive to shift production and employment to the current period, so that production and employment remain at current levels. In fact, expectations of permanent inflation might cause businesses to increase their investments in new productive capacity. By increasing productive capacity, they expect to make more profitable sales in a future of ever-rising prices.

Needless to say, correctly identifying wage-price inflation as temporary or permanent is difficult, if not impossible. In fact, if businesses mistakenly identify temporary inflation as permanent, they might invest too much, building too much productive capacity relative to long-run demand for their products. A long time would have to elapse before spending for new products actually increases enough to justify excessive current investments. In the meantime, firms will make fewer new investments, so that production, income, and employment may even fall. Lucas worries that expectations of permanent price inflation could bring on a prolonged period of rising unemployment and unwanted inventory accumulation.

Expectations of permanent inflation are most clearly associated with too rapid growth in the money supply. Remembering Milton Friedman, we know that money growth in excess of growth in real production (turnover remaining constant) causes prices to rise. All of which leads to the not-so-surprising conclusion that expansionary monetary policy to increase income and employment will not be successful. Indeed, throughout the 1970s annual money growth averaged 6.5 percent, almost double Friedman's recommended rate. Over the same decade unemployment averaged 6.2 percent, in part because of inflation averaging 8.4 percent. The experience of the 1970s suggests that in a world of rational expectations, expansionary monetary policy only feeds producers' and workers' expectations of permanent inflation. Expectations of permanent inflation create no incentive to increase current production and employment and, therefore, no tendency to eliminate the business cycle.

When Policy Loses Its Effectiveness

This is Lucas's "policy ineffectiveness proposition," and it states two reasons why expansionary monetary policy is ineffective against business cycles. First, because it affects all prices, expansionary monetary policy does not create price differences across markets. When prices are increasing across all markets, businesses and workers cannot distinguish between those markets with higher-than-normal demand and those without. Businesses are not encouraged to shift production into markets with higher-than-normal prices. Second, expansionary monetary policy is not effective because it generates permanent inflation and, therefore, provides no incentive to shift production and employment into the current period. Who will rush to produce for sale today what might be sold for higher prices tomorrow?

Businesses and workers might be fooled initially into believing that wages and prices are higher-than-normal only in their particular markets. Eventually, however, rational people come to understand inflation and that their higher prices and wages reflect only general price increases. With this realization, businesses and workers return production and employment to their customary levels. Thus, expansionary monetary policies intended to increase production and employment are effective at most only in the very short term.[13]

The bottom line is, therefore, this: After years of experience with the effects of expansionary policies, workers and businesses come to view such policies as potentially inflationary. Behaving rationally, they respond to expansionary policies by immediately adjusting prices and wages upward, while making absolutely no changes in current production and employment. Such behavior destroys the inverse relationship between unemployment and inflation (one might say that it verticalizes the Phillips curve) and discourages increases in employment.

Some observers have drawn a rather astonishing policy conclusion from the theory of rational expectations: that the only way government policymakers can achieve their employment-expanding objectives is to design monetary and fiscal policies so perversely that workers and businesses misread their implications. Confused about current policies, workers and businesses might come to behave in a way consistent with policymakers' objectives—but only until they realize their mistake, at which point their behavior will return to normal. According to this interpretation, the way for policymakers to achieve their employment-expanding objectives is to create such chaos in their policymaking that people are unable to behave rationally!

This is not economists' recommendation, of course. The rational expectationists' more sensible recommendation is that policy be made fairly predictable, so as to reduce the uncertainty of workers and businesses and reduce the inefficiencies associated with costly mistakes. The effect of predictable money growth is to enable businesses and workers to identify the wage-price changes that truly indicate changes in demand in their particular markets. Correct interpretation of wage-price changes will prompt businesses and workers to make the adjustments that allow markets to clear, without the sorts of disruptions that might call for more government involvement in the economy.

In essence, Robert Lucas's critique of active monetary and fiscal policy implies a return to Milton Friedman's steady-money-growth rule, growth at the same rate as growth in productive capacity and, therefore, noninflationary. Believers in rational expectations doubt the effectiveness of broad, sweeping macroeconomic policies. Instead, they believe the rational responses of businesses and workers can weaken the effects of macroeconomic policies and may even turn such policies in unintended directions. The correct policy for business cycles is no policy at all.

Lucas himself was so confident that his contribution to modern economic thought merited a Nobel Prize that, it is said, he included in his divorce settlement a pledge to share the expected future award with his soon-to-be ex-wife, a rather extreme example of rational expectations!

How Rational Are Our Expectations?

Even rational expectations theory is subject to question, of course. To the skeptics, Lucas's theory of rational expectations requires that businesses and workers constantly weigh alternatives and correctly choose optimal behavior. No doubt, a certain amount of rationality does govern our behavior. However, much of our rationality is embodied in the institutions that we have established to standardize and regularize our routine decisions. Without ever consciously thinking about alternative courses of action, we are guided by such institutions toward rational behavior. A skeptic might find rather ironic the fact that we behave most rationally when we are not thinking about our behavior at all!

Spending From Lifetime Income

Franco Modigliani offers another interpretation of rationality and the determinants of consumer spending. Modigliani received the Nobel Prize in 1985 for his analyses of saving and investment behavior.

Modigliani was born in Rome, Italy. His father was a pediatrician and wanted Franco to study medicine. But while working as a translator of German articles, Franco learned about price controls, enough to write a prize-winning essay and to stimulate a lifelong interest in economics. During Italy's war with Ethiopia in the 1930s he administered his government's price-control program. Facing growing anti-Semitism in Italy, in 1939 he emigrated to the United States where he became embroiled in the controversy over monetary and fiscal policy. Modigliani demonstrated his willingness to swim against the tide by challenging the apparently self-evident orthodoxies of the time, including the Keynesian explanation for business cycles.

Modigliani suggests that the cyclical behavior of consumer spending (and, therefore, saving) depends not so much on current income as on the relationship between our current incomes and our expectations of an entire lifetime of income.[14] Modigliani's lifetime-income theory allows for no permanent increase in personal wealth but assumes that people accumulate wealth solely as a means of smoothing out their lifetime consumption: consuming less than income in our middle, most productive years so as to finance consumption in our early and later years. In his view, "the purpose of saving is to allow families to redistribute the earnings they get (and expect to get) over their entire life cycle so as to secure the most desirable pattern of consumption over life."

If Modigliani is correct, monetary policy affects total spending, not by affecting business investment spending, as Friedman believes, but by affecting the value of consumers' accumulated savings. By changing the value of consumers' accumulated wealth, monetary policy causes changes in consumers' ability to spend.

To understand his point, consider the effect of steady money growth in a booming economy. With steady money growth, rising incomes and prices will cause interest rates to rise as well. Friedman would expect rising interest rates to discourage investment spending and slow down the booming economy. Modigliani points out that rising interest rates also reduce the value of bonds purchased when interest rates were lower. A reduction in the value of their accumulated wealth threatens consumers' ability to spend in their later years and forces them to reduce their current spending. On the other hand, in recessions, as incomes, prices, and interest rates fall, the value of consumers' accumulated wealth increases, allowing us to increase current spending.[15] In both cases, changes in consumer spending help reverse unwanted changes in income and employment.

The "wealth effect" on consumer spending, along with leakages from income for taxes and import payments, reduces the significance of current income for determining consumer spending. With current spending responding very little to changes in current income, consumers' respending rate is also low, and the multiplier that affects total income is low as well. (Some estimates put the U.S. spending multiplier at only slightly greater than one.) A small spending multiplier translates into small swings in income, which can be accommodated fairly readily without episodes of extreme unemployment or inflation—and, in turn, without the need for large infusions of monetary or fiscal policy.

Economists' interest in the wealth effect on consumer spending arose again in 1999 when skyrocketing stock prices unleashed a flood of spending for luxury autos, homes, jewelry, and assorted accoutrements of the lavish lifestyle. High consumer spending contributed to unprecedented increases in income and employment, while at the same time raising concerns that, should stock prices fall, consumer spending could collapse and bring on recession. All of this contributed to Federal Reserve Chairman Alan Greenspan's fears about what he called the "irrational exuberance" of investors in the U.S. stock market. Recent econometric estimates of the wealth effect on consumer spending range from $0.02 to $0.10 for every $1 in increased wealth, boosting annual consumer spending by as little as 2 percent or as much as 10 percent.

Reprise

I have described the economists in Part 4 as macroeconomists: concerned with broad levels of economic activity, production, income, employment, and price levels. In reality, such a sharp distinction between macroeconomics and microeconomics is not possible. Whatever happens in the broader economy has its origins in individual markets, in the spending and saving decisions of individual consumers, in the work and leisure decisions of workers, and in the producing and investing decisions of businesses. To the extent that individual markets adjust freely in response to the incentives contained in neoclassical theory, markets clear, with demand equal to supply at relatively stable prices. Then changes in demand or supply bring on price and wage changes that smoothly and incrementally adjust production and employment to accord with the new conditions. By this reasoning, and provided there are no unexpected shocks to labor or product markets, the primary responsibility of government is to ensure sufficient purchasing power to support the level of payments decided by individual buyers and sellers.

In the real world, things do not always proceed so smoothly. The real world includes institutions that interfere with the smooth adjustments required in neoclassical theory. Labor unions bargain for wage increases, large firms negotiate price increases, psychological factors sweep through product and money markets and distort consumer and business spending. Returning to John M. Keynes, in the long run markets may clear, he said, but "in the long run, we are all dead." Rather than await the inevitability of death, we might better in the short run allow policymakers to weigh the ill effects of market disequilibria—the unwanted changes in production, employment, and prices that disrupt lives—against the potential costs of government policies to restore noninflationary, full-employment levels of economic activity.

Perhaps James Tobin best expresses the defense of government involvement in economic affairs. It makes no sense, he says, for any society to endure "immediate and tangible sacrifices to avert an ill-defined, uncertain, eventual evil."[16]

Chapter 18

HOW DOES ECONOMIC POLICY WORK IN THE REAL WORLD?

O ops! is not an expression often used in economics but it probably should be—for all those times when logical explanations and simple policy solutions run up against the realities of the world.

Some people find economics frustrating for this very reason. No matter how earnestly one studies, how committed one is to finding the optimal solution to economic problems, one can never know for sure whose theoretical explanation is correct—whose theory correctly explains the infinitely complex relationships that underlie whatever result is observed in the open economy.

Public discussion of the various theories that underlie economic policy is a recent occurrence. In fact, only in recent decades has economic policy been regarded as a legitimate function of government. Only after depression and world war have people come willingly to the notion that, perhaps, economies cannot always run themselves efficiently—without any sort of specific guidance from government. Since passage of the Employment Act of 1946, the U.S. government has played a more or less active role in the economy, depending on the politics and ideologies of the administration currently in office. But whatever actions have been taken have been more on the order of experiments, hopeful attempts at creating benefits and limiting costs, than confident programs with predictable consequences.

The first explicit use of Keynesian fiscal policy in the United States occurred in the 1960s, when President John F. Kennedy's advisers persuaded him to cut taxes in spite of a government budget that was already running a deficit. This was something his predecessor President Dwight Eisenhower had refused to do—Eisenhower's strong commitment to orthodox economic theory probably playing a part in the two recessions that occurred during his administration. In part because of the tax cut ultimately implemented by President Lyndon Johnson, economic activity did pick up in the United States and the government's deficit did shrink. Later in the 1960s, however, heavy government spending for the Vietnam War and mounting inflation complicated policymakers' choices, and the 1970s brought further discredit to Keynesian theory and stabilization policy.

The problem of the 1970s was christened *stagflation* to denote the combination of economic stagnation (high unemployment) with inflation—a combination that believers in the Phillips curve thought could not happen. One problem or the other, they said, but not both at the same time. A combination of 6.5 percent unemployment and 0.9 percent inflation (in 1961) or 3.4 percent unemployment and 5.1 percent inflation (in 1969) would yield a tolerable "misery index" of around 8 (6.5 + 0.9 = 7.4 or 3.4 + 5.1 = 8.5). A combination of 7.6 percent unemployment and 9.3 percent inflation (in 1976) yielded a misery index that was not tolerable by anyone's definition.

To be sure, exceptional conditions in the 1970s affected Phillips-curve variables, probably increasing tendencies toward both inflation and unemployment. Two serious energy crises raised prices and rendered obsolete many manufacturing processes, businesses, and entire occupations.[17] The massive entry into the labor force of females and teenagers reduced average labor productivity, which increased businesses' production costs, pushed up prices, and worsened unemployment. And the collapse of the international exchange-rate system brought uncertainty to international transactions and asset values. Such untypical circumstances were partly responsible for what many saw as a rightward shift of the Phillips curve—higher inflation and higher unemployment at the same time.

Keynesian stabilization policies could not be expected to deal with such untypical influences on spending and production, pleaded the Keynesian economists. If that is so, countered policymakers, then how better can we ensure stable employment at stable prices?

To which the followers of Milton Friedman were pleased to provide an answer. Untypical influences on spending and production are beyond the power of humans to predict, they declared. Therefore, whatever policy actions are based on the discretion of fallible prognosticators are doomed to, at best, ineffectiveness or, at worst, absolute failure.

And so, beginning in the 1980s, both the United States and Britain embarked on an experiment in monetarism: adherence to Friedman's steady-money-growth. In the United States, Paul Volcker at the Federal Reserve resolved to bring money growth down from more than 8 percent annually at the end of the 1970s to a rate more nearly consistent with growth in production of real goods and services, which was running closer to 3 percent over the same period. Only by following a steady-money-growth rule, it was said, could the Fed avoid costly mistakes.

Things did not work out quite as expected. As money growth slowed, interest rates rose to 20 percent, bringing on severe recession. Irate farmers sent Chairman Volcker bags of rotting food, builders sent chopped bits of 2 by 4s, and one disturbed individual even brandished a machete in the Fed's boardroom. Concern that worsening recession in the United States would bring on global financial collapse led to an increase in money growth in 1983.

In Britain, Prime Minister Margaret Thatcher's government was also committed, politically and ideologically, to reducing government's involvement in the economy. There and on the European continent, policies to reduce total spending brought rising unemployment with the threat of permanent deterioration of worker skills.

The monetarist experiment created other problems. Throughout the industrialized world, nations' resolve to gain control over money growth was undone by the gradual freeing of international financial markets. When savings are free to flow across national borders, any shortage of money engineered by one nation's monetary authorities can be quickly offset by an increase in money flowing into that nation from other nations. Or the reverse, with outflows of money quickly eliminating an increased supply engineered to increase a nation's spending.

Other inconvenient realities weakened the effectiveness of the steady-money-growth rule. To control total spending by controlling the money supply works only if money turnover doesn't change. Money turnover is constant only if people hold a constant fraction of their incomes as cash and checking accounts. This requires that consumers and businesses continue the same habits and attitudes toward payments that have governed money turnover in the recent past. To expect this to happen, one would have to expect no response on the part of financial markets to new opportunities opened up by changing technologies. Of all participants in the economy, financial institutions are probably the most responsive to such opportunities—and respond they did.

Following the inflation of the 1970s and the erosion in the value of cash and checking accounts, savers looked for interest-earning opportunities outside the typical banking services. New kinds of checkable savings accounts, mutual funds, and credit union accounts are as spendable as traditional cash and checking accounts but are not counted in the usual definition of money. Moreover, all these new types of financial instruments have been changing too fast to be precisely defined and measured. When bank customers can shift their wealth freely among various forms of financial assets, the rate of money turnover fluctuates widely. A monetary authority that attempts to control spending by regulating the supply of cash and checking accounts is simply flummoxed by the complexity.

The problem could be explained this way: Suppose people's demand for cash and checking accounts is shrinking, as we convert more of our traditional money to nontraditional financial assets. As businesses issue more stocks and bonds, interest rates begin to rise. The monetary authority might see rising interest rates as a sign that money is scarce and the supply should be increased. The problem is that if nontraditional types of financial assets are also increasing, increasing cash and checking accounts would provide too much more money. Holders of the increased cash and checking accounts would buy still more nontraditional assets, providing still more money for businesses to spend. The effect is the same as continuing to add boiling water to a scalding bath because the temperature gauge is upside-down.

Some economists excuse the unemployment and inflation of the 1970s and 1980s as simply a return to business as usual. Conditions for stable employment and prices were unusually favorable in the first decades following World War II, they say. The technological catch-up after the war and the increasing worldwide liberalization of trade and investment, combined with the postwar resolve to maintain full employment, probably stimulated business investment during those years. By the 1970s, these favorable conditions had ended, and a relapse was inevitable. None of the usual explanations better explains the combination of high unemployment and inflation that characterized the 1970s.

Since the policy confusion of the 1980s, the governments of industrialized nations have adopted various combinations of the Keynesian and monetarist approaches to economic stabilization. They have sought an optimum set of "feedback rules," which would dictate appropriate policies, independent of the sorts of political and ideological pressures that tend to influence policymakers.

The United States has fared better than many other industrialized nations in its lower inflation and unemployment and, very likely, a shift of the Phillips curve back from its rightward position to more tolerable levels of both variables. Still, throughout the 1980s and into the mid-1990s, the United States continued to experience ballooning budget deficits, especially troublesome because they occurred at nearly full employment. Deficits at full employment cannot contribute to economic stability, since at full employment the spending made possible by deficits is not needed to promote recovery from recession. Unless the excess spending created by government deficits is diverted to foreign markets, through imports greater than exports, it can exert inflationary pressures in the domestic economy. Moreover, government deficits at full employment absorb saving that might otherwise be borrowed for private investment. Investment is essential for the economic growth that can ultimately yield the tax revenues necessary for balancing the government's budget. Fortunately for U.S. investment, inflows of capital from foreign savers have (thus far) ameliorated the shortage of domestic savings and helped maintain usual rates of investment spending, so that productive capacity has continued to grow. By the end of the 1990s, relatively stable growth in the United States had yielded enough of an increase in federal tax revenues to produce at least a temporary shift from deficit to surplus.

PART 5
THE MODEL BUILDERS

Richard Stone • *Gerard Debreu* •
Kenneth Arrow • *Maurice Allais* •
Wassily Leontief • *Lawrence Klein* •
Simon Kuznets

M uch as understanding the internal combustion engine requires a model of pistons, valves, ignition systems, and so forth, understanding an economic system requires an economic model. Like the model of an engine, a macroeconomic model duplicates the basic structure of an interactive system, concentrating on the system's main functioning parts while omitting its less critical details. A macroeconomic model shows how economic units—consumers, businesses, and governments—interact to determine total spending, prices, production, employment, saving-investing, and other variables that bear heavily on our standard of living. Armed with a macroeconomic model, an economist can simulate random changes in spending—for residential housing, business plant and equipment, or government programs—and random changes in conditions underlying production—changes in the money supply, the seasons, or technology or the availability of certain natural resources. Simulations help economists understand the economy's typical responses to change and project the likely effects of policies designed to offset unwanted changes.

Chapter 19
EVERYTHING DEPENDS ON EVERYTHING ELSE

M odel airplanes typically don't fly as well as real planes. Nor (sadly) does model clothing typically look or fit on our bodies as it does on the store's mannequin. Nevertheless, our lives are enhanced by both—as we attempt to approximate the real with the contrived. Our efforts toward understanding our economic system are likewise enhanced by economic models.

The better the model, the better the policy recommendations that emerge from it. Unfortunately, even using the best economic theory and empirical evidence, models are imperfect representations of the real thing. No macroeconomic model can precisely duplicate economic relationships, such that policymakers can precisely project economic activity and unfailingly project the consequences of economic policies. An absolutely perfect macroeconomic model would require much finer breakdowns of information and much more complete descriptions of economic relationships than is practical.

Still, even with their imperfect models economists have made much progress toward more complete understanding of economic activity, with some evidence of success in the use of government policy to smooth out the peaks and valleys of business cycles. In fact, data collected by the National Bureau of Economic Research reveal much less severe cycles in the half-century after World War II than in the century before, at least in part because of the more effective use of government policies to offset cyclical behavior.

Accounting for a Nation's Income

World War II compelled participating nations to mobilize all their resources to achieve maximum war-fighting capability, and after the war to ensure quick recovery and peaceable growth. Efficient mobilization of resources requires information about the structure of the economy and the relationships among consumers, businesses, and government—all in all, a good definition of a macroeconomic model.

As far back as 1664 William Petty, a physician, scientist, and adviser to the British government, set out to model the income and wealth of Britain, with the goal of making British tax policies more equitable. Petty began with a basic idea, that a nation's expenditure and income are identical, expenditure by one person necessarily being received as income by another. He estimated British expenditure-income at 40 million pounds, of which 8 million was yielded by land and 7 million by "other Personal Estates." The remaining 25 million pounds of income Petty attributed to the "Labour of the People." Divided among its 6 million people, Britain's income amounted to about 7 pence per capita per day, the current equivalent unknown to this writer but suspected to be not very much. Eventually other national accounts were produced to estimate the portions of British savings that were attributable to each of what were identified as 26 social classes. Half of the population, with more than three-quarters of the nation's income, provided virtually all its saving for investment.

During the same time that Petty was working in Britain, accountants in France were producing similar estimates and concluding that France's tax policies were injurious to the welfare of the country and needed to be reformed. This information was unacceptable to King Louis XIV and was, therefore, suppressed. In 1758 King Louis XV's physician François Quesnay made perhaps the most fundamental contribution to macroeconomic modeling with his *tableau economique,* a table that describes how spending and income flow through the various economic sectors—much as blood flows through the organs of the human body.

The depression and wars of the twentieth century made understanding flows of spending and income especially urgent. In the Soviet Union (following the teachings of Karl Marx) and in Britain (through the influence of John M. Keynes) increased attention was paid to accounting for the nation's income. One of the first contributors to this effort was Britain's Richard Stone, winner of the Nobel

Prize in 1984 for his contributions to the measurement of economic activity. Stone was an assistant to John M. Keynes at the British Treasury during World War II. His boyhood passion was building models, particularly models of trains and boats. Through his experience with model building, he came to believe that understanding the structure of something was a first step toward making that structure work better.

Stone describes a nation's economic activity in terms of its "stocks" and "flows." Stocks are a nation's capital resources, he says, buildings and equipment, as well as materials intended for use as intermediate inputs today or as finished products in the future. Flows are additions to and subtractions from stock, including, respectively, newly produced capital resources and depletions of existing capital resources. Stone drew up a set of income accounts, in which he shows additions to capital stock as revenue received and depletions as costs paid. A healthy level of economic activity yields an excess of revenue received over costs paid, he concludes, thereby increasing the nation's stock of capital resources and, in consequence, the people's capacity for improved material standards of living.[1]

Another of the post–World War II macroeconomic modelers we have already met: Kenneth Arrow, whose contributions to social welfare theory were discussed in Part 2. There, Arrow was most concerned with the ways people express their values through votes for particular allocations of collective resources. Here, Arrow is most concerned with the ways people express their tastes through their behavior in markets.

Working with Kenneth Arrow was Nobel economist Gerard Debreu, Nobel laureate of 1983 for work that integrates all economic behavior into a comprehensive model of economic activity. Debreu was born in France and came to the United States in 1950. His background in mathematics and physics equipped him well for testing economic theory using real data. Indeed, Debreu rejects any economic theory that requires assumptions contrary to real experience. It is not possible, he says, to arrive at realistic conclusions if the assumptions that underlie those conclusions contradict what happens in real life. All of which is reminiscent of the joke about the engineer, the minister, and the economist marooned on a desert island with nothing to eat but a can of beans. When the engineer and the minister are unable to open the can, the economist proposes to save the day by suggesting, "Assume a can opener." Debreu would not be amused. Our theories are strong, he says, only to the extent that the assumptions that underlie them are plausible.

More immediate for our purposes here, Debreu wanted to build a model of economic activity to help plan economic reconstruction after World War II. Essentially, his model would duplicate Adam Smith's "invisible hand," which describes how a host of buyers and sellers, acting independently, can coordinate an entire nation's productive activity, all without any guidance from government. Previous attempts at duplicating the invisible hand combined equations describing demand and supply in many markets and solved them simultaneously to yield market-clearing quantities and prices, not without problems, as it turned out. In fact, solving those earliest demand and supply equations occasionally yielded negative values—negative quantities or negative prices, not a very helpful result.

Together with Kenneth Arrow, Debreu developed a set of conditions for demand and supply equations that would always produce nonnegative results. The conditions were that large size should yield no cost advantage (no economies of scale), buyers and sellers have perfect information about market conditions, and an array of futures markets exists for everything, including labor—assumptions that violated Debreu's own standards for realism, but we won't be picky. Nevertheless, while producing a model well short of replicating Smith's "invisible hand," the method Arrow and Debreu developed constituted a major step toward more realistic macroeconomic modeling.

Because of their logic and simplicity, the Arrow-Debreu equations are often described as "elegant." Their product demand equations show how consumer demand for a particular good or service depends on its price. The relationships between quantity demanded and price measure the trade-offs consumers experience when they choose particular products: the intensity of their demand for, say, broiled lobster over chipped beef. The resource demand equations are written similarly, with demand for labor and capital resources depending on their prices and productivity. Labor whose price is low and productivity high enjoys higher demand than otherwise. Likewise, demand for a capital resource depends on the current cost of capital (typically the interest rate) and the resource's productivity. Again, low cost and high productivity mean greater demand for a capital resource.

All of this helps explain why college graduates have more job opportunities than high school graduates, and why computer-controlled machines have replaced human workers for producing certain kinds of Oriental rugs. These are the sorts of relationships about which economists can produce countless equations and virtually indecipherable graphs. But the basic relationships confirm the internal logic of Adam Smith's invisible hand.

Demand equations are useless without supply, and Arrow-Debreu also produced supply equations based on markets' ability to offer resources and finished products for sale. In resource markets, supply depends on workers' willingness to give up leisure in return for a paycheck and savers' willingness to give up liquidity in return for a financial asset. In product markets, supply depends on producers' ability to assemble the necessary resources and apply existing technology for producing pretty much anything consumers could possibly want.

Combining all the Arrow-Debreu demand and supply equations yields market-clearing quantities in all their separate markets, which in turn affect demand and supply in all other markets (hence, the title of this chapter). After all necessary adjustments are made in all product and resource markets, the economy reaches what Arrow and Debreu called general equilibrium. A general equilibrium model indicates the market-clearing quantities of all the products currently produced to satisfy consumer demand and all the resources currently employed for producing those quantities. While risking the charge of grandiosity, we might describe a general equilibrium model as combining all the tastes of consumers and all the requirements of production, thus revealing how an economy allocates its resources to produce all the goods and services its consumers want to buy. Well, why not?

Solving simultaneously all the Arrow-Debreu equations also yields the relative prices of all products and resources. Relative prices are important because they reflect, in the case of products, consumer tastes, and in the case of resources, resource productivity. Product prices are the signals that guide manufacturers toward efficient production. Resource prices determine costs of production and, ultimately, incomes paid to owners of those resources. Resource owners then use their incomes to purchase the products supplied in product markets, thus completing the never-ending cycle of spending, income, and more spending.[2]

The Significance of General Equilibrium Models

Economists differ in the significance they attach to the Arrow-Debreu general equilibrium model. Some see its significance in the support it gives to laissez faire, to their ultimate confidence in free markets for allocating resources efficiently. Others see general equilibrium modeling entirely differently, as a guide to government planning. Because a general equilibrium model incorporates information about consumer tastes and resource productivity, they say, it enables government to plan the efficient allocation of resources without any market activity.

Depending on certain conditions, either laissez faire or a certain amount of government planning might be the more correct approach to resource allocation. For laissez faire to yield the most efficient allocation, there would have to be perfect markets for all products and resources, and there would have to be complete information about market conditions. Consumers would have to understand all available products, and producers, all production technologies. Where markets are imperfect or information is incomplete, there might be a role for government: to determine a set of taxes and subsidies that shift resource allocation in a way that improves efficiency and increases social welfare. Government can do this, some economists say, if it has information not available to private buyers and sellers. Indeed, the World Bank and International Monetary Fund currently use macroeconomic models based on Debreu's for efficiently allocating aid to poor nations.

How Understanding Past Experience
Helps Project Future Conditions

Probably the Nobel economist who best expresses the significance of general equilibrium models is Maurice Allais, Nobel laureate of 1988. Allais spent his youth in France during World War I, later studied mathematics and physics, and eventually went to work as an engineer, supervising France's mines and railway systems. During the Nazi occupation in World War II, Allais worked in Paris as Director of the Bureau of Mine Documentation and Statistics. His work as a government engineer, his experience of the Great Depression, and his sensitivity to the social problems created by economic distress prepared Allais well for a lifetime studying the interrelationships that constitute a nation's macroeconomy.

Allais taught himself economics, largely through reading the work of the masters of economic theory. He wrote his first major work at age 32 when he was, in his words, a "passionate amateur," the ranks of which include many of the world's most insightful scientists. Through his writings Allais seeks to explain the basic structure of an economy: to explain, in his words, the "permanent regularities, particularly quantitative, from the history of civilizations, dealing with economic systems, standards of living, technology, monetary phenomena, demographic factors, inequality and social classes, the respective influences of heredity and environment, international relations, exogenous physical influences on human societies, and political systems."[3] Wow! What an ambitious objective and what a clear expression of what a comprehensive macroeconomic model might accomplish.

Allais's way of thinking is described as inductive, thinking that draws from real world data an "explanatory thread without which [facts] appear incomprehensible and elude effective action." His background in physics equipped him to use the scientific method for explaining economic phenomena, while also persuading him of the importance of experimentation and correct interpretation of experimental results. Interestingly, while working as a physicist, Allais studied the periodic behavior of pendulums, a physical phenomenon that we have already seen applied to economic phenomena by the early econometricians.

Allais is particularly interested in the dynamics of money: how the demand for and supply of money changes with historical and psychological changes; how changes in money demand and supply generate business cycles; and how monetary conditions affect employment and prices. Without a stable monetary policy, he says, there is neither economic efficiency nor equitable distribution. In all Allais's investigations he reveals remarkable "*structural regularities in social phenomena* [italics in original] which are as striking as those we observe in the physical sciences." He concludes that *"everything happens as if,* irrespective of the institutional framework, contingent historical situations, and their particular aspirations, people react in the same way, as it were mechanically, to identical complex sequences. *They show that we are conditioned by our past."*[4] This is a profound conclusion, suggesting that complete understanding of past responses to economic conditions can help us deal effectively with similar conditions in the future.

Above all, Allais emphasizes the importance of synthesis. Economic theory, he says, is merely usable, condensed synthesis of past economic experience. Another remarkable insight! Even more sweeping, economics is a synthesis of all the social sciences, including psychology, sociology, political science, and history. Economics synthesizes such disparate human relationships as the workings of democracy, the balance among different levels of economic power, competition for power, the role of social elites, and social mobility. Economic models provide a way to synthesize real and monetary phenomena, theoretical and applied economics, and economics and the other social sciences. By synthesizing knowledge, Allais says, one gains understanding of the interdependencies and complementarities that link all aspects of human life. And one can give proper consideration to the human and historical contexts in which economic decisions are made.

Allais admits to a "passion for research," a "thirst to know more," a zeal to explore the unknown. To him, research is a sort of "adventure full of risks, but a fascinating adventure." He acknowledges that occasionally the results of research may conflict with established thinking and, therefore, subject the innovative thinker to the "active ostracism of the 'establishment.'" He continues, "Only slowly, after lengthy effort, does the intimate interdependence between parts begin to reveal itself. Slowly, the difficulties subside, the whole becomes clear and limpid, like the countryside viewed from the top of a high mountain."[5]

Economics has been compared to poetry. Both seek to strip massive amounts of information down to its essentials, to use only essential words to convey essential meaning. No poet could express the essential role of economics more vividly than does Maurice Allais.

Chapter 20
FILLING THE
THEORETICAL BOXES

E ven before Stone, Arrow, Debreu, and Allais had laid down the
theoretical guidelines for macroeconomic modeling, Wassily
Leontief was implementing their basic ideas and actually applying an
economic model to solve practical economic problems. Without
practical applications, he said, economic theory loses its relevance,
its practical impact on real events. Practical applications require
empirical data. Indeed, Leontief was offended by complicated theoretical models that arrive at profound conclusions about economic
behavior without ever collecting real data. He was not shy about con-
demning abstract theorizing, saying: "In no other field of empirical
inquiry has so massive and sophisticated a statistical machinery been
used with such indifferent results."[6]

That is, until Leontief arrived on the scene. Leontief filled the
empty boxes of economic theory with empirical content, an accomplishment that earned for him the Nobel Prize in Economic Sciences
in 1973.

Leontief's Grid

Wassily Leontief was born in St. Petersburg, Russia, and witnessed
the gunfire that began the Russian Revolution. While a student at

the University of Leningrad, he was arrested for nailing anti-Communist posters on the wall of a military barracks and placed in solitary confinement. After his release, he continued his anti-Communist activities and was arrested over and over again, until at age 20 he was allowed to leave the Soviet Union. He earned his doctorate at the University of Berlin and then came to the United States, teaching for 44 years at Harvard and later at New York University. Until he died at age 93, he continued to question established authority, to the occasional annoyance of the academic institutions he served.

Leontief's driving ambition was to understand the mechanics behind a modern economy, the nuts and bolts behind the end results. He especially wanted to understand how changes in one part of a vast economic engine are transmitted from one sector to another, with consequences for its overall performance. Toward that understanding, he divided all the nation's economic activity into 42 major sectors. Then he collected data measuring the flows of goods and services among the sectors. For this task, he reached beyond economics, consulting engineering sources for information about the technical requirements of particular types of production. The result of his effort is a statistical picture illustrating specific transactions among all his 42 economic sectors. Indeed, Leontief's statistical picture defines the links that weave together consumer tastes in all a nation's various product markets with purchases of raw materials and component parts in all its resource markets.

To display his statistical picture, Leontief constructed a rectangular grid, whose cells display the value of transactions between producer sectors listed down the left-hand side and user sectors listed across the top, as shown in Figure 5.

The sectors listed down the left-hand side of Leontief's grid are the suppliers of resource inputs, including raw materials and semifinished parts. The sectors across the top are the producers of finished output, using the raw materials and parts supplied by suppliers listed on the left. Reading down a column, one learns the specific resource inputs required from suppliers listed at the left for producing the finished product named at the top. For example, in a typical input-output grid, a column headed Primary Metals would list resource inputs amounting to 6.9 units from the sector supplying primary metals, 0.9 units from petroleum and coal products, 0.18 units from chemicals, 0.35 units from coal, gas, and electricity, 0.21 units from stone, clay, and glass production, and 0.52 units from railroad trans-

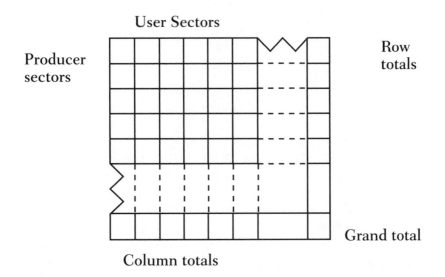

Figure 5

portation. The Primary Metals column would also include cells recording the intermediary's markup, taxes paid, and payments to workers and stockholders in this sector. The sum of all resource inputs would be the value of total output in the Primary Metals sector and would be shown at the bottom of the column.

Reading across a row one learns how the raw materials and component parts produced in a particular supplying sector are distributed among the various user sectors. Thus, in the Primary Metals row, the cells would record all the sectors that use primary metals in production (including, as we have noted, Primary Metals itself). The last user cell in the row would record the quantity of this resource that is supplied to final users. The sum of all the user cells in a single row is the total output of that sector and would be shown at the end of the row. For any sector, the distribution of output to all users must be equal to that sector's total output. Therefore, the sum of a particular sector's row must be equal to the sum of that sector's column.

The sum of all the column totals in an input-output table indicates total production for the year in all the nation's producing sectors. This sum is necessarily equal to the sum of the row totals, which represents totals of all the resource inputs used in production.

We might think of Leontief's input-output grid as a map of the processes described in an Arrow-Debreu general equilibrium model.

The columns represent Arrow-Debreu demand equations, each cell defining demand for a particular resource required in production, and the sum defining total demand for the product produced in that sector. The rows represent components of supply, each cell defining quantity supplied to a particular user. Thus, the values in the cells are at the same time demand from one sector for inputs produced by another and the supply of one sector's output to satisfy another sector's demand.

Just as is true in an Arrow-Debreu general equilibrium model, every value in an input-output table is linked, directly or indirectly, with every other value. Changes in a single value can cause multiple changes in all the other values, such that adjusting the values can quickly get out of hand. Take as an example an increase in consumer demand for autos. To satisfy an increase in demand for autos requires, first, increases in the resource inputs indicated in each of the cells in a column headed Motor Vehicles and Industrial Equipment: that is, ferrous metals, iron/steel foundry products, machine tools, electrical equipment, iron and steel, nonferrous metals, textile mill products, rubber, and so forth. But to increase quantities of each of these resource inputs requires further increases in their sectors' columns—which require increases in all the cells in those columns. Using a single table to describe all the increased resource requirements that result from an increase in demand for autos yields complications that are only resolvable by high-speed computers.

Leontief describes his input-output grid as an illustration of the economy's "interlocking interdependencies," including both the direct dependence of each sector on every other sector, and also the indirect dependence based on the indirect requirements for expanding production in supplying sectors. Leontief himself says it best: "[T]he auto industry's purchases of glass are dependent in part upon the demand for motor vehicles arising out of the glass industry's purchase from the fuel industry."[7]

The first major application of input-output analysis was during World War II, to identify the resource requirements for increasing production for the war effort. To know in advance, for example, the ferrous-metal requirements for producing 100 more military aircraft would help avoid bottlenecks and production delays. When faced with critical resource shortages, the input-output table would reveal opportunities for substituting more abundant resources. After the war, the input-output model helped predict the necessary sectoral growth to support growth in civilian production. For example, Leontief's grid could be used to answer such questions as "How would an increase in public expenditures for primary education affect demand for sulfuric acid?" Not at all, you might say, until you remember that primary education requires textbooks, which require printing stock, which requires wood pulp, which requires in its production—you guessed it—sulfuric acid.

An Illustration of Leontief's Grid

Applying an input-output model for all these purposes requires, first, correct information and, second, mathematical manipulation. As an example, consider Leontief's original table, which includes the following data about the distribution of output from the steel industry. It says that, of every $1000 of output produced by the Steel Industry in 1939, the indicated quantities (in tons of steel) were supplied to other industries:

Steel Industry User Sectors

Con- struc.	Metal Fabri.	Motor Vehic.	Trade & Restau.	Chem- icals	Rubb. Prod.	Food Proc.	Fuel & Power	Lumb. & Papr.	Agri & Fish	Trans- port	Other
1.65	2.90	2.50	0.23	0.30	0.20	0.23	0.22	0.46	0.15	0.28	0.66

Likewise, Leontief's original table includes information on the resources demanded by the Motor Vehicles and Industrial Equipment sector. The following data represent the current dollar cost of the resource inputs that were required in 1939 to produce $1000 worth of motor vehicles and industrial equipment.

User Sector

Motor Vehicles and Industrial Equipment

133.60	=	(value of ferrous metals used) +
44.90	=	(value of iron/steel foundry products)+
29.20	=	(value of electrical equipment) +
22.30	=	(value of textile mill products) +
64.60	=	(value of rubber) + . . .
		et cetera, until all inputs are recorded
	=	total value of resources purchased for production

Mathematical manipulation of an input-output table requires that the values in the rows and columns be expressed as algebraic equations. By manipulating the equations it is possible to propose a change in final demand for one column's output and determine the resulting changes in demand for all the inputs listed in that column's cells.

These changes understate the effect on total demand, however, because they include only the direct requirements of increasing production in a single column. They do not consider the indirect effects on production in all the sectors that supply that sector with resource inputs.

To write equations including both the direct and indirect requirements of increasing production in one sector calls for a mathematical procedure called *matrix inversion*, a process that (like making laws and sausage) is best left unobserved. Suffice it to say that matrix inversion combines all direct and indirect requirements along an almost infinite chain of adjustments, yielding finally the total requirements from each row sector per dollar of each column sector delivered to final demand. The values produced by matrix inversion constitute a "total requirements table," which includes all the consequences of a single change in demand for all the supplying sectors in the table.

Useful Applications

A valid input-output table has a raft of uses. The total requirements table is especially useful for projecting the consequences of structural change, in particular, a change in technology that affects the individual input requirements in the initial table.

During World War II, military planners used input-output analysis to assess the significance for Germany's war effort of various resource inputs and concluded that the most critical resource was ball bearings. Ball bearings are tiny balls made of hard metal that are used in many devices to reduce friction between moving parts. They are essential for many pieces of military equipment. With this information, allied military planners identified the major producers of ball bearings and pinpointed their locations for allied bombers, with devastating consequences for Germany's military production.

The input-output format is easily transferable from the national economy to state and regional economies. An input-output table for the state of Georgia in the 1970s, for instance, revealed the composition of that state's economic activity. With state output of more than $34 billion, Georgia's manufacturing output was valued at $14 billion and service output at $11 billion, percentages of 26 and 25.6 percent, respectively. Compared with the national average of 28.9 percent in manufacturing and 26.9 percent in services, Georgia's lower percentages reflected the state's relatively modest stage of industrial development in 1970.

A useful by-product of Leontief's input-output table is the computation of multipliers. We are already familiar with Keynesian spending multipliers, used for estimating the multiple effects on total income of a $1 change in spending. In the input-output context, the multiplier emerges from the fact that a $1000 increase in final demand for motor vehicles requires (as shown in the previous section) $133.60 worth of ferrous metals, $44.90 worth of iron/steel foundry products, $29.20 worth of electrical equipment, and so forth. Producing $133.60 worth of ferrous metals requires another list of intermediate inputs (one of which is very likely to be motor vehicles, necessary for transporting materials and parts). All these second- and third-stage requirements stimulate production in many other related industries, so that ultimately the $1000 increase in demand for motor vehicles has multiple effects on all related industries (including the motor vehicle industry itself). When all related sectors increase their output to satisfy the increased demand for a particular product, the ratio of the change in total output to the initial $1000 expenditure defines the input-output multiplier, relating changes in demand for a single product to changes in a host of supplying industries.

This is the multiplier that is often used in *economic impact* studies, which estimate the consequences of certain occurrences: for example, the consequences for Alaska's economy of the regular visit of cruise ships or for Virginia's of the Pentagon's order for a new nuclear submarine. As expenditures for tourist souvenirs or nuclear control devices begin to percolate through the state's economy, all the sectors that supply equipment, materials, and component parts must increase their production, proportionally increasing their own requirements from all the other sectors that supply raw materials and parts.

Economic impact studies were especially critical in the mid-1970s to project not increasing economic activity but potential economic distress. The problem in the 1970s was a threatened reduction in total output, the result of oil embargoes that created energy shortages in many industries. Understanding the potential economic impact of energy shortages can guide policymakers toward policies that offset the most objectionable effects. If the primary goal of economic policy is to minimize unemployment, for instance, policy might be directed to cutting back energy use first in the highest energy-using industries that also employ the fewest workers.[8] Using Leontief's input-output model, economists were able to estimate the economic adjustments likely to result from energy shortages, the industries most severely threatened, the potential increase in unemployment, and so forth. In fact, input-output models estimated that a 12 percent cut in oil supplies would push both unemployment and inflation rates into double digits, primarily through production cuts in sectors producing chemicals and synthetics, transportation, drugs and soap, agriculture, mining, construction, metal containers, iron and steel, electronic equipment, utilities, and oil refining. The industries judged to be least affected by the oil shortage were photographic equipment, retail and wholesale trade, telephone communications, motor vehicles, household appliances, construction equipment, farm equipment, rubber, and paper. Geographic regions specializing in the most affected industries did suffer from energy shortages much as was predicted through economic impact studies based on Leontief's input-output model. And inflation did move into double digits in the years of severest oil shortages.

Chapter 21

THE BUILDING BLOCKS OF INCOME, EMPLOYMENT, AND PRICES

Whereas Wassily Leontief bases his model on the microeconomic relationships linking resource inputs with product outputs, Lawrence Klein combines microeconomic data into summary equations describing broad classes of spending. Solving simultaneously all of Klein's equations produces estimates of total spending, income output, and employment in the entire macroeconomy. Klein's aggregate measures serve as indicators of the nation's economic efficiency. Like Leontief's input-output model, Klein's model can project the future behavior of these efficiency indicators and the likely consequences of government policies aimed at improving them. For this achievement, Lawrence Klein was awarded the Nobel Prize in Economic Sciences for 1980.

(In addition to guiding government policymakers, models derived from Lawrence Klein's original work have contributed to a commercial forecasting industry that now produces income amounting to hundreds of millions of dollars each year.)

The world in the mid-twentieth century provided an ideal environment for macroeconomic modeling. The world economy had emerged from crushing depression and devastating war, with some confusion and uncertainty about its future direction. At the same time, world politics had moved sharply toward democracy, with governments increasingly committed to satisfying the wants of their people. The world's people wanted improved standards of living, more and better housing and consumer goods, more easily obtainable health care and education, better job opportunities and improved technologies at work. It is understandable that after decades of uncertainty and worsening standards of living, the world's people would want a more prosperous and secure world for themselves and their families.

Economists wanted all those things, too, and many drew upon their wartime experience to apply in peacetime some of the tools that had helped win the war. They saw planning for a peacetime economy as not too different from planning production of military equipment, logistics, and strategy.

Building a "Structural" Model

During World War II Lawrence Klein was a student at the University of Chicago, where he became acquainted with some of the scientists there developing the atomic bomb. After the war he moved to the Wharton School at the University of Pennsylvania, which gave its name to his first macroeconomic model.

Economists describe the Wharton model as "structural," in contrast with other models described as "naive." A naive model simply extrapolates economic activity from the recent past onto the future. In years of fairly stable growth, naive models forecast rather well, but structural models are better for forecasting business cycles. By focusing on the individual components of total spending, structural models can incorporate such changes in spending as result from families' long-term move to the suburbs, the introduction of automated information processing in manufacturing, and the growth of trade with the world's emerging market economies. Not even structural models can forecast erratic events, however, and erratic events can have significant economic consequences. Events such as a strike in a major industry, a crop failure in a major farming region, and a political upheaval in a major trading partner can have unpredictable effects on a nation's markets and confound even the most nearly perfect structural model.

To construct his model, Klein combined the theoretical concepts of John M. Keynes with the econometric techniques of Jan Tinbergen. He began by writing a system of equations describing fundamental spending flows—consumption, investment, government spending, and net exports—along with their interactions and feedbacks. He used historical data and multiple regression to estimate equations describing the responsiveness of total spending to a number of causal variables (income, interest rates, and so forth). Then he substituted projected values of the causal variables and solved his equations simultaneously, using—one's head pounds at the thought—"laborious hand calculation with a desktop machine." The ultimate result was estimated values for significant macroeconomic variables, including national income and output, employment, interest rates and investment spending, tax revenues, and international payments.

Klein characterizes the individual components of spending as the "building blocks" of the economy, summarized in what he calls *structural equations*. The estimated relationships within his structural equations are the *dial settings*. In his structural equation for consumer durables, for instance, total spending for durable goods rises by $0.116 for each $1 increase in income, falls by $0.0209 for each $1 worth of consumer durables owned in the previous period, and rises by $0.0552 for every $1 in planned purchases of durables—the numerical values being the dial settings.

Consumer spending plans vary from year to year, and durable goods last for several years, all of which makes spending for durable goods an especially volatile component of total spending—which isn't news to workers in auto and appliance plants. Spending for non-durable goods, such as food and fuel, is more stable. Richard Stone conducted similar investigations in Britain to model total spending for food, as dependent on consumers' income and food prices. Through multiple regression, he estimated the responsiveness of food purchases to changes in income and prices to be, respectively, +0.53 and −0.58. These results say that a 1 percent increase in income increases (+) spending for food by 0.53 percent, and a 1 percent increase in food prices reduces (−) spending for food by 0.58 percent. The fact that the spending responses are less than 1 is significant. It means that total spending for food rises or falls by a smaller percentage than (in fact, only about half as much as) a rise or fall in incomes or prices. (We all have to eat regularly whatever our incomes and prices, but most of us don't often eat lavishly.) Spending for other nondurable goods also responds less than proportionally to changes in income and prices, making for a relatively constant level of spending for nondurable goods—and relatively constant employment for workers in food processing and fuel delivery.

Klein's other structural equations describe business investment spending and include four categories: inventories, plant and equipment, regulated-industry and mining investments, and residential construction. Investment spending in each category depends on such economic factors as you might expect: consumer spending in the previous year, manufactured output over the previous several years, businesses' average cash flow, interest rates on business borrowing, and the previous year's stock of capital goods in manufacturing. The model shows business spending for inventories as quite volatile, accounting for more than half of postwar volatility. Spending for business plant and equipment depends on consumer spending in previous periods and, therefore, tends to lag behind the business cycle. Spending for residential construction tends to change in the opposite direction from other kinds of investment spending, suggesting that home building is a residual that uses resources when they are not currently being used to produce inventories and business plant and equipment.

The Wharton model treats government spending as largely exogenous, depending on factors not directly included in the model. Exports are exogenous, too, depending on conditions in the world economy that affect spending in other nations. In contrast, spending for imports is endogenous, depending on domestic incomes, relative prices, and trade in the previous year. Not surprisingly, we purchase more foreign cars, cruises, and fine jewelry when we've had a good year. The nation's total employment depends on current output and recent changes in output, consumer spending, and wage rates. The general price level depends on the share of wages in total income, consumer spending, the previous year's prices, and changes in the productivity of capital resources. The model also includes equations describing how taxes and transfer payments affect spending.

In all, Lawrence Klein's original Wharton model includes 47 structural equations. To estimate his equations, Klein used 12 U.S. data series covering the years 1948 to 1964. Then he tested his regression results by tracking the U.S. economy, correctly forecasting the recessions that actually occurred in 1954, 1958, and 1960.

The Effects of Stabilization Policies

The Wharton model's primary application is for forecasting the likely effect on national income of changes in any of the separate components of spending—the types of changes described by Paul Samuelson—as well as the effects of government policy to offset too fast or too slow growth in private spending.

In particular, the Wharton model is useful for estimating multipliers associated with any sort of change in government policy. For example, the Wharton model estimates the Keynesian spending multiplier at about 2. A multiplier of 2 is based on an economywide respending rate of about half. Consumers actually spend on average about $0.93 of every $1 change in take-home pay. But because taxes reduce take-home pay by roughly 0.30 of earned income, consumption is only $0.93 \times (\$0.70) = \$0.64$ of every additional $1 earned. Businesses spend about $0.07 of every sales dollar for new investment goods, which increases the nation's respending rate; but spending for imports amounts to about $0.16 of every $1 change in income, which reduces it. In general, the greater are the respending rates of spenders and the greater is disposable income relative to earned income, the larger is the multiple effect of a change in spending. The greater the tendency to import relative to export, the lower is the multiplier effect.

Changes in tax rates have smaller multiple effects on income in the short run than do changes in government purchases, since a change in taxes initially affects consumers' saving rather than spending. The effect of a decrease in corporate income taxes is only 0.5, suggesting that a cut in corporate taxes increases the nation's income by only half as much as the tax cut. In the long run, however, changes in taxes and government spending have almost equal effects on income, changing GDP almost dollar-for-dollar with changes in the amounts government puts into or takes out of the domestic spending stream. For this reason, increased government spending may be more effective than tax cuts for correcting recession; but tax reductions may be more favorable for long-run growth, encouraging increased investment spending and increased growth in productive capacity.

The Wharton model gives monetary policy a multiplier of about 2 and suggests that its largest effect is not generally felt until at least a year after implementation. Monetary policy affects prices before it affects production because its effects on investment lag and delay the implementation of new capital investments. Monetary policy affects prices most strongly in industries with relatively fixed productive capacity.

The Wharton model is also used to estimate multipliers associated with variables other than total income: for example, the multiple effect on government's tax revenues of changes in tax rates and government expenditures. This type of information is especially critical for forecasting budget deficits and surpluses—as members of the U.S. Congress were discovering at the end of the 1990s. Interestingly, the Wharton model estimates that increases in government expenditures generate almost enough added tax revenue after six months to offset the increased government spending. In contrast, cuts in personal income taxes generate only about one-third of the tax revenue necessary to offset the tax cut. A good example is provided by the Korean War, which lasted three years and required defense expenditures of about $40 billion. Defense expenditures were only partially financed by increasing tax rates, but still the government ran budget surpluses averaging $3 billion during the war. When defense spending was reduced after the war, the budget moved into deficit by $3 billion. Apparently, the reduction in incomes from lower defense spending reduced tax revenue by more than the cut in spending. As a general rule, fiscal policy has more significant effects on economic activity than on the government budget—all this is revealed by the Wharton model.

The model can also estimate such things as how changes in world trade affect exports, how government's agricultural policy affects farmers, how selective credit controls affect borrowing, and how a variety of other changes affect resource productivity.

Using the Wharton model, Klein was moved to make certain recommendations regarding economic policy. First, he says, government spending should be decided according to the international and domestic needs of the nation, as determined by the President and Congress. Second, having determined the optimal level of government spending, the President and Congress should adjust tax rates to bring the nation's total spending to a level that yields the desired level of employment and price stability. If a balanced budget is also desired, whatever changes in tax revenue are necessary can be achieved most efficiently by changing the corporate income tax.

An Update

In 1968 Klein participated in construction of a global economic model, labeled Project LINK. LINK uses data from industrialized nations, developing countries, and centrally planned economies, ultimately including 72 country-area groups and 15,000 dynamic equations. LINK is useful for tracing the effects in particular nations of changing trade relationships and of changing supplies of capital resources. Not surprisingly, LINK failed to predict the major worldwide recession of 1974, a consequence of OPEC's oil embargo. That recession had especially damaging consequences for Asian economies, since cutbacks in the production of oil reduced production of oil-based fertilizer, sorely needed in Asian agriculture.

Chapter 22

DOCUMENTING NATIONAL INCOME AND GROWTH

To list as one's accomplishment collecting data may seem trivial and to some people, boring. Economists' fascination with data is probably one reason they are not invited to many parties. However, without data scientific analysis is impossible, and the macroeconomic models described thus far are nothing but abstract theories, practically useless for guiding economic policy. For efficient policy-making, even the most careful, the most precise macroeconomic models require empirical testing and, for that purpose, real data. Simon Kuznets received the Nobel Prize in 1971 for establishing the means and the format for collecting the empirical data necessary to complete and make usable the macroeconomic models described thus far in this book.

Kuznets was born in czarist Russia and emigrated to the United States after World War I. This was a time when the world's industrialized nations were losing interest in colonial empires and exploring ways to lift their domestic populations from social, political, and economic backwardness. It was a time that cried out for information concerning the status of nations' economies and the likely consequences of policies intended to improve them.

Providing the Information for Making Economic Decisions

Kuznets' most fundamental contribution to macroeconomic modeling was to construct the *national income accounts:* an arrangement of aggregate economic data that describe a nation's total production and that determine its employment, prices, interest rates, and so forth. The national income accounts begin with information measuring the four types of spending defined in Keynesian theory: consumption, investment, government spending, and net exports. Taken together, spending in all these categories yields gross domestic product (or GDP), which is the final value of all goods and services produced for sale in a nation during a particular year.[9] This is the amount that is actually spent and that is received by business firms as sales revenue. It is thus a measure of a nation's current production of new wealth. In 1998, U.S. spending in the respective categories was (in trillions) $5.8 + $1.4 + $1.5 − $0.2, for GDP of approximately $8.5 trillion.

Not all of GDP produced in any year actually increases the nation's wealth, however. Because some portion of business investment spending simply replaces capital equipment that wore out during the year, an estimate of depreciation must be subtracted from GDP to yield net domestic product (or NDP). Replacement investments in 1998 amounted to about two-thirds of total investment in the United States, or $1 trillion, making NDP approximately $7.5 trillion.[10]

Not all of the year's production of new wealth actually becomes income to those of us who supply labor and other resources to businesses. Some amount of business sales revenue must be paid to local, state, and federal governments in the form of general sales taxes and excise taxes on cigarettes, alcoholic beverages, gasoline, and certain transportation and communication services. These taxes are described as *indirect taxes* because they affect taxpayers through what they buy rather than directly through their incomes.[11] Business revenue remaining after sales and excise taxes is called *national income* and represents income earned by suppliers of all the labor, land, capital, and entrepreneurship needed for producing new goods and services. The fractions of national income attributable to these basic resource categories have shown no discernible trend in the

United States during the past half century and in 1998 were approximately 70 percent for workers' wages and salaries, 2 percent for rent, 8 percent for interest to suppliers of financial capital, and 20 percent for the profits of corporations and proprietorships.

Before businesses can distribute all these forms of income, however, certain other payments must be subtracted from national income. Social Security contributions (FICA) must be subtracted from workers' pay before it is distributed. Corporate income taxes must be subtracted from corporate profits before dividends are distributed to stockholders, and corporations also retain a portion of current profits as corporate saving. All these subtractions reduce the portion of national income that is actually paid to resource suppliers. On the other hand, some amounts are paid to persons who have not actually contributed to current production. Such transfer payments as Social Security benefits, welfare benefits, unemployment compensation, and farm subsidies are added to income but are not earned through contributions to current production.

Making all the necessary subtractions and additions yields the value of income received, which is called *personal income*. Personal income may be larger or smaller than national income depending on the magnitude of subtractions relative to additions.

Again, not all of personal income is available for spending, since some portion must be paid in personal income taxes, which amounted to more than $1 trillion in the United States in 1998. After personal taxes are subtracted from personal income, the remaining income is called *disposable income*. In 1998 U.S. disposable income totaled $6 trillion, or an average of $22,500 for every man, woman, and child in the nation—a number that noneconomists generally find more interesting than most other economic data. This is the amount that the nation's consumers can allocate to new spending for consumer goods and services or to saving. In the first case, consumer spending returns continually to the nation's spending stream and is included in subsequent measures of GDP. In the second, saving is made available to businesses for investment spending, which also returns to the nation's spending stream in the form of spending for buildings, equipment, and inventories.

Data describing all these spending and income flows began to be collected and organized systematically only after World War II and have since provided valuable information for analyzing economic performance and guiding economic policy. Scientifically determined policies have been responsible at least in part for the fact that business cycles since World War II have been shorter and less severe than those that came before.

A Look at U.S. Economic History

To understand where we're going, it is helpful to understand where we've been. Much of what is true today of the U.S. economy has emerged from its historical development: its growth over time and the structure and spread of growth across sectors. Simon Kuznets contributed to this understanding by piecing together production data describing the preceding two centuries of our nation's history, a time when the United States was transforming itself from a fragmented agricultural economy to a unified, advanced industrial economy.

During its first hundred years, our nation's settled land multiplied almost 8 times. Population ballooned more than 85 times, a range of magnitude far greater than Europe's, where population only quadrupled over the same period. Both birth and immigration rates were high in the United States, immigration being especially high for the years before and immediately after World War I. Rapid population growth was a natural response to the newness of the nation, its plentiful resources, and the absence of economic and institutional constraints on marriage.

U.S. income increased fairly steadily, too, both in total and average (or per capita) amounts. The first half-century of the U.S. nation brought 1 percent annual growth in average income, followed by almost 1.5 percent annual growth in the second half-century. Then, in the century from 1880 to 1970 average income grew annually by almost 2 percent. Growth at that rate increased average income by a factor of 5 in less than a hundred years. Over the entire two centuries of Kuznets' data, accelerating productivity growth brought an elevenfold increase in average income. With a population growth factor of 85 and an income growth factor of more than 11, the scale of the economy as a whole (in terms of total income produced) increased almost 1000 times!

Such rapid economic growth in the United States is explained in part by the nation's relatively late entry into industrialization and the fact that it was formed at about the same time the Industrial Revolution was transforming the world economy. U.S. scientists and engineers could learn from preceding generations of scientists and engineers, those who had created what Kuznets calls "epochal innovations" like steam and electric power. Another reason for our rising prosperity was a high initial level of income, which translated high percentage rates of growth into even higher absolute growth. The United States has also been fabulously lucky, benefiting enormously from nature's "gift" of ample resources: verdant forests and rich farmland, plentiful water and mineral sources, a temperate climate and convenient seaports. Steadily increasing industrialization has provided opportunities and incentives for businesses to apply new scientific and technical knowledge in their manufacturing processes. U.S. businesses came to be known for their ability to adapt new technologies, the better to use efficiently the nation's unique resource endowments. U.S. scientists, technicians, and (not least!) ordinary workers have created technological innovations that have enlarged vastly the productive capacity of human labor. Technological innovations are critical for economic growth because—in contrast with resource endowments and even human learning capacity, both of which have absolute limits—there is no limit to the growth possibilities that flow from technological innovations.

Typically, a nation's rate of technological innovation is limited only by constraints imposed by its own institutions. New technologies require new economic and social institutions. Consider Kuznets' epochal innovations, steam and electric power. Both required "large-scale plants [that are] not compatible with family enterprise, illiteracy, or slavery."[12] Such necessary changes in work and living arrangements change relationships among social groups, often with painful consequences. The usual example is the pain experienced by small-scale producers of buggy whips when mass produced automobiles displaced horse-and-buggy rigs. A more recent example is the displacement of neighborhood book shops by nationwide chains and Internet stores like amazon.com. Unless a nation's people are willing to make painful and difficult changes in their economic and social institutions, technological change cannot occur and economic growth could slow or stop.

Applying Macroeconomic Analysis to Current International Events

Tumultuous events in the last half of the twentieth century turned the world's attention to growth prospects in Europe and Asia. In Europe, the advance and then decline of Soviet power overturned established economic relationships in nations formerly affiliated with the Soviet Union and stimulated a search for new ways of organizing economic life. With GDP per capita less than one-tenth of that of the United States, Russia struggles today with a brand of "cowboy capitalism" that threatens to isolate its young and vigorous entrepreneurial class from aging adherents to central planning. In Asia, declining support for central planning is forcing a reassessment of goals, opportunities, and policies that affect billions of the world's people. None of the impending changes will be accomplished easily or without pain. All bring the possibility of social conflict, with more of the sorts of turmoil that divert global resources from wealth-producing activities.

Perhaps the greatest threat to global stability today comes from the world's most populous nation. China has a 5000-year history of technological achievement, with natural resources capable of reviving its ancient standing in the global economy. But a half-century of central planning has reduced China's per capita GDP to less than one-twentieth that of the United States. China's current government is looking for ways to benefit from new forms of economic organization while minimizing the costs imposed on its 1.2 billion people, with some success.

Indeed, China's formerly communist government has recently joined the worldwide retreat from central planning and has declared its intention to transform its economy to a system of "democratic socialism." Don't ask for a precise definition of the term—most likely some combination of Karl Marx with Adam Smith. In fact, it is said that China's Prime Minister Zhu Rongji has books by Friedrich von Hayek on his bookshelf. China's transformation will doubtless require a shift from a state-run economy to a combination state-and-market economy, with the first order of business to convert large government-owned enterprises to private ownership. Subjecting newly privatized businesses to market forces can be traumatic for Chinese workers. Under central planning, the Chinese government distributed subsidies to businesses to enable them to employ all available workers, whether or not their products could actually be sold. Without subsidies, privately owned businesses will have to compete for sales. Managers will seek ways to improve product quality and cut costs, with the likelihood that inefficient workers will be laid off. Layoffs in 1997 amounted to 10 million workers. Without adequate job training and new job opportunities, such massive layoffs could cause "social unrest." Because almost one-fourth of the world's population is involved, China's shift to a market economy is of great concern to other nations.

China's most urgent economic problem is to sustain current rates of economic growth. Population growth and advances in technology have been increasing the nation's productive capacity by almost 9 percent annually. Unless spending increases at the same rate, new technologies and new entrants to China's workforce cannot be put to work. Unfortunately, 9 percent growth in spending cannot be guaranteed from Chinese consumers and businesses, since there is as yet insufficient wealth in the private sector. This means that much of China's spending growth must come from increasing exports, and indeed China has succeeded in exporting more highly valued products to developed and less developed nations alike. But exports cannot serve as China's sole source of spending growth, in part because other nations resist sacrificing their domestic markets to Chinese products. Indeed, the U.S. annual trade deficit with China has ballooned to $50 billion and is an increasing source of friction between the U.S. and Chinese governments.

All of this leaves the Chinese government as an important source of the spending needed to ensure growth in employment and incomes. China's government recognizes this requirement and has embarked on major infrastructure investments—the Three Gorges electric power complex being a spectacular example. But dependence on infrastructure investment for spending growth risks the possibility that ill-considered projects will divert valuable resources into inefficient uses.

Foreign investors have been eager to make long-term investments in China, the prospects of marketing sodas and sport shoes to 1.2 billion Chinese consumers being infinitely compelling. Already China has received billions of dollars of foreign investments for producing consumer goods, as well as investments in such high-tech industries as aerospace, electronics, and telecommunications. Nevertheless, in a perverse restraint on growth, the Chinese government has placed limits on foreign investors, including such requirements as partial domestic ownership and caps on local sales of the products of foreign investment. Current trade negotiators are working to persuade China to remove such restraints.

PART 6
ECONOMIC GROWTH
AND DEVELOPMENT

*Robert Solow • Theodore Schultz •
Arthur Lewis • Robert Fogel •
Gunnar Myrdal*

Business cycles bring misery in one form or another to almost every man, woman, and child in society. The downswings of business cycles bring unemployment (or, at the very least, underemployment), which slashes income, obliterates skills, and disrupts families. Upswings bring the risk of inflation, which redistributes wealth and complicates all our economic choices. The lives of many people are diminished by short-term deviations from generally expected economic conditions.

All this is true. But perhaps more important than business cycles for affecting economic opportunity and living standards are a nation's economic growth and development. To grow is to increase in magnitude—more jobs, more production, more income, and so forth. To develop is to change—with different jobs, different products, and income from different sources. (Need I say that in all these cases "different" implies "better"?) When a natural tendency toward business cycles is combined with a tendency to grow, the effect is to often the negative impact of cycles: to shorten and moderate the downswings and lengthen and strengthen the upswings. A nation that experiences general growth in prosperity can tolerate occasional lapses into recession. Indeed, the greater a nation's tendency toward economic growth, the less miserable are the effects of recession.

Chapter 23

THE THEORY UNDERLYING ECONOMIC GROWTH

What we are dealing with here is in essence the difference between short-run events and a long-run trend—all of which raises an interesting question regarding the length of the long run: Is the long run perhaps just a longer version of the ups and downs that occur rather frequently in a person's working life—a very long business cycle that isn't recognizable as a cycle until long after it has passed?

The great Austrian economist Joseph Schumpeter (1883–1950) suggested that this might be so, describing periods of growth as simply the upswings of giant technological waves, each one bringing rising prosperity as a new technology is implemented, followed by slower growth and even decline after the technology is fully diffused throughout the economy. For example, James Watt's steam engine in the eighteenth century ushered in the technological wave we call the Industrial Revolution, and Cornelius Vanderbilt's railroad network in the nineteenth opened the resource-rich North American continent to settlement and economic exploitation. In the early decades of the twentieth century, Henry Ford's automobile was another catalyst, all such inventions spurred a raft of activities that supported or benefited from the pathbreaking technology: steel production, mechanical devices and instruments for controlling them, energy systems, new business and residential construction, and countless more. The most recent technological wave to affect the industrialized world has been the one based on electronic information processing, and that wave may now be fading into a new one based on bioengineering.

All technological waves have roughly the same shape. They begin with a fundamental innovation—scientific, technological, or organizational—which is gradually applied in more and more diverse ways as the innovation catches on. In the meantime, workers learn to operate new machines, entrepreneurs conceive new products, and more sectors of the economy enjoy better living standards from improved methods of production. Indeed, technological innovations set in motion processes that feed on themselves, creating ripple effects that open new opportunities and extend the life of the technology that began the great upsurge in economic activity.

Long-run growth, whether a true trend or the upswing of a long technological wave, raises another question that is even more critical for future standards of living. It is the familiar dichotomy between exogeneity and endogeneity: the question whether growth falls upon a nation like "manna from heaven" or whether actions taken by ordinary men and women—planners and policymakers in business and government—can affect a nation's ability to grow. Is there something ordinary men and women can do to tilt upward the growth plain? Can ordinary people find a way to promote growth and ensure the hoped-for results: improved job opportunities, increased output and income, and ultimately higher standards of living that growth brings? Moreover, if they can do all this, is the gain likely to justify the pain that may accompany growth?

Perhaps a worthy objective for any nation should be not unlimited growth but growth at an efficient rate, a rate that achieves its maximum benefits net of the costs associated with too rapid growth.

Determining a Nation's Potential for Growth

The Nobel economist who pioneered modern growth theory is Robert Solow, Nobel laureate of 1987. If one were asked to select one word to describe Solow it would be "modest": modest in his personality and modest in his expectations of economic theory. His motto might be "Don't take yourself too seriously." And: Don't take too seriously the ability of economic theory to explain economic behavior fully.

Not that Solow lacks respect for the logic that underlies economic theory. On the contrary. One of Solow's college tutors was Wassily Leontief, who taught him respect for disciplined theory supported by empirical testing. Neither Solow nor Leontief would tolerate vague generalizations unsupported by facts. Still, Solow understands that economic activity is only one part of an enormously complicated web of human behavior, difficult to explain simply and comprehensively and subject to change unforeseen by the most precise economic model. In fact, he says, sometimes economic models are merely "nature's way of helping you to recognize nonsense when you see it."[1]

All this suggests that economics might never rightly be regarded as a hard science. To qualify as a hard science economics would have to be capable of analysis through scientific modeling, and scientific modeling is just not possible in economics. How economic systems really work—how real people respond to all the pushes and pulls to which real life subjects them—will always be beyond the limited understanding of mere mortals. Ruefully, Solow admits that economists' limited understanding of actual behavior does not generally compel them to answer questions with "I don't know" or, better yet, "Nobody can know."

Solow was a teenager in the United States while the world economy languished in the Great Depression and while fascism/nazism was capturing European governments. To Solow the high school student, it seemed as if all of society had broken down economically and, in consequence, politically as well. He began his career as a professor of economics and distinguished himself as an outstanding teacher. His teaching experience was beneficial in his intellectual development, he says, since teaching forced him to figure out how to explain clearly and to have a feel for a topic's shape, organizing principles, message, relationship to the rest of economics, and relationship to real life. He had ample opportunity to demonstrate those skills while serving on the staff of President John F. Kennedy's Council of Economic Advisers in the 1960s. This was a time when U.S. policymakers were wrestling with the problem of slow growth and persistent unemployment. To his colleagues on the CEA, Solow emphasized the difference between growth brought about by increases in spending and growth brought about by increases in productive capacity. Economists use different words to describe the different types of growth: *expansion* describes increases in spending, relative to a given productive capacity, and *growth* is used to describe increases in productive capacity. While the first type of growth merely closes a gap between actual and potential output, the second brings permanent increases in living standards. The first is strongly affected by a nation's monetary and fiscal policies, but it is the second that most interests Robert Solow.

According to Solow, there is no single rate of economic growth that is efficient for all nations but a wide range of possible growth rates, each one depending on the particular nation's preference for growth versus stability or perhaps, for a few, even decline. Indeed, the most fundamental determinant of a nation's growth potential is probably its people's belief that their human condition is not dictated by mysterious powers beyond human understanding but actually amenable to change guided by the thoughtful decisions of ordinary men and women. A school for commissars or ayatollahs, he suggests, will not produce engineers.

People express their preference for growth in their willingness to sacrifice current consumption, to save today for the sake of investment to be followed by even greater consumption tomorrow. A nation expresses its preference for current versus future consumption in the relative weights it places on, to use a common analogy, fresh strawberries and cream today versus strawberry jam tomorrow. Many factors enter the choice of preference weights, most notably the urgency of current wants. For a desperately poor nation, a meal today is more than just a preference but an absolute necessity; investment for future consumption must take a back seat to feeding and sheltering people today.

For nations beyond such desperation, growth becomes a real possibility. Such nations create social, political, and economic institutions that reflect their preference for current versus future consumption. Thus, through the institutions they create, nations glorify current consumption, or they reward thrift; they permit infanticide, or they establish preschool learning programs; they base individuals' incomes entirely on their contributions to current production, or they supplement current incomes with grants that, it is hoped, will plant the seeds for increasing productive capacity in the future.

New contributions to economic theory generally mean new jargon for describing new concepts, and Solow's growth theory does not disappoint. His new concept is described as the *steady state,* a term that sounds like stagnation but actually means growth at a certain constant rate. A nation's steady-state rate of growth is determined by basic factors unique to each nation—factors describing, first, its propensity to save and invest and, second, the resources it requires for producing output. The resources required for producing output depend on available technologies, often expressed in terms of the nation's capital/labor ratio. A nation that produces, say, petroleum-based chemicals requires a significantly greater quantity of capital per unit of labor than a nation that produces simple crafts, making for a significantly higher capital/labor ratio.

Saving and Investment in the United States

Despite our high incomes, we Americans are not big savers. Personal saving in the United States has fallen fairly steadily as a fraction of disposable income, from around 8 percent in the decades immediately following World War II to only about 2 percent in recent years. Business saving has grown, however, from about twice personal saving in mid-twentieth century to four times personal saving at century's end. (Business saving includes undistributed profits and allowances for depreciation.) The sum of business and personal saving was approximately $1.1 trillion in 1998, which represents about 13 percent of the year's GDP—a small percentage compared with saving in Germany, Switzerland, and, most especially, Japan.

Concern that the low U.S. saving and investment rate will cause a slowdown in economic growth has so far proved unfounded for one important reason: While U.S. savers are saving less, the United States is also the beneficiary of significant saving from abroad, the response of foreign savers to investment opportunities in the United States. Foreign saving added almost $200 billion to U.S. domestic saving in 1998.

For much of the past half-century, part of domestic saving in the United States has gone to finance spending by the federal government, reducing the amount available for private investment. (The larger part of the federal government's annual deficit is financed by borrowing from local and state governments, which generally run budget surpluses.) In 1998, however, a federal surplus added to the nation's savings and made possible private investments totaling almost $1.5 trillion. About two-thirds of investment spending in 1998 was required for replacing depreciated capital goods and equipment, keeping the U.S. capital stock in roughly the same ratio with respect to the U.S. labor force. In fact, the average capital/labor ratio for all manufacturing industries in the United States is currently about $55,000, which tells us that each year's saving and investment must be sufficient to maintain that amount of capital goods and equipment for every worker employed.[2]

Solow's Three-Legged Growth Stool

Solow likens the determinants of economic growth to a three-legged stool. The first leg of the stool is the rate of saving and investment (and thus indirectly the growth rate of the nation's capital stock). Second is the rate of population growth (and thus indirectly the growth rate of its labor force). And third is the rate of technological progress (and thus indirectly the productivity of combinations of capital and labor). Taken together, a nation's saving-investment rate and population growth determine the quantities of capital and labor available to produce output. Given its existing technical knowledge, the nation's available quantities of capital and labor make possible a certain quantity of output, thus determining simultaneously its capital/labor ratio, total employment, and output per worker. Output per worker determines income per capita and, in turn, the nation's average standard of living.

In Solow's steady state, a nation's saving and investment provide precisely the quantity of new capital resources required to replace depreciated capital and employ annual additions to the labor force. With steady-state growth, output and employment do grow. But the rate of growth is limited to the rate of population growth, with saving and investment just sufficient to maintain the current capital/labor ratio. With steady-state growth, output per worker and income per capita remain constant, as do average standards of living. Indeed, the nation's standard of living remains the one that precisely satisfies its people's preference for strawberries today versus jam tomorrow.

The Bottom Line

Now we come to an important conclusion of Solow's growth theory thus far.

- If growth in a nation's capacity to produce depends only on growth in population and growth in capital resources, a result of the population's propensity to save and invest, and
- If growth reaches a certain steady rate, which then prevails, then
- With Solow's steady-state rate of growth, growth in a nation's capacity to produce is linked to growth in population.

Under these conditions, growth in production cannot exceed growth in population. If a nation's growth stool has only two legs, production cannot grow faster than population, with the result that production per worker and income per capita cannot increase. Living standards don't improve.

Of course, we know that production does grow faster than population and living standards do improve, the reason being the third leg on Solow's growth stool: the nation's rate of technological progress.

The Importance of Technological Progress

Improvements in technology affect a nation's growth by changing its capital/labor ratio. Consider a high-saving nation, for which an ample supply of saving tends to push down the cost of capital. For that nation the cost of technologies requiring large amounts of capital is low, encouraging businesses to shift production toward products that require a higher capital/labor ratio. We call such technologies capital-intensive, and we expect a high-saving nation to specialize in such products. Germany's specialization in producing machine tools is a good example. On the other hand, we expect a low-saving nation, such as Turkey, to specialize in products that are more labor-intensive, like textiles or pottery.

The most obvious examples of technological progress come from advances in scientific knowledge, from inventions of new products or new manufacturing processes, or from improved methods of organizing resources for production.

Technological progress is the essential ingredient for overcoming Solow's limitations on economic growth. Consider this: Increasing capital resources precisely in line with population cannot by itself bring increases in output per capita, since each new worker has the same quantity of capital as previous workers. But without technological progress, neither does increasing capital resources faster than population bring increases in output per capita. The reason is that increasing capital resources faster than population, technology remaining the same, ultimately yields diminishing returns to capital. If textile workers, for example, have more machines than they can operate effectively, their average output per machine falls, limiting prospects for growth from increasing capital resources.

Having ruled out growth in labor and capital resources as single sources of growth, we are left with only one sure way toward better living standards: advances in technology. Advances in technology change the quantities of labor and capital required for production. And advances in technology make possible new types of capital investment, with increases in total output and employment and without diminishing returns.

The implications of Solow's analysis so far are profound. They suggest that a nation tends toward an aggregate standard of living that is dictated by its own future orientation: its people's willingness to forgo strawberries today for the sake of jam tomorrow. A nation can improve on that standard of living only through technological progress that augments the productivity of its workers. At this point, we might pose a tentative answer to the question raised early in this chapter: the question of whether ordinary men and women—planners and policymakers in business and government—can improve prospects for growth in living standards. The answer lies in the ability of a nation's men and women, first, to change their own future orientation and, second, and perhaps more important, to create labor-augmenting technological progress.

Solow's Formal Growth Model

Solow's growth model is easily understood through use of a simple formula, showing the contributions his three growth-promoting factors make to a nation's growth rate. He used historical data to estimate the contributions to growth of the three growth determinants and arrived at the formula below:

two-thirds the growth rate of the labor force	(1)
plus	
one-third the growth rate of the capital stock	(2)
plus	
the growth rate of technical knowledge	(3)
equals	
the growth rate of total output	(4)

The fraction two-thirds describing labor's contribution to growth is based on the fact that workers' share of total output is roughly two-thirds; likewise, capital's share is about one-third. Solow uses those fractions in his growth formula because the share of output paid to each resource is the best indicator we have of that resource's contribution to production.

The starkest reality underlying Solow's growth model has to do with output per worker. Consider growth in real output, the value shown as (4) in Solow's growth formula. Each 1 percentage point increase in labor's growth rate (1), other variables remaining the same, yields only two-thirds of a percentage increase in total output (4). With total output (4) increasing by less than the labor force (1), income per worker must fall. This result is not surprising if we imagine the entire labor force as if it were employed in a single factory. Then, imagine a 1 percent increase in the number of workers. Unless capital resources are also increased by 1 percent, the added workers cannot increase production enough to maintain the same output per worker. For the economy as a whole, the stark reality is that when the labor force grows, capital resources (2) must grow at the same rate if growth in output is going to keep pace with growth in the labor force.

Even so, equal growth in labor and capital is sufficient only to maintain existing living standards. Growth of 1 percent in both labor and capital yields only 1 percent growth in real output. More workers, more factories, more output, but the same output per worker and the same living standards. Under these conditions, to improve living standards requires an increase in the third component of growth—the third leg of the stool—technical knowledge, shown as (3) in Solow's growth formula. Technical knowledge is generally expressed as *total factor productivity* (TFP) and describes the part of total output that is attributable to the quality of the interactions between labor and capital in current production. Unless total factor productivity (3) increases, increases in output (4) will not exceed equal percentage growth in labor (1) and capital (2).[3]

Dissecting Total Factor Productivity (TFP)

Total factor productivity is not easy to measure, since improved interactions between labor and capital have many disparate sources. Suppose a farmer employs satellite imagery and global positioning technology to manage his fields more efficiently and produce more output. Is growth in the farmer's output attributable to the additional capital equipment now in place, the advance in knowledge supplied by the new technology, or perhaps an improvement in the education and training of the farmer himself? It is impossible to say. Recognizing these difficulties, government statisticians actually calculate TFP as a "residual" after inserting best possible estimates for (1), (2), and (4) in Solow's growth formula and solving for (3). That process has yielded estimates of TFP averaging almost 2 percent annually over the period 1948 to 1973, but less than 0.5 percent annually from 1973 to 1990. Considering only manufacturing industries, TFP has increased more markedly in the 1990s, exceeding levels reached in the early post-war years and suggesting prospects for healthy growth of per capita income.[4]

Is There a New Industrial Revolution?

The recent vigor of the U.S. economy is often attributed to the improved technology of information—what some economists have dubbed the "steam engine" of the new millennium, the innovation that is sparking a second Industrial Revolution. To these economists, the development of IT exemplifies a shift from an exogenous source of growth to an endogenous source. Indeed, the tremendous power of IT to stimulate economic growth comes less from scientists' exogenous discovery of the behavior of electrons embedded in a silicon chip than from the endogenous responses of highly competitive businesses to new opportunities for improving the design, manufacture, finance, and marketing of the things today's consumers want to buy.

Along with successive implementations of IT, today's growing firms are increasing their investments in capital resources and pressuring governments to support R&D, education, and worker mobility—all essential elements of TFP. And all essential for broadening and extending basic IT to more and more uses. Achieving maximum benefits from new technologies depends on large, prosperous markets, which provide the incentives for firms to develop new products and new technologies for producing them. Large markets and improved technologies lessen the risks of failure and strengthen entrepreneurial incentives.

Indeed, some growth economists have suggested that IT has created a "new economy," in which the old laws of economics no longer hold. The supposed new economy enjoys a higher growth path and offers workers higher-paying jobs than did the old economy. Moreover, because of its higher productivity and lower costs, the new economy has moved the Phillips curve farther to the left, thereby reducing tendencies toward either unemployment or inflation.

Other economists are not so sure. Productivity gains from IT have occurred mainly in computer manufacture, which represents only about 1 percent of the total U.S. economy. Although firms like Dell Computers and Cisco Systems handle large percentages of their orders on the World Wide Web, these firms are exceptions. Firms in other industries are actually experiencing decreases in productivity. Probably most firms use IT to plan production, control inventory, reduce lead times, and improve distribution. But it isn't clear that such uses of IT actually yield more output, being necessary merely to ensure survival in today's highly competitive markets.

Another downside to IT has been the failure to develop new "killer products," products like Coca-Cola, the Sony Walkman, and Post-it notes that resist market saturation and continue to fuel growth. Today's product innovations tend to become obsolete fairly quickly, so that firms must constantly renew their core products and production processes if they are to remain profitable. Some economists worry that today's competitive environment forces firms to concentrate more on short-term cost cutting than on developing the new products and processes that will increase productivity in the long run.

Government's Role in Economic Growth

Considering government's role in economic growth brings to mind an anecdote told about President Lyndon Johnson in the 1960s. When Johnson's economic advisers gathered around, pontificating about a current economic problem with all their supporting graphs, tables, and equations, the President would listen (not patiently, we are told) and finally reply: "Therefore . . . ?" He wanted to know what was being suggested by the discourse, what recommendation was being made, what he was supposed to do about the situation. In effect, the President wanted to know the answer to the age-old question of government's role (or potential role) in affecting the nation's economy. In particular, he wanted guidance as to appropriate government policy (including always the absence of any policy at all, a dim possibility but a possibility nevertheless) to affect economic growth.

Government has had less experience with growth policy than with policy for correcting short-run deviations from a given growth path. Policy to correct business cycles has not been perfected, of course, but years of experience have provided a measure of guidance for this sort of policy. Policy to affect growth is newer and much more complicated. For output to grow faster than population requires increases in total factor productivity, including improvements in technical knowledge, worker skills and motivations, and organizational efficiency. Some increase in TFP is virtually inevitable, societies as a whole generally learning more than they forget. But even highly trained psychologists don't claim full understanding of the components of TFP, which suggests something about the difficulties facing government policymakers.

One growth-enhancing process in which government might play a role is the nation's saving-investment rate.

Balancing Private With Public Investment

Achieving the efficient rate of saving and investment, however, is complicated by the difficulty of defining investment.

Defining investment appears simple, but, in fact, distinguishing between current consumption and investment for the future can be difficult. When we think of investments, we think about such obvious purchases as machines, buildings, and the like. To be correct, we should also think about investments in knowledge, including expenditures for research, job training, and education. But, you ask, if we include these expenditures in our definition of investment, why not include current expenditures for health care, child nutrition, even prenatal care? Surely such expenditures also contribute to our ability to produce for future consumption. Where should we draw the line between the more obvious means toward future production and the less obvious means that also increase current consumption?

Government's role in saving-investment decisions is actually carried out through its transfer payments, taxation, and spending programs. We might describe those responsibilities as contributing, respectively, to the nation's consumption, saving, and investing—although we must admit the impossibility of drawing precise lines between the categories. Transfer payments provide recipients the means for current consumption and have no direct consequences for future productivity.[5] Taxes qualify as saving, to the extent that tax collections exceed current government outlays, and combining government saving with private saving yields total domestic saving. Government spending programs that increase productivity qualify as public investment—highway construction and publicly supported research, job training, and education being the most obvious examples. Thus, a government's mix of transfer payments, taxes, and spending plays a major role in the nation's mix of consumption, saving, and investment.

Government can compensate for too little saving and investing in the private sector by increasing public saving and investment—increasing taxes and using tax revenues for making public investments. In this case, government's saving and investment substitutes for insufficient saving and investment in the private sector. On the other hand, if the private sector is saving-investing too much relative to current consumption, government can bring about the efficient mix for the nation as a whole by reducing its own saving-investment—by reducing taxes and/or increasing transfer payments until society as a whole is consuming, saving, and investing in the efficient proportion. This theory is the basis for the policy recommendations the U.S. government has offered high-saving Japan.

A Word of Caution

None of our theories about economic growth guarantees that growth will actually take place—or that it will occur at the efficient rate. As Robert Solow himself acknowledges, the growth process is complex, depending on many characteristics that interact within a nation and making broad generalizations impossible. In fact, probably all growth economists would agree with Solow about the practical difficulty of explaining economic growth and deciding growth policy. Having devoted most of their professional lives to studying the issue, having accumulated mountains of data, having run complicated regressions and simulations to test theories and forecast results of alternative policies, having done all these things and more, growth economists often find slipping from their grasp any semblance of certitude about their subject. The more they discover, the more they see yet to learn.

Solow has described this professional angst with an account of a personal experience. Walking near the Boston Federal Reserve Bank, no doubt following a conference on weighty issues, he spotted graffiti spray-painted on a board fence. In apparent despair, someone had proclaimed in clear block print: "I don't know. I just don't know." It is impossible to describe more eloquently than that the frustration of economists attempting to get a firm grip on the complex issue of economic growth.

Chapter 24

ACCOUNTING FOR HUMAN CAPITAL INVESTMENT

In Chapter 23, we considered only part of the issue: only growth, not development. Growth implies more of the same, but development implies fundamental changes in economic relationships, in methods of production, behavioral patterns, and, most fundamental of all, people's beliefs about their lives and prospects for the future. While Robert Solow despairs of fully understanding the determinants of economic growth, Theodore Schultz examines the kinds of economic change some economists find even more difficult to explain.

In fact, some economists regard economic development as more "social" than "science" and, therefore, even less subject to scientific analysis than economic growth. Theodore Schultz believes differently, that the standard tools of economic analysis are just as applicable to development as to other economic phenomena. Standard economic principles describing, for example, the benefits and costs of alternative resource allocations, incentives to save today and invest for tomorrow, and the advantages of decentralized decision making by informed buyers and sellers are perhaps even more applicable to economic development than they are to economic growth.

Schultz was awarded the Nobel Prize in 1979 along with Arthur Lewis for their research into economic development, in particular, the development problems of the world's poorest countries.

The Link Between Land and Entrepreneurship

Studies of economic development usually begin with that most basic of all resources: land. Even more important than land, however, are the farmers who work on the land. According to Theodore Schultz, economists tend to overrate the importance of the land over those who work the land. They are captivated by the land theories of the classical economists, developed two centuries ago when land was indeed the most critical resource for sustaining much of the world's population. The classical economists regarded land as a fixed resource and, therefore, a constraint that limits production of the means to human survival. The great classical economist David Ricardo warned that the world's limited supply of fertile land would make for differences in productivity and differences in the rents that could be paid on land of varying quality. Ricardo expected that shortages of fertile land would gradually nudge rents higher and higher, so that national income would be distorted increasingly in favor of landowners. Since landowners have little incentive to invest their ever-rising incomes in new productive capacity, the inevitable result would be an end to economic growth.

Such has failed to come to pass, of course, and today rent actually consumes only a tiny share of national income (only 2 percent in the United States in 1998). What the classical economists failed to anticipate was the behavior of enterprising users of land, those ordinary farmers who have developed ways of making erstwhile unfertile land fertile and of substituting for their limited supplies of land other more readily expandable resources. Rather than "lowly cultivators," as so regarded by the classical economists, Theodore Schultz sees farmers as "calculating economic agents." Rather than "indifferent to economic incentives," they are "fine-tuning entrepreneurs."

When nations fall behind in the process of economic development, says Schultz, it is not through want of land but through want of the kinds of incentives that build entrepreneurship.

Schultz worries that the entrepreneurial qualities so vital to economic development are weakened by government policies that distort price incentives. Without valid price signals, farmers' natural entrepreneurial behavior becomes confused and ineffective. In particular, Schultz cites government policies to favor urban over rural populations, including price controls that reduce the price of food and trade restraints that increase the price of manufactured goods. Through such policies, governments in many of the world's poorest countries reduce the benefits and increase the costs of entrepreneurial behavior on the farm.

Some African governments provide pertinent examples.

Africa's Commodity Boards

Development economists sometimes have difficulty explaining why resource-rich nations of sub-Sahara Africa[6] have developed so slowly, while relatively resource-poor nations of Southeast Asia are fast becoming economic powerhouses. One likely reason for the difference is Africa's commodity boards, which were established by many African governments after their nations emerged from colonialism in the 1960s. The idea was that commodity boards would help farmers market their coffee, cacao, cotton, cashews, and tobacco, because many African nations lack transportation and institutional arrangements for getting these valuable commodities to export markets. The commodity board would pay farmers a portion of the export revenue, which they would use to expand production, while the government would use the remaining revenue for building roads and ports and subsidizing business services and credit facilities so essential for further development.

The result has been different from expectations—which is often the case when a government bureaucracy takes over activities normally handled by private entrepreneurs. Instead of using export revenues to promote development, corrupt governments used it to build spectacular government facilities, facilities that would, no doubt, employ the friends and relatives of government officials. In the meantime, farmers were paid less and less for their crops, so farming that had previously been lucrative became much less so. Many farmers abandoned their land, and coffee and cacao production fell to less than half its previous level. Some farmers were forced to make their living smuggling or engaging in black market sales.

Some African governments attempted to reverse the decline in agriculture by buying up the land and establishing state farms, which were notoriously inefficient. The result is that today a continent of 300 million farmers imports close to half of its food. Food shortages have brought on inflation and social unrest and have increased the influence of local warlords. Riots and civil war have further diminished the allocation of resources to real production. Exports have shrunk. Revenues for saving and investment have disappeared. And farmers, who have historically demonstrated the entrepreneurial drive so essential to economic development, have been stripped of their entrepreneurial incentives.

The Complex Complexion of Capital

Economic development depends on entrepreneurship. And entrepreneurship depends on economic incentives and the human qualities that drive entrepreneurs continually to respond to changes in the benefits and costs of economic behavior. Theodore Schultz would expand Solow's definition of capital to include those human qualities (perhaps adding a fourth leg to Solow's growth stool). Much more than the usual suspects—the buildings and machines, materials and inventories that businesses purchase and replace when depreciated—Schultz's definition of capital includes human skills and knowledge, such intangible resources as require investments in education, health, and workers' ability to move about seeking opportunities for a better life.

Some people criticize Schultz's treatment of human beings as capital, or as marketable assets, suggesting that the comparison offends human dignity. Others find this criticism misguided, since human capital exists for the benefit of people themselves. "By investing in themselves, people can enlarge the range of choice available to them. It is the one way free men can enhance their welfare."[7] To believe otherwise is to suggest that inanimate objects—buildings and machines—are more valuable than living human beings. Today's military certainly recognizes the value of human capital. By substituting "smart weapons" for the indiscriminate sacrifice of military personnel, today's military protects its most valuable resource.

Investments in human capital are similar to investments in non-human capital in that acquiring both types requires saving. Workers must sacrifice current consumption to improve their education, health, or job mobility. Western nations encourage workers to make these sacrifices, so much so that in Western economies the human capital stock has grown even faster than the stock of nonhuman capital. With investments in human capital come improvements in the quality of the population working on the land. Total factor productivity increases; any scarcity of land is remedied by substituting more plentiful resources; output grows in excess of population growth; and opportunities increase for even more investments in nonhuman capital. This is the way Western nations have achieved steady improvements in average levels of living.

Again, sub-Sahara Africa provides a counterexample. In the decades following the end of the colonial period, these nations significantly reduced their investments in human capital. Per-student spending for education fell by one-third, and primary school enrollment today reaches only two-thirds of eligible children. One-third of Africa's college graduates have left the continent, depriving African nations of the benefits of their technical capabilities. One-fourth of Africa's children are malnourished. Many lack the most basic health care, including vaccinations and sanitary water, and many suffer from anemia, stomach parasites, and debilitating diseases. AIDS is killing Africa's young adults in their most productive years, as well as orphaning Africa's children and depriving them of the parental guidance and support so necessary for encouraging development of human capital.

Investing in Human Capital

Theodore Schultz experienced firsthand the importance of human capital. The oldest of eight children of a farm family in South Dakota, he failed even to complete high school. Nevertheless, he pursued bachelor's, master's, and doctoral degrees in agricultural economics and became a college professor, first at Iowa State College and later at the University of Chicago. The story is that Schultz was asked to leave Iowa State because he defended a colleague's publication of research that recommended margarine as a wartime substitute for the scarcer butter—a sensible recommendation but one not likely to win friends among Iowa's dairy farmers.

To document the importance of human capital, Schultz cites a fundamental riddle of economic growth. The riddle is that Western societies have consistently grown faster than could be predicted solely on the basis of population growth and growth of capital resources. In fact, less than half of the increase in national income over the half-century studied by Schultz is explained by increasing quantities of labor and (conventionally measured) capital resources. Schultz's explanation is that the data for measuring capital include only part of a nation's true capital stock, the nonhuman part. It is natural to emphasize nonhuman capital, he says, because this is the capital that is easier to measure. Still, the part of the capital stock that contributes most to economic growth is human capital.

One problem with measuring human capital stems, in part, from the difficulty in separating investments in human capital from spending for consumption. What types of spending build human capital? The obvious answer is spending for education. And in fact during the second quarter of the twentieth century, spending for education in Western nations rose about twice as fast as spending for nonhuman capital.[8] What about spending for food? Doubtless, some spending for food is done strictly for enjoyment, but some also contributes to workers' human capital. During many decades in the southern United States, a staple of rural diets, rhapsodized in country music, was "an R-C Cola and a Moon Pie," hardly sufficient for supporting the healthy development of workers' physical and mental abilities.[9] Only when industrial jobs brought higher incomes to their parents did many children of the rural South receive adequate nutrition for building the job skills necessary for escaping poverty.

Even spending for education cannot be classified entirely as investment, but in part as consumption—contributing not only to the educated person's productivity on the job but also to his enjoyment of life. The fact that a part of education is not investment but current consumption helps account for the fact that the cost of education has risen faster than income from increased education. Even so, Schultz reports that "the returns to education were relatively more attractive than those to non-human capital"[10]—which is music to the ears of educators everywhere.

Another critical form of investment in human capital is spending for on-the-job training, which amounts to more than half of the amount spent on formal education. Typically, the costs of capital investments are paid by the party that expects to receive the benefits, in the form of income on owned property, and in years past the costs of on-the-job training were generally paid by employers. But because today's workers move more freely from job to job than did workers of the past, today's employers risk losing whatever gains in productivity are made possible by on-the-job training. Unable to claim ownership of the human capital they help create, many employers lack the incentive to finance on-the-job training.

With the virtual disappearance of employer-financed on-the-job training, whatever training most workers receive today must be paid for by the workers themselves. The cost is not trivial and includes the cost of forgone income, now the fastest growing component of costs and the hardest cost for some workers to pay. Individual investors in human capital expect to earn a return on their investment; and indeed workers' investments in their own skills and job mobility are generally rewarded by significant increases in earnings. Still, it is difficult to calculate the true return on human capital investments, since the income from human capital investments is inseparable from increases in income that result from many other causes: workers' innate talents, personal qualities, personal access, and, occasionally, luck. Who among us does not know of a school dropout who went on to become spectacularly successful using some personal ability his schoolmates (and teachers) had no inkling he possessed?

Investments in education and on-the-job training yield greater income when workers enjoy longer years of work life. The ability to work longer years depends significantly on workers' health—another example of a human capital investment that also provides benefits in the here and now. To the extent that advances in health care extend average life expectancy, they permit more years of productive work. Greater productivity over longer years of work increases the income from investments in education and encourages workers to make the current sacrifice.

All these forms of human-capital investments depend to some extent on smoothly functioning capital markets. Typically, capital markets provide loans for investments on the basis of collateral produced by the investment. But investments in human capital lack any sort of appropriable collateral (indentured servitude being widely frowned upon!). Funds for investing in human capital are limited also because of uncertainty among lenders about the talents and productive capabilities of potential borrowers. The fact that private capital markets operate imperfectly when it comes to lending for education provides some justification for public investments in education—Pell grants and Hope scholarships being prime examples. Public investments to ease worker mobility may also enhance prospects for economic development, particularly in industries and regions with declining job opportunities. Indeed, helping surplus labor move off the farm to where it is needed in industry can increase workers' productivity in both sectors.

The Negative Effects of Certain Government Policies

If, as Schultz asserts, economic development depends significantly on building human capital, a fruitful policy for sustaining development is for government to encourage human-capital investments. Regrettably, even some of today's advanced economies continue policies that actually discourage such investments. Government regulations that interfere with prices distort the market signals that would identify the most productive human-capital investments. Tax laws discriminate against human-capital investments by failing to grant human-capital investments the same tax advantages granted to nonhuman capital. Human capital is like nonhuman capital in that it depreciates, becomes obsolete, requires maintenance. To equalize the tax treatment of human and nonhuman capital would call for allowable tax deductions to replenish depreciated human capital: through continuing education and skill development. Human capital investments are also discouraged by limitations on the free choice of professions, the result of discrimination, professional associations that limit membership, and restrictive licensing requirements.

Whatever the cause, insufficient investments in workers' knowledge and skill reduce a nation's potential for growth and development. Differences in workers' human-capital investments makes for differences in worker productivity and, ultimately, income. Widening income inequality increases the likelihood of social conflict and stiffens resistance to change.

Changing government policies to increase human-capital investment cannot yield overnight results, because it takes time for workers to respond to new opportunities. Fruit pickers cannot quickly become bioengineers. Also, human-capital investments are generally slower to yield increases in income than are investments in nonhuman capital. All of this may make it impossible for some nations to achieve the current saving necessary to make the investments—a major reason for poor countries' neglect of human capital.

Chapter 25

BRINGING ECONOMIC DEVELOPMENT TO POOR NATIONS

Theodore Schultz's co-prize winner in 1979 was Arthur Lewis. Lewis applies what is known and knowable about economic development to policy issues in today's less developed countries, often known as LDCs. We're speaking now of countries like Bangladesh, Congo (Kinshasa), Ethiopia, Ghana, India, Kenya, Pakistan, and Tanzania, with annual GDP per capita less than $500. Located mainly in sub-Sahara Africa and southern Asia, the LDCs are desperately seeking help to lift their people from poverty. Lewis admits that enhancing the development of poor countries might not seem worthwhile to rich nations like the United States. But, he says, helping such nations develop their resources and secure higher living standards for their people is a moral obligation of the world's developed nations.

Like Schultz, Arthur Lewis experienced firsthand the problems that later consumed his professional interest. Born on the island of St. Lucia in the Caribbean Sea, Lewis was one of five sons of a widowed mother. He had the good fortune to receive early tutoring from his father, however, which moved him ahead of other students in his age group and ultimately earned him a scholarship to the London School of Economics. He received his doctorate from that institution in the 1930s when there was lively interest in Keynesian macroeconomic theory and policies to correct business cycles. Lewis was less interested in business cycles than in economic development, however, and was attracted to the development philosophy of the neoclassical economists.

Lewis found some weaknesses in neoclassical economics, however, particularly in what he saw as its optimistic conclusions regarding the self-regulating powers of a free-market economy. Observing the world economy in the 1930s Lewis saw not the full employment, economic growth, and rising living standards predicted by the neoclassical economists, but stagnation. Consequently, he rejected the neoclassical confidence in laissez faire as a means of promoting economic development. Although laissez-faire may have brought economic development to European nations, he said, laissez-faire could leave today's LDCs with no development at all.

The Problem of Insufficient Saving and Investment

Economic development requires capital resources, and accumulating capital resources implies the ability to save and invest. But saving and investing are impossible when incomes are below the minimum necessary for subsistence—when people must consume all they produce if they are to survive. For nations too poor for *all* incomes to be above subsistence, neoclassical theory calls for significant income inequality, so that at least *some* are. In fact, according to neoclassical theory as few as 10 percent of income earners, those at the very top of the income scale, are all that is needed to save enough to yield the capital resources necessary for economic development. To test the neoclassical conclusions regarding saving and economic development, Lewis studied the Industrial Revolution in Europe and was surprised to discover a cause-effect relationship precisely opposite from the relationship assumed in neoclassical theory. Instead of higher saving leading to economic development, he found the reverse to be true: that economic development brings the higher incomes that make possible higher saving.

If neoclassical theory incorrectly explains economic development, then policymaking for the world's LDCs cannot be based on laissez-faire. More correctly, says Lewis, development requires active policy, policy decided and implemented by governments that understand the sociological and political factors that underlie economic development. "In trying to understand how a society, as distinct from its individual members, learns, chooses new directions, creates new loyalties, faces up to costly tasks, and so on, we come up to the limits of the mechanical analogies normally used by economists."[11]

Lewis's Two-Tiered Model of Development

Lewis was motivated to study economic development by two mysterious circumstances he observed in the world around him. One was the disparity between the price of steel (which many LDCs import) and the price of coffee (which they export). The high prices paid for steel imports and low prices received for coffee exports keep LDCs poor, he found, and indebted to the world's richer countries. The other mystery involves wage and profit trends. According to neoclassical theory, economic development increases the demand for labor and, therefore, wages; at the same time, greater accumulations of capital reduce its marginal product and, therefore, profits. As nations develop, the theory continues, income distribution shifts from profits to wages. The mystery is that the Industrial Revolution brought no such shift but, in fact, precisely the opposite trends in wages and profits.

Studying the conditions underlying these mysterious circumstances, Lewis arrived at one answer that he believes explains both.

The answer involves the LDCs' relative supplies of labor and capital. Applying Solow's growth model, Lewis finds that the LDCs have plentiful (indeed almost infinite) supplies of labor and very little capital. The image of hordes of peasant farmers gathering and processing coffee beans by hand leaps to mind. LDCs' skewed distribution of resources means that labor's marginal product (the added production of the last farmer working on a given plot of land) is virtually zero. Labor's marginal product might even be negative if the last farmer added to an already crowded field damages the coffee plants. Because of labor's low marginal productivity in farming, poor nations could move surplus farm labor into more productive jobs without suffering any loss of current production. Labor, therefore, is without cost, a finding that occupies a central position in Lewis's development theory.

Lewis divides an LDC's economy into two sectors: an emerging capitalist sector and a traditional subsistence sector. The capitalist sector enjoys an infinite supply of cheap labor fleeing the subsistence sector (exemplified by coffee plantations) for jobs in industry (typically mining or small manufacture). The effect of LDCs' labor surplus is that, except for a small class of highly skilled workers, wage rates in the capitalist sector remain at the level of subsistence. In fact, the capitalists have an interest in keeping productivity low in the subsistence sector, since low pay in that sector reduces workers' opportunities and reduces wage demands in the capitalist sector. A worker on a coffee plantation must accept a subsistence wage, since unemployed workers stand ready to take his job if he refuses. With expansion of the capitalist sector, he can move into an industrial job—but at the same wage for the same reason.

Many African nations seem to fit Lewis's description, having a sharp division between a highly capitalized mineral or energy sector operating side by side with a peasant sector of hardscrabble farms, primitive crafts, and petty traders. In many of these nations, wages in the capitalist sector exceed subsistence only to the extent that living costs in congested industrial centers exceed living costs in rural areas. With its low wage costs, the capitalist sector enjoys high profits and an increasing share of total income. Then the capitalists use their high profits to accumulate more capital, increasing the productivity of industrial workers and increasing industrial jobs. New capital investments also embody new technological knowledge, so that employment, output, and income increase until finally there is no more surplus labor remaining in the subsistence sector.

In Lewis's two-tiered model, saving and investment are not the cause of development but are the result of the development process, emerging from the capitalists' profits. (This is true, of course, unless profits in the capitalist sector are used for building mansions and importing luxury automobiles, which have also characterized Africa's LDCs.) To the extent that the capitalists' profits are siphoned off by landowners in the form of rent, less remains for saving and investment. If land is the LDC's scarcest resource, landowners can extract all of the surplus product, leaving the capitalist sector with insufficient profits for making capital investments. An established class of landlords (generally including moneylenders, priests, soldiers, and princes) is less likely than a capitalist class to make new investments, so that capital formation slows. The way to increase capital formation and promote development in the capitalist sector is to shift income distribution from rent to profit.

Government Policy for Development

For LDCs that lack capitalist profits for investment, Lewis recommends development through other means: specifically, through government projects that employ surplus farm labor to build roads, bridges, irrigation channels, and port facilities, construction of which requires much labor but very little capital. Such investments are called "infrastructure" investments and are critical to the eventual industrialization of the domestic economy.

With surplus farm labor and without a profitable capitalist sector to provide sufficient saving, government may have to create additional money to finance infrastructure investment. Creating additional money keeps consumer spending from falling and reduces the sacrifice of consumer products in the short run, while increasing the capacity to produce in the long run. But creating additional money also raises the possibility of inflation. Lewis concedes that consumer prices may rise during construction of infrastructure, since workers' incomes will rise without a proportional increase in the supply of consumer goods. But he predicts that when new infrastructure is finally in place, supplies of consumer goods will increase, along with increases in capitalists' profits and an automatic tendency toward more private savings and investment. Then inflation will return to normal. To minimize the inflation associated with infrastructure investment, government should invest in programs that quickly yield gains in total production. Water projects and seed farms, for example, might best be undertaken before school buildings.

More Pitfalls

In Lewis's two-tiered economy, economic development continues as long as labor costs absorb such a small fraction of the capitalists' income as to leave sufficient profits for new capital investment. Nevertheless, at some point increasing labor costs are bound to reduce prospects for further investment, so that economic development grinds to a halt.

When growth in the capitalist sector has finally absorbed all the surplus labor from the subsistence sector, market wages must rise above subsistence. Capitalistic employers might postpone the effects of labor shortage by going outside the domestic workforce for workers, perhaps through inducements to immigration or by relocating production facilities to labor-surplus areas abroad. Immigration can so augment the domestic labor supply as to prevent an increase in wage rates, a possibility that is understandably unpopular with local workers. Relocating factories abroad is no less unpopular, since it reduces domestic capital formation and reduces job opportunities for the domestic labor force. But relocating production facilities has the advantage of introducing new technologies and new resources to other LDCs and exploiting whatever favorable cultural and economic conditions may prevail outside the domestic economy.[12]

In spite of all the pitfalls, Lewis is optimistic about the use of active government policy for economic development. By building up high-quality institutions, he says, a poor nation can ultimately raise the productivity of its farmers and industrial workers. Examples of such successes can be a guide and an inspiration to other nations aspiring to growth.

In his words: "Growth occurs whenever there is a gap between capability and opportunity."[13] The role of government should be to create opportunities for private individuals to fill the gap.

Two Tigers

Creating opportunities for private individuals to fill the gap between capability and opportunity was the objective of the governments of two Southeast Asian "tigers."

The island nation of Singapore is the center of what has been called the Asian *miracle*. Singapore emerged from colonialism a mere three decades ago, resource poor, with no major industries and with only scattered low-skill workshops. Beginning in the 1980s, Singapore's founding prime minister Lee Kuan Yew resolved to make whatever changes in Singapore's physical and social institutions were necessary to bring economic development to its people. By the early 1990s Singapore's living standards were surpassed in Asia only by those of Japan.

The steps toward Singapore's transformation are simple to state but difficult to accomplish. Primarily, they have involved infrastructure investments that encourage high-tech manufacturing firms from other countries to bring their production facilities to Singapore. Singapore's investments in a modern airport and seaport facilities, roads and communications networks made the island nation especially attractive for producers of such products as computers, computer software, and precision instruments. But Singapore's principal infrastructure investment, the one that is most attractive to foreign manufacturers, is an educational and training system that produces in Singapore some of the world's most productive workers. Along with its skilled workers, Singapore offers foreign businesses help with research and development and a "culture of innovation" that readily accepts change. Singapore's appeal to "brain-intensive industries" brings high-wage jobs, so that today Singapore tops some global rankings in terms of both output per capita and personal freedom.

Along with Singapore, South Korea has also experienced an economic miracle, rising from third-world status only two decades ago to become a major producer of high-tech exports. Also like Singapore, South Korea has allowed substantial governmental involvement in its development policies—in the form of an Economic Development Board charged to think about where the economy should go and what incentives might help businesses get there. Adhering to a series of official five-year plans, South Korea's government has built industrial parks and subsidized utilities for new businesses. It has provided tax rebates and low-cost loans to Korea's industrial conglomerates, or *chaebols,* for expanding exports and investing in selected new industries. It has sent students to U.S. universities, hired technical advisers from Japan, and licensed foreign technologies for use in high-growth industries.

The philosophy of Korea's Economic Development Board is, first, to increase output and, second, to invest extra profits in developing brainpower (not difficult in a Confucian culture that gives high priority to education). Korea wants its engineers to think several years ahead and its workers to think like entrepreneurs, tailoring their microwave ovens, TVs and VCRs, video cameras, and CD players to foreign tastes, so as to capture niche markets for their exports. Korea's disciplined workers put in 70-hour weeks to make their high-quality products leaders in world markets.

Output per capita in South Korea has more than doubled since its development program began less than 20 years ago. Today its average living standards are higher than living standards in Argentina and roughly comparable with those of the Czech Republic.

Chapter 26

USING ECONOMETRICS TO EXPLAIN ECONOMIC DEVELOPMENT

Historians can chronicle the experience of development, and theorists can weave their explanations, but a true understanding of economic growth and development requires empirical data and econometric analysis. The role of Nobel laureate Robert Fogel has been to apply econometric methods to the real experience of growth and development. For this accomplishment Fogel was awarded the Nobel Prize, along with Douglass North, in 1993.

Fogel is more precisely known as a *cliometrician,* where the prefix *clio* comes from Clio, the Greek Muse of History. Thus, Robert Fogel is an economic historian who uses econometrics to test theories of history.

His main use of econometrics has been to measure the impact on economic growth and development of key science and technological innovations, key government policies, and key environmental and institutional changes. For example, Fogel began one study to measure the effects of good nutrition on the health of the aged, but he ended by revealing the effects of good nutrition on economic growth. Based on his econometric analysis, he concluded that half of Britain's growth since 1790 can be explained by improved nutrition.

Fogel's education prepared him well for the tasks of economic history. He was born to Russian immigrants to the United States and spent several of his young years as a Communist youth organizer. His family operated a small business and was virtually penniless. Young Fogel first attended the public schools of New York City, where his talent and obvious dedication to learning moved his teachers to encourage him to aspire to a career in science. Along with science, Fogel exhibited a love for literature and history. This particular combination of talents, plus the hardships his family suffered during the Great Depression moved him to focus on the sorts of institutional change that are necessary for ensuring economic stability and equity.

Later at Columbia University one of Fogel's professors was conducting research into the effect on economic development of infrastructure investments, in particular, construction of U.S. railroads and canals during the rapid growth years of the nineteenth century. Such venerable economists as Joseph Schumpeter and Texan Walt W. Rostow had asserted that a major technological innovation, such as the railroad, is critical for a nation's takeoff into sustained economic development. Without empirical support, however, Fogel questioned the validity of a single spur to development, and he resolved to seek scientific verification.

Railroads in U.S. Economic Development

The U.S. railroad network was begun in the early 1800s, not intentionally to promote economic development but rather to provide low-cost transportation for moving heavy freight from America's farms and mines to cities and seaports. Railroads were initially intended merely as a supplement to canals, which at that time were considered the more efficient means of carrying freight. The initial view had changed by mid-century, however, when railroads were represented as so fundamental to U.S. prosperity as to merit financial support from the federal government.

Fogel's econometric analysis supports the importance of rail transport but disputes the idea that any single innovation was indispensable for economic development in the United States. In fact, Fogel suggests that by uncritically accepting the necessity of a railroad network for U.S. economic development, the U.S. government left itself open to extortion—in the form of too generous rewards to builders and operators of railroads.

Even mature nations occasionally offer government support for investments expected to enhance further development, and transportation is a popular candidate. Take for example European governments' support for Airbus, production of which is intended to broaden and deepen technical capabilities in the four European nations that supply the fuselages, engines, and electronics for the finished airplanes. Government subsidies to Airbus have been justified as compensation for the low rate of return expected from a new enterprise in competition with established aircraft manufacturer Boeing. Defenders of Airbus subsidies expect that their cost will be recovered eventually in the increased opportunity for economies of scope and learning throughout European industry—much as the railroad no doubt provided opportunities for industrial development in the United States.

The railroad network affected U.S. growth and development both directly, through lower costs for transporting heavy freight, and indirectly, through the economic boost building railroads gave to industries supplying construction materials and equipment. Nevertheless, if railroads are to be accepted as indispensable to U.S. economic development, it must be shown that their direct and indirect contributions to U.S. output exceeded significantly the potential contributions of alternative means of transportation, including wagon haulage, water transportation, and motor vehicles (the latter of which Fogel suspects would have developed sooner in the absence of rail transport).

To test the indispensability of railroads, Fogel first estimates the "social saving" in 1890 associated with the cheap transport of basic agricultural commodities. He defines social saving as the difference between the cost of shipping wheat, corn, pork, and beef by rail and the cost of shipping exactly the same commodities between exactly the same locations over navigable waterways. Considering first the long-haul transport of wheat, Fogel found negative social savings of about $38 million: in other words, rail transport actually cost $38 million more than comparable water transport. He modified his initial conclusion, however, to account for certain difficult-to-measure costs of water transport, including cargo losses, transshipment costs, wagon haulage costs to markets not on waterways, capital costs not reflected in water rates, time lost from using a slower mode of transportation, and the cost of being unable to use water routes during the winter months. After adding estimates of these costs to water transport costs, Fogel concludes that transporting wheat by rail cost less than half transport by water, yielding positive social savings of $73 million from long-haul transport by rail.

Savings from short-haul rail transport are more difficult to calculate, since short hauls serve more diverse locations and require more connecting means of transport. Still, Fogel concludes that social savings from short-haul transport by rail are even greater than from long-haul because railroads require less wagon haulage than is required to transport freight to and from existing waterways. To measure the social savings, Fogel constructed an econometric model where the cost difference depends on (1) the volume of freight, (2) average freight rates by wagon, water, and rail, (3) the distance freight must be moved from its source to water and rail shipping points, and (4) the distance from end shipping points to primary markets. The resulting equation yields positive social savings of $213 million on rail short hauls.

Fogel modified his initial cost estimates, using his own judgment and historical knowledge. Then, because his data include only about one-fourth of the commodities actually transported in 1890, he multiplied his estimated social savings by four. Finally, he arrived at total social savings from rail transport of more than $800 million, or 7 percent of the nation's total output of $12 billion in 1890. Seven percent of the nation's total output is a substantial amount, equivalent in 1998 to what U.S. consumers and businesses spent for all information processing equipment, about twice as much as U.S. new-home buyers spent for new homes, or all of corporate profits in that year.

Even so, we have considered so far only the direct social savings of rail transport: that is, the lower costs of transporting freight by rail. The total social savings from railroads include also the indirect effects, in particular, the economic stimulus to new industries and the new technologies and worker skills that developed specifically to support railroad construction. (Leontief's grid is helpful here.) Defenders of government subsidies claimed that rail construction was crucial to the development of many industries not directly affected by cheap rail transport, chiefly iron, coal, lumber, transportation equipment, and machinery. However, when Fogel investigated the railroads' use of these products, he was surprised to find rather insignificant purchases (only 2.8 percent of the total output of these industries). Interestingly, Fogel found that the years of significant railroad construction (1850–1872) do not correspond to the years of most rapid industrial development in the United States—that construction of the railroad network actually occurred after the nation began its growth spurt in the 1820s.

While surely beneficial, Fogel concludes that construction of the U.S. railroad network was not absolutely essential to U.S. economic development. Rather, he asserts that the phenomenal growth of the U.S. economy actually resulted from the great body of scientific knowledge acquired in the seventeenth, eighteenth, and nineteenth centuries. In fact, he argues, economic development arises out of a "multiplicity of solutions along a wide front of production problems." It is not from a few lucky decisions that growth emerges, he says, but from "a broad supply of opportunity created by the body of knowledge accumulated over all preceding centuries."[14]

Economic Growth as a Public Good

Our discussion of government support for railroads brings us back full circle to that age-old question with which we began Part 6: the role, if any, government should play in economic growth.

Economists sometimes justify a governmental role because of their characterization of economic growth as a "public good." The distinguishing characteristic of a public good is that the individual or group that produces it pays the entire cost, while the benefits flow to individuals and groups who have not paid. The creator of one of Simon Kuznets' "epochal innovations," for example, receives as a reward only a tiny fraction of the benefits the society as a whole enjoys from his efforts. (James Watt and Thomas Edison hardly lived fabulously wealthy lives.) Likewise, an individual or group that undertakes a growth-promoting endeavor pays the entire cost. But because the benefits of growth extend to the society as a whole, the persons responsible receive only a small share of the gains made possible by their efforts. The builder of a railroad and the manufacturer of an Airbus engine pay the cost and assume the risk of operating a new enterprise, while many other businesses benefit indirectly from the income and the learning that flow from it.

As is true of public goods in general, a rational comparison of the private benefits and costs of growth and development might discourage individuals and businesses from making the effort. This is the kind of reasoning that underlies a general failure privately to protect and enlarge natural fisheries, broaden the reach of education, preserve natural ecosystems, and so forth. The failure of private businesses to undertake these sorts of activities leaves a role for government, with government-sponsored programs that combine the efforts of occasionally reluctant individuals toward achieving lasting benefits that all of society can enjoy.

Economists have identified technological innovation as essential to economic growth. But technological innovation is another of those growth-promoting endeavors with characteristics of a public good. The long years of forgone income, failed prototypes, and apparently useless laboratory experiments that precede a successful innovation are too costly for most individuals to assume—indeed too costly for all but the largest privately owned businesses. To effect technological progress may occasionally require either institutional support for innovators or direct innovation by collectivized institutions—in a word, government.

A decision to invest in a technological innovation is similar to any other investment decision, in that it is based on a comparison between benefits and costs. Because the costs of innovation occur mostly in the present and benefits accrue in the future, future benefits must be discounted at a rate dependent on their distance in the future and the likely return from alternative uses of investment funds. Investments and (especially) technological innovations also suffer from the risk of failure and loss, which must be incorporated in the benefit-cost calculation. Given the uncertainty of returns, the perceived future benefits from technological innovations are likely to fall short of current costs. Under these circumstances and absent some sort of special inducement, technological innovations may not be undertaken by private businesses.

Technological innovations have another characteristic that creates a gap between private and social benefits: economies of scale. Large-scale technological innovations may open more opportunities for success, and large-scale applications may yield more possibilities for adaptations, refinements, and eventual evolution into still more new technologies. Technological innovations build upon one another. If the cost of all the preceding scientific-technical steps had to be included in the cost of one more step, that next step might not be taken. A nation can ensure that next steps are actually taken by assuming collectively (through tax-supported subsidies) the costs of creating the basic scientific knowledge necessary to support techno-logical innovations. In this way, a nation imposes on current innova-tors only the costs associated with their single contribution to eco-nomic growth and development.

Kenneth Arrow and James Buchanan provide insights here. The issue underlying technological innovation involves appropriability: the ability to claim as personal reward the benefits made possible through one's own endeavors. Some of the rewards of technological innovation are indeed appropriable, in the profits that flow to inno-vating firms. But if only the technological innovations that yield appropriable benefits are undertaken, the world would be short of innovations whose social benefits more than justify their costs. This is particularly true of innovations that provide benefits over wide dis-tances and time periods, some of which are currently unknown and largely unknowable. Today's public investments in, say, education or childhood nutrition are not easily linked with the technological inno-vations of tomorrow's biogeneticists. The technological innovations of tomorrow's Nobel Prize–winning scientists are not easily linked to their grandparents' investments in trips to natural history museums!

Chapter 27

DEVELOPMENT ISSUES FOR THE MATURE ECONOMY

G unnar Myrdal's concerns about growth and development focus on the opposite end of the spectrum from the economists discussed so far, on the time when a nation has passed through the difficult process of economic development to reach economic maturity. A mature nation has acquired so much productive capital that the rate of return on new investments has fallen, and economic growth has settled down to Solow's steady-state.

Indeed, Myrdal did his major work at a time when Western nations had arrived at what might be described as maturity. With annual GDP per capita greater than $25,000, Austria, Belgium, Denmark, France, Germany, Japan, the Netherlands, Norway, Switzerland, and the United States[15] are beyond such immediate concerns of food and shelter as those that compel the attention of the world's LDCs. Their prosperity enables today's mature nations to shift their attention from growth and development to issues bearing on the ethics of their economic institutions: issues involving equality of opportunity, equitable income distribution, and social responsibility toward the less fortunate. Myrdal and Friedrich von Hayek were awarded the Nobel Prize in 1974 for their analysis of the connectedness of economic, social, and political phenomena.

Deciding policy toward issues facing mature economies continues the old debate: whether mature nations should rely on free markets alone to allocate resources or whether the magnitude of global problems calls for some sort of central planning. Myrdal comes down on the side of planning—planning that is not comprehensive, he says, but pragmatic—flexible enough to adjust to changing economic conditions. Myrdal's support for central planning is quite different from the views of his co–Nobel Prize winner. The gossip is that the Prize Committee initially intended to award the prize to Myrdal but was persuaded to balance his support for significant government involvement in the economy by choosing Hayek to share the prize. Ironically, Hayek's views have been more enduring than Myrdal's, such that many of today's policy recommendations—to developed and less developed nations alike—stress the disadvantages of central planning for guiding development.

An aside: Gunnar Myrdal is probably unique among Nobel Prize winners in that he is married to another winner. His wife Alva won the Nobel Peace Prize in 1982.

The Case for the "Welfare State"

Before the Industrial Revolution began in the eighteenth century, economic activity was regulated by trade associations called guilds. Blacksmiths, cobblers, and bakers, for example, conformed to the standards set by their respective guilds. Then for nearly two centuries following the Industrial Revolution, widely dispersed enterprises operated largely without any formal controls, with government's involvement in economic affairs limited to temporary responses to particular crises. Only in the twentieth century did government's role in the economy become more pervasive and better coordinated. World War I brought a cataclysmic change in economic relationships, calling for massive government involvement in the economy and such fundamental changes in public attitudes that many government regulations were not removed after the war ended.

Throughout history wars have always brought sudden and violent change, the sorts of change that lessen people's respect for the status quo and all the institutions that support it. One prewar institution that succumbed to wartime disrespect was the gold standard. The gold standard derived its support from the fact that it operated without any sort of government control to balance flows of spending among nations. The problem with the gold standard was that while achieving balance in a nation's international payments, it ignored the damage achieving international balance might bring to the nation's domestic economy. Specifically, the gold standard required a nation to adjust its money supply to bring international payments into balance, regardless of the effect this might have on domestic incomes, employment, and prices. Adjusting its money supply to balance its international payments might subject a nation to too much money and rampant inflation or not enough money and recession.

Having endured the horrors of World War I and the Great Depression, the people of the world's mature nations became less willing to tolerate wide swings in prices and employment. For many, the willingness to endure domestic instability was replaced by support for rational government planning—planning that they hoped would bring more order to their lives. Of course, these are just the notions Friedrich von Hayek so forcefully rejects.

Other forces were also at work pushing mature nations toward central planning. Advances in technology and business management were integrating formerly scattered markets and strengthening businesses' control of output and prices. Giant firms in mining, food processing, transportation, and finance were challenging governments' powers of taxation, while at the same time strengthening popular support for laws to curb the power of big business. Large labor unions were clamoring for the right to bargain collectively and for macroeconomic policies to guarantee full employment. In turn, programs to increase employment were increasing government's need for tax revenues and increasing public support for progressive taxation. Political parties were identifying broad constituent groups and pressuring government toward policies supporting group interests.

To the surprise of its critics, increased government involvement did not immediately "ruin the economy" but in many cases actually accelerated economic growth. Contrary to the critics' worst fears, increased government involvement in the economy brought no pressure for large-scale nationalization of industry—no slide down the proverbial "slippery slope to socialism." Indeed, rather than actively controlling businesses, more powerful central governments generally limited their involvement in business to rather loose regulation and oversight of business practices.

Defenders of an increasing role for government pointed to a long history of increasing government involvement in markets. Government's increased role in economic affairs was not consciously planned, they said, but evolved as a political ideal, to be revised and reworked along with changes in fundamental economic conditions. What critics had dubbed "the welfare state" did not grow out of any sort of socialistic ideology, its supporters claimed. On the contrary, it had emerged from a long evolutionary process, simply because people had grown accustomed to market restraints and liked them. People came to see government regulations not as the decrees of a too powerful central government but as the outcome of democratic processes intended to protect the rights of ordinary men and women.

International Implications

The welfare state has a downside, of course. As mature nations expand their welfare state, they become less interested in and less committed to a healthy international economy. Why should a nation get involved in international problems, when international involvement brings fewer benefits than does a more concentrated attention to domestic problems? International relations are inherently more uncertain and less controllable than domestic relations. People tend to react to uncertainty and loss of control with self-centered behavior and hostility toward outsiders. Thus, instead of providing the means and the motivation for mutually beneficial international cooperation, the domestic welfare state may foster isolationism, hostility, and even aggression.

Indeed, at the same time that the welfare state brings mature nations sustained economic prosperity, the LDCs are likely to sink more deeply into poverty. With increasing population growth and insufficient investment many nations of Africa and southern Asia face a long future of economic backwardness. Wide divergences between the prospects of poor and rich nations weaken support for international law and foster narrow nationalistic interests at the expense of policies that could foster economic development.

Mature nations' indifference to the problems of LDCs instills in poor nations the belief that their poverty is the fault of the international system. Within the LDCs, popular hostility toward mature nations becomes a way for unscrupulous politicians to benefit from anti-West sentiment, promoting flag burnings and the kinds of terrorism associated with the governments of Pakistan and Sudan. In a sort of international blackmail, LDCs can make life extremely difficult for mature nations.

Myrdal's remedy: To replace international disintegration with international harmony requires not a welfare state but a "welfare world": a world in which excessive nationalism is replaced by international economic planning.

A Welfare World

The goal of international economic planning would be to coordinate and harmonize economic activity among all nations, in support of the universal ideals of liberty, equality, and brotherhood. Toward this goal, Myrdal's welfare world would promote the narrow interests of the world's LDCs relative to those of mature nations. For example, because of their small domestic markets, LDCs lack sufficient demand for building manufacturing industries. If they are to develop a healthy industrial base, they must be allowed to levy tariffs against imports and pay subsidies for producing exports. Mature nations must be denied these trade advantages. Moreover, to begin development the LDCs must have savings for investing in physical and human infrastructure and for building modern productive facilities. Mature nations must be encouraged to grant financial assistance toward these goals. Involvement in an international economic plan can create hope among the people of LDCs and encourage sacrifice for the sake of a better future.

More important, Myrdal's international economic planning would ensure international peace and social harmony. The world's irresponsible groups typically become responsible, he says, when they are finally vested with legitimate power. Thus, the way to tame international conflict is to create institutions that bring free and equal opportunity to all the world's people. This is a better way to ensure good behavior among nations than through sanctions, military force, and bribes to petty dictators. Such coercive measures only feed the frustrations of disadvantaged groups and encourage international terrorism.

Society's Moral Dilemmas

Some of Gunnar Myrdal's critics regard him as a kind of "scold," a nuisance who persists in calling people's attention to their faults, their shortcomings, their failure to live up to the highest ethical standards of behavior. Myrdal would probably agree with his critics—and proceed undeterred to do more of the same.

Myrdal has devoted his life and career to examining issues that overlap economics and ethics. Too often, he says, economists excuse their failure to deal with ethical issues on the grounds that ethics has no place in their economic models. Indeed, the neoclassical economists' goal of maximum net benefits promotes a policy of "triage" toward global economic problems. Originating as a way to classify battlefield casualties, triage divides needful people into three groups and dictates the allocation of resources toward the one group that can be helped most with the least expenditure. The effect is to withdraw attention from the most needful group—evidence, to Myrdal, of the sacrifice of ethics for the sake of economic efficiency.

The Hazards Ahead

Despite Myrdal's admonitions, it is difficult to be optimistic about the development prospects of today's LDCs. Nations like the United States that developed a century ago had an easier time of it. For the United States, a conglomeration of factors—geographic and climatic, social and political, religious and psychological—came together in such fortunate combination as to initiate and sustain fundamental changes in patterns of production, exchange, and consumption. Over a relatively short period in world history a relatively small part of the earth's surface transformed itself from a self-sufficient (most of the time) farming and rigidly hierarchical social structure to a collection of versatile, flexible, liberal societies, whose concerns are no longer economic conditions that are simply survivable but economic conditions that continually improve. During the century when today's mature nations were completing their economic development, today's LDCs languished in such backwardness that their people's current living standards are below those that prevailed in today's mature nations before their great advance began.[16]

Documenting the experience of development in today's mature economies can help identify the necessary factors and provide some guidance for development policies in LDCs. Regrettably, much of a particular nation's experience is unique to that nation's geography, people, and culture and untransferable to other, also unique, nations. Many of the factors influencing development are linked only indirectly, loosely, and partially with growth consequences. Whereas a particular social and economic structure may be essential for development whatever the nation, within that structure a particular nation must create its own combination of elements to fit its traditions, possibilities, circumstances. In its particular development process, a developing nation may play around the edges of a process common to other nations, but it must itself follow a unique process.

Perhaps the greatest advantage enjoyed by today's mature nations has been their people's freedom to communicate without fear. If people fear reprisals from failed experiments, they tend to suppress the sorts of knowledge that might help transform old ways of behavior. Absent such fear, people become more willing to take risks, to attempt new methods and generate new knowledge. Once having enjoyed the benefits of knowledge, having bitten from the forbidden fruit, people strive to learn more. Indeed, from the start of the worldwide knowledge revolution in the eighteenth century, the romance of the new has come to dominate today's mature nations— initially in the application of new science to industrial technology and today in the scientific revolution of information systems.

And herein may lie a fundamental impediment to development in today's lagging economies.

Information is so easily transmitted today that it can outpace knowledge. Today's LDCs are discovering that the free dissemination of scientific and technical information is not sufficient in itself to effect economic change. In fact, without the social, cultural, political, and material underpinnings that have enabled Western nations to apply information, the expectations of today's lagging economies cannot be fulfilled. Dashed expectations yield frustrations and disruptions that stifle enterprise and productive change. All of this suggests an even more urgent and less certain role for today's mature nations in promoting the fundamental changes essential for LDCs to join the community of developed nations.

PART 7
FINANCING GROWTH-PROMOTING INVESTMENTS

Harry Markowitz • William Sharpe •
James Tobin • Franco Modigliani •
Paul Samuelson • Merton Miller •
Robert Merton • Myron Scholes •
Bertil Ohlin • James Meade •
Robert Mundell • William Vickrey •
James Mirrlees

The close links that economists perceive between their academic pursuits and the "real world" are not always apparent to Joe and Jane Six-Pack. Whatever achievements economists claim in economic theory are often dismissed by ordinary people as solutions to mind games with no relevance at all to life's real problems. The perception is not so negative when it comes to the work of financial economists, however. Financial economists are generally seen to be tuned-in to real events in real markets. Perhaps more so than is apparent with other types of economists, financial economists bring the principles of economics to bear on things people really care about.

(It is a bit ironic, therefore, that "true" economists tend to be rather snobbish toward financial economists. Perhaps they are offended by what they perceive as financial economists' willingness to "dirty" their hands with such mundane tasks as making money.)

Financial markets are a monumental achievement of market economies. To say that financial markets comprise the nerve center of a market system may be trite, but the analogy is appropriate. Like the body's nerve center, their main function is to receive and relay information and in so doing determine the types and level of economic activity today and the prospects for growth tomorrow.

Chapter 28

HISTORICAL PERSPECTIVES

A big reason people around the world want to come to the United States is, of course, political freedom. U.S. immigrants want to escape the constraints on behavior exercised by the heavy hand of government. But just as important, immigrants are seeking to participate in the great wealth-producing machine that is the U.S. economy. They want access to the immense material and financial wealth that is made possible by our rich natural resources and highly motivated workers.

Until early in the twentieth century, a nation's wealth was denominated in terms of precious metals. Beginning with the Age of Exploration, nations began accumulating stocks of gold and silver, frequently to fund their war-making endeavors. Successful wars brought more territory under control, along with jurisdiction over its material and human wealth. In those years, the true act of saving was performed by the small farmers and shopkeepers who sacrificed current production to fight the wars of their feudal masters. The true act of investment was not so much to create new capital resources as to capture and exploit resources already existing in other countries.

Nations added to their wealth through so-called favorable terms of trade: trade that brought higher income from exports than they paid out for imports. Under the system known as *mercantilism*, nations set limits on imports in order to ensure a surplus of in-payments, manifest in a continuing inflow of gold and silver. Needless to say, for one nation to limit its own imports necessarily limited other nations' exports and threatened to stall trade altogether. It was the likelihood of a collapse of world trade that motivated Adam Smith to write *The Wealth of Nations* in 1776. A nation creates wealth, said the venerable Scot, by using its resources efficiently to produce the things consumers want to buy, whatever the location of those consumers—U.S. airplanes for all the world's tourists and Asian cellular phones for all its commuters, although these examples would have been science fiction to him. Resource allocation is most efficient, Smith went on, if markets are free to trade whatever imports and exports people want, without any form of government restraint.

True to Adam Smith's promise, freer world trade did bring increases in production and rising living standards. Financing a growing volume of trade soon required more spending power than was available from existing supplies of gold and silver, however, so that transactions came to be carried out using paper currency representing specific quantities of those precious metals. The use of paper money required international cooperation to ensure consistency in value, a requirement that forged closer interdependencies among nations. At the same time, ensuring consistent value for a nation's currency required limitations on its growth with, as a result, slower growth in economic activity and smaller gains in living standards. Closer interdependencies among nations and slower economic growth within them led to occasional frictions, increasing both the frequency of wars and the costs associated with them.

Markets for Investment Funds

The world's wisest leaders sought peaceful means of economic growth—through freer trade, along with increased saving and investment. Achieving such aims calls for efficient markets, especially markets for saving and investment. Secure and informative financial markets encourage investors to offer their savings to business firms for acceptable compensation. And they ensure that firms allocate scarce investment funds to projects whose rates of return exceed their cost. Businesses affirm their obligations to investors by issuing securities: either bonds, which promise to pay interest at specified rates and principal at a stated maturity date; or stocks, which pay higher or lower dividends (or no dividends at all) depending on the success of the firm's investment projects. We might think of bonds and stocks as intermediate assets that parcel out among investors the return and risk from production according to investors' preferences for, one, a guaranteed return specified in a bond or, two, the possibility of an exceptionally high return on a stock.

Firms market their securities through financial institutions. Buyers attempt to pay the lowest price for securities; sellers attempt to obtain the highest. The price paid and received is the inverse of the interest rate. Thus, investors who pay $95 for a new bond promising to pay $100 at the end of a year receive (approximately) 5 percent interest for allowing the issuer to use their funds. In turn, the issuer of such a bond must create capital resources capable of producing value at least 5 percent over costs in order to make good on the promise. If investors pay only $90 for a $100 bond, the implied interest rate is (approximately) 10 percent, and the requirement to use the funds productively is even more urgent. At maturity, the bond's face value ($100) must be paid to the bondholder. But before maturity the bond may be resold in secondary markets for a price higher or lower than its face value, depending on its attractiveness to other investors relative to newly issued securities. If new bond issues are paying 10 percent, for example, holders of the 5 percent bond above would see its market value fall until its price is competitive with prices of newly issued bonds, and vice versa.

Efficient financial markets nurture investors' confidence, encourage saving, and provide freer access to funds for business firms, which then create growth-promoting capital resources. Financial economists contribute to the efficiency of financial markets by providing information relevant to investor and business decisions, information regarding the potential profitability of investment projects and the true value of securities. Improved information helps ensure that savings flow efficiently to the types of capital investments that contribute most to economic growth.

Balancing Return and Risk

The story of financial economics usually begins with the French mathematician Louis Bachelier around the beginning of the twentieth century. Mathematicians are always looking for real data for conducting their experiments, and Bachelier seized on data from financial markets. He first identified patterns in stock prices and then attempted to apply the laws of probability to predict their future trends. Finding too many determining factors at work (in the language of statisticians, too much "noise"), Bachelier concluded that stock prices are impossible to predict. In fact, he concluded that stock prices are just as likely to fall as to rise, so that the average return to stock pickers over the long haul is zero. A 10 percent return in a good year is offset by a 10 percent loss in a bad year. Bachelier's work was ignored for half a century in the hopeful expectation that perhaps "experts" using more sophisticated analysis could improve on his conclusions, that they might indeed predict stock prices and receive ample compensation for their superior performance. Bachelier would have shaken his head sadly.

At mid-century, interest in securities took off. The prosperity that followed World War II and the establishment of tax-deferred retirement accounts had created rich sources of investment funds and called for new procedures to reduce the cost and smooth the flow of financial transactions. The Cowles Commission had been established in the 1930s to conduct research in economics, and after the war it encouraged financial economists to investigate the behavior of financial markets. In fact, most of the U.S. Nobel Prize winners in Economic Sciences were at one time or other affiliated with the Cowles Commission.

One was Harry Markowitz, whose pioneering article, "Portfolio Selection" was published in 1952 when he was a 25-year-old graduate student at the University of Chicago. Markowitz's article was the first attempt to do more than simply describe the behavior of securities prices but to use statistics to guide investors' choice of securities. In particular, Markowitz's article explains how investors can better satisfy their investment objectives by assembling a portfolio of different securities, instead of picking a single security on the basis of dubious predictions about price trends—in other words, that distributing one's eggs among numerous baskets might be a better approach to investing than the reverse.

Markowitz's portfolio theory was aided by the statistical techniques of his teacher, Tjalling Koopmans, who developed linear programming. In its original application, linear programming enables a decision maker to identify the optimal combination of certain preferred characteristics by trading off quantities of one preferred characteristic in exchange for quantities of the other. Markowitz's innovation was to change Koopmans' linear programming model to substitute a dispreferred characteristic for Koopmans' second preferred characteristic. When assembling a portfolio of securities, the preferred characteristic is its expected rate of return. A future rate of return cannot be known for certain, of course, making the second (dispreferred) characteristic the risk that the actual return might just as well be exceptionally low as exceptionally high. A portfolio investor wants to achieve the optimal combination of expected return and risk, maximizing the first characteristic while minimizing the second.

When Markowitz submitted his doctoral dissertation explaining portfolio selection to his dissertation committee, one committee member, Milton Friedman, criticized the content on the basis that it was "not real economics." Fortunately, the majority of the committee thought otherwise, and the dissertation was accepted. Otherwise, Markowitz might have become not a 1990 Nobel Prize–winning financial economist but a violinist or cryptographer, both interests having consumed his adolescent years.

Measuring the Value of a Security

In addition to regular payments of interest and dividends, the return on a financial asset depends on what other investors will pay for it at some time in the future. What other investors will pay for a security depends on their assessment of the value of the firm that issued it, which raises another question attacked by the financial economists: How do you measure the value of a business firm? The first answer that comes to mind might be: A firm is worth what it owns minus what it owes, a value similar to the one an individual might calculate of his own personal worth—exclusive of charm, intellect, and general lovableness, of course. Following this reasoning, a firm's value would be determined by looking at its balance sheet, which lists the value of all the firm's assets and liabilities, or outstanding claims against those assets. The difference between the two values is the firm's *net worth:*

the value of assets owned in excess of amounts owed to various claimants—again, analogous to our own personal net worth.

Net worth might be an appropriate measure of a firm's value except for the fact that net worth is affected by a firm's decision to issue stocks or bonds. By issuing stocks a firm can fund additional holdings of real assets without increasing outstanding claims against those assets, thus increasing its net worth. On the other hand, by issuing bonds to pay for additional assets the firm at the same time increases claims against those assets, so that its net worth does not change. Evaluating different firms on the basis of their net worth can lead to very different conclusions, whether or not there is any difference in the firms' ability to produce income for its stockholders and bondholders.

This doesn't seem helpful. Moreover, balance sheet analysis focuses on a firm's solvency, its ability to pay its debts. A sufficient excess of assets over liabilities is essential, of course, if a firm is to remain in business. By the middle of the twentieth century, however, rather general economic prosperity had reduced investors' concerns about firms' ability to pay their debts and increased concerns about firms' potential for growth.

Information about a firm's growth prospects is more clearly contained in its income statement. An income statement lists sales revenue and costs of production during a particular period of time, with the difference between total revenue and total cost labeled the firm's *net revenue*. By this method, the behavior of net revenue relative to the firm's obligations to stockholders and bondholders provides information about its potential for growth and, therefore, its value. Indeed—and this is a critical point—for as long in the future as a firm is expected to collect sufficient net revenue to satisfy its obligations to bondholders and pay healthy dividends to stockholders, its value increases, along with the value of its securities.

We can illustrate the practical difference between the two ways of evaluating firms by the initial experience of IBM's stock. The fledgling producer of desk calculators that eventually became IBM was initially shunned by investors because of the "poor quality" of its assets. The firm really didn't own much and it owed a lot! Failing to foresee the firm's tremendous earnings potential probably cost many timid investors the chance to make a fortune on its securities. (An early investment of $100 in IBM stock would be worth, after numerous stock splits, more than $200,000 today.)

This said, it isn't easy to evaluate a firm in terms of its prospective net revenue. It isn't easy to estimate future streams of revenues and costs and the dates in the future when all those payments will occur. Neither is ever precisely what one expects. Moreover, estimated net revenues have to be discounted according to investors' willingness to wait for their rewards, another uncertain prospect. After discounting and summing projected net revenues, we have an estimate of the firm's value. Then, when we purchase its stock, we are buying shares of its value entitling us to receive shares of net revenue in the form of dividends. When we purchase a firm's bonds, we are buying the right to receive the indicated interest payments. The total amount we receive in excess of the price we pay determines our return on the stock or bond.

None of these values is known for certain when we choose our investments, of course, and this is why Markowitz's theory of portfolio selection was so important. Still, for two decades after its publication, his 14-page paper received little attention. In most of those years stock prices rose, sometimes spectacularly, for an average annual increase of almost 5 percent after adjusting for inflation. Until stock prices plummeted in 1973, investors must have thought they had finally—now and forever—conquered risk and had no need to worry about Markowitz's trade-off.

More About Risk

Risk sounds like a terrible burden, a barrier to enjoyment of all the good things that humans crave. Nobel economist Kenneth Arrow is sometimes described as the father of risk management, occasionally quoting from the poetry of Omar Khayyám to describe risk: "The moving finger writes; and having writ, moves on; nor all your piety nor wit shall lure it back to cancel half a line; nor all your tears wash out a word of it." Sad but true.

Looked at more positively, risk is a marvelous benefit to the human species, a part of life that frees us from inevitability. If the future were truly known, where would we find the opportunities to choose, to analyze, to develop those human capabilities that distinguish us from other animals? Because we cannot know the future, we must use our intelligence and all available information to function best in that unknown.[1] Our decisions matter! Furthermore, understanding and protecting against risky future possibilities makes us more willing to engage in risk-taking activities, without which there is no possibility of economic growth and development. And performing that function is helped by Harry Markowitz's adaptation of Tjalling Koopmans' linear programming model.

Markowitz first distinguishes between the risk of a single security and the risk of a portfolio of securities. He defines a single security's risk in terms of the variability of its return: the tendency of the issuing firm's net revenue (and hence the value of its securities) to swing at times wildly above and at times wildly below its long-term average. Investors in stocks with highly variable returns might enjoy lofty gains, but they risk crushing losses. When we assemble securities together in a portfolio, the portfolio's risk depends not on the risk of its individual securities, but on their tendency to move together. Portfolios of securities that move up or down together make for an especially risky combination. (Statisticians would say the covariance of their returns is $+1$.) A less risky combination would contain securities that move precisely in opposite directions. (Their covariance is -1.) For the latter combinations the occasional below-average returns on some securities are offset by the above-average returns on others. The result is an average return on the entire combination that follows roughly the return on the market as a whole. This is the fundamental principle underlying portfolio diversification, the contribution of Markowitz to financial economics.

Articulating the principle is sometimes a far cry from implementing it. Calculating the risk of individual securities requires significant computing capacity: measuring every firm's net revenue for every past time period, calculating its average rate of return over time, and then measuring all its short-run deviations above and below its average return. This mind-boggling process was simplified by William Sharpe, who shared Markowitz's 1990 Nobel Prize and who, like Markowitz, characterizes himself as a computer nerd. Sharpe came naturally to the "joys of learning," he says, his father a college president and his mother a high school principal. He began his education expecting to become a physician but discovered an aversion to science. He switched to business but discovered an aversion to accounting, too. Finally, he switched to economics, which, he said, employs the discipline of science and examines a broader world than does accounting. Today, Sharpe operates a Web site for investment information at www.financialengines.com.

Following Markowitz, Sharpe developed a computer method for measuring a security's deviations above and below not its own average return but above and below the return on the market as a whole—obviously a much easier value to calculate. This measure he called *beta*. Securities issued by firms with significant earnings volatility, relative to the market as a whole, have high betas, so that their investors face the possibility of returns either exceptionally above or exceptionally below the market return. Securities whose betas have opposite signs move in opposite directions relative to the market. Thus, two securities with betas of +0.80 and −0.80 move up and down, respectively, 80 percent as far as the market moves up and down. Combining the two securities in a portfolio implies an expected return equal to the market's return—no more, no less.

Consider a stock with a low (positive) beta, one that swings with the market as a whole but not as far in either direction as the market. Risk-averse investors will increase their purchases of such stocks, adding a premium to the stock's price and pushing down its rate of return. Therefore, low beta is associated with low risk and low return. Following the Markowitz-Sharpe guide to portfolio selection, low-beta stocks would come to rest in the portfolios of investors whose preference for low risk is associated with a low expected return. Exceptionally high-beta stocks move farther than the market—in both directions—and come to rest in the portfolios of investors with greater tolerance for risk. In return for their willingness to hold high-beta stocks, these investors expect to receive relatively high returns. Once investors have ranked all stocks according to their behavior with respect to the market (their betas), the expected return on stocks in the same risk category would tend toward equality.

The Capital Asset Pricing Model

Together with Sharpe, Markowitz developed what they called the *capital asset pricing model*, often spoken of by its shorter name CAP-M. CAP-M provided the basis for a veritable explosion in such financial institutions as mutual funds, index funds, insurance funds, and other institutions that combine a variety of securities into portfolios that are less risky than their individual securities.

CAP-M first assembles all conceivable combinations of available securities into hypothetical portfolios and ranks them in terms of their overall expected return and risk: low-risk portfolios including mostly low-return securities, and high-risk, high-return. Then it identifies the portfolios that provide the very highest expected return at every level of risk. Those portfolios Markowitz and Sharpe pronounce *efficient*. Given the set of all efficient portfolios, Markowitz and Sharpe advise investors to define their own personal tolerance for risk and select the efficient portfolio at their preferred level of risk. Typically, the wealthiest and most secure investors tolerate greater risk and purchase portfolios with greater expected return, while the least secure investors opt for lower returns, with greater assurance the return will actually materialize. Choosing a properly balanced portfolio enables individual investors happily to walk that "thin line between greed and fear."

A Fundamental Distinction

Much of a security's risk is irrelevant to portfolio risk.

A security's risk arises about equally from three causes: unique characteristics of the industry or sector represented (a sleepy utility or a high-flying Internet company), unique characteristics of the issuing firm (the competence and strategic vision of its managers), and the variability of the market as a whole. Combining securities of about a dozen firms into a single portfolio erases the unique effects of industry and firm and leaves almost all (Sharpe believes about 90 percent) of the variability of a portfolio to be determined by the variability of the market as a whole—the betas of the securities contained in it.[2]

In his words, the securities that make up an efficient portfolio are related "only through common relationships with some basic underlying factor,"[3] that is, the behavior of the market as a whole. The behavior of the market as a whole is determined by broad economic conditions and creates *systematic risk*. Thus, systematic risk is the variability of return that results from economic conditions in general and is the only type of variability that is relevant when assessing the risk of a security.

Risk not associated with the variability of the market is irrelevant for selecting securities because it can be diversified away. *Diversifiable,* or *unsystematic, risk* arises from the issuing firm's unique characteristics, including its size and industry, the liquidity of the market in which the security trades, and whether the security is owned primarily by institutions or individuals. Unique characteristics explain as much as 70 percent of a security's performance. But when securities having widely differing characteristics are combined in one portfolio, their behavioral patterns offset each other, affecting the overall performance of the portfolio not at all.

By emphasizing portfolios rather than individual securities, the Markowitz-Sharpe capital asset pricing model threw a bombshell into the financial community. Along with the work of other financial economists, CAP-M threatened the careers of the "noise traders," all those investment advisers who claimed expertise in picking individual stocks. Stock pickers claim the ability to identify firms with prospects of exceptionally high returns, but, as Louis Bachelier had warned at the turn of the century, the expected return for stock picking tends toward zero. Because firms are as likely to experience losses as they are to experience gains, in the long run the losses from stock picking will offset the gains. Therefore, the optimal behavior for investors is not to buy and hold particular stocks (those promoted by the "noise traders") but to assemble a portfolio of stocks that are sufficiently diversified so that their performance differences cancel out. Different portfolios will have higher or lower risks and rates of return depending on their particular combination of high-beta and low-beta stocks—the tendency of their stocks to vary more or less than the market as a whole.

Securities as a Part of Total Wealth Holdings

The work of Markowitz and Sharpe was extended by another Nobel economist whom we met in Chapter 16, James Tobin. Remember that Tobin's chief interest is in macroeconomics, and in particular, the tendency for changes in total spending to bring on business cycles. Changes in total spending are intimately related to (in fact the mirror image of) changes in money holdings: primarily cash and checking accounts. In his article "Liquidity Preference as Behavior Towards Risk," Tobin linked a particular investor's choice of a particular efficient portfolio with the allocation of that investor's total assets between securities and cash.

Tobin's contribution to portfolio theory was to replace an array of efficient portfolios for risk-averse and risk-tolerant investors with a single efficient portfolio for both types of investors. The one efficient portfolio duplicates as nearly as possible the market as a whole—all the securities offered for sale. To Tobin, the important question then becomes how an investor combines the one efficient (but at least somewhat risky) portfolio with (less risky) cash and checking accounts. Some investors want to avoid risk and, therefore, allocate a smaller portion of their total wealth to securities, holding the larger portion in cash, checking accounts, or their closest equivalents, insured savings accounts and U.S. Treasury bills. Other investors prefer a higher expected return with greater risk and so allocate more of their wealth to securities. These latter investors may even purchase securities in excess of their own wealth by borrowing the necessary cash. We may think of such investors' portfolios as containing some positive and some negative assets.

Thus, Tobin's so-called separation theorem separates an investor's decision regarding the optimal portfolio from the decision regarding the allocation of his total wealth. It permits all investors to hold identical combinations of securities while at the same time satisfying their particular preferences for risk.

From Tobin's separation theorem it was a natural step to investigate the quality of investors' investment choices: in short, whether investors use their funds to increase the nation's productive capacity or simply to transfer the ownership of existing investments. The first activity creates new wealth; the second merely shifts the ownership of existing wealth. Whether investors allocate their funds to create new capital investments or to acquire existing capital investments depends on the investments' rates of return. The return on existing investments depends on their current market price relative to their replacement cost—which fact was noticed by James Tobin and which earned for him a further distinction (in addition to that of being a Nobel laureate). Indeed, James Tobin has the interesting distinction of being the only economist (perhaps the only person) for whom a letter of the alphabet is named, Tobin's q.

Tobin's q = current market price ÷ replacement cost
of existing capital investments

A value of $q < 1$ indicates a lower market price than replacement cost and favors the purchase of existing capital investments. As investors allocate their funds toward purchases of existing capital, investments in new capital fall. A value of $q > 1$ dictates the reverse.

Toward the end of the 1990s, the run-up in stock market valuations in the United States pushed stock prices as much as 70 percent above the replacement costs of the issuing firms' underlying assets, a greater spread than before the stock market crash of 1929 and any other time since. As predicted by Tobin's q, high stock prices stimulated a burst of new capital investment, which increased significantly the nation's productive capacity.[4] The recent surge in capital investment is in sharp contrast to the 1970s when stock prices fell, both in nominal and real terms (DJIA). By early in the 1980s, for example, Gulf Oil's stock price was less than half the value of the company's recoverable oil reserves. The plunge in Tobin's q reduced incentives to make new capital investments and probably had much to do with the many corporate buyouts that occurred in the 1980s.

Replacing Social Security

Virtually all U.S. workers own shares in the world's largest investment portfolio, the one belonging to the U.S. Social Security trust fund.

The Social Security trust fund collects FICA taxes from U.S. workers and pays benefits to retired workers and their survivors. Current contributions from the horde of baby-boom workers exceed benefits paid to the much smaller group of retired "depression babies," so that during the 1990s alone close to $700 billion was set aside in a portfolio of U.S. government securities, drawing interest for ultimate distribution to retired boomers. Many boomers also contribute to individual retirement accounts, such as 401(k) plans and IRAs, which provide tax incentives to encourage thrift.

The correlation between the taxes workers pay in FICA and the benefits they ultimately receive is not perfect, so that some workers receive more and some less than they pay in—a natural consequence of a program intended to provide a basic minimum standard of living for all the nation's retirees. If workers were allowed to invest their FICA taxes individually, some would undoubtedly earn more on their investments than they receive in retirement benefits under the current system. And this prospect has given rise to a political movement to abolish the Social Security system.

If the Social Security program were abolished, thrifty workers could use their FICA taxes to purchase Tobin's efficient portfolio, along with insured savings accounts and U.S. government securities according to their preferences regarding risk. The expected rate of return on the combination would be a weighted average of the return on the stock-and-bond portfolio and the return on the risk-free assets. Since those returns are critical to the workers' standard of living in retirement, let's reason through their likely behavior.

Taking the portfolio's return first: We must expect the average return on a stock-and-bond portfolio to mirror the productivity of the economy as a whole. Where else could value come from except from increases in the net revenues of all the firms that contribute securities to Tobin's efficient portfolio? The behavior of firms' net revenue depends on Solow's TFP (Chapter 23), which includes technological progress, organizational improvements, worker skills, etc. This makes TFP of particular significance to a worker's retirement income.

What about the return on insured savings accounts and U.S. government securities? The existing Social Security trust fund holds government securities, which as risk-free assets earn a lower rate of return than the stock-and-bond portfolio. Changing the Social Security system to allow workers to allocate their own funds would likely drain funds out of risk-free, low-return savings accounts and government securities and into risky, higher-return stocks and bonds for, one hopes, a higher-weighted-average return.

But let's not be too hasty about this conclusion. A major shift of funds out of government securities will require government to offer a higher return to finance its borrowing. Meantime, a major shift of funds into stocks and bonds will enable business firms to obtain financing at lower cost. In fact, a tenfold run-up in stock prices over the past two decades has already cut the average dividend yield on stock from almost 6 percent to barely 1 percent. With an increase in the return on government securities and a reduction in the return on stocks and bonds, the weighted-average return on workers' individual portfolios may be no greater than the current return on the Social Security trust fund, particularly after adjustments are made for the higher costs associated with administering individual portfolios.

If workers are given responsibility for their own retirement investing, it must be assumed that some will not behave prudently, so that their investments will fail to provide acceptable living standards in retirement. Like as not, government will be called upon to bail out imprudent investors, raising costs to taxpayers and possibly even encouraging more imprudent behavior. (Economists refer to people's perverse response to perverse incentives as *moral hazard.*)

Now for the bottom line. Our standards of living in retirement depend on all our contributions during our working lives to the nation's TFP, increases in productivity that yield growth in per capita GDP, and higher average incomes in the years of our retirement. Shifting funds from one portfolio to another increases per capita GDP only if one allocation of retirement savings yields more technological progress, organizational efficiency, worker skills, etc., than all the other possible allocations.

Chapter 29
EXPLAINING A FIRM'S FINANCING DECISION

The next major contribution to financial economics comes from the team of Franco Modigliani, whom we have already met, and Merton Miller, corecipient of the 1990 Nobel Prize with Harry Markowitz and William Sharpe. Modigliani and Miller address a question that is the mirror image of the question addressed by the developers of portfolio theory in Chapter 28. Instead of exploring how investors decide on the optimal combination of stocks and bonds for their portfolios, these economists look at financing decisions from the side of the issuing firm, exploring the process through which firms decide on the lowest-cost combination of stocks or bonds to issue in order to fund their investment projects.

Whether to issue bonds or stocks is essentially the question of whether to borrow against the firm's assets or to sell ownership claims to those assets. Borrowing requires the issuance of bonds and increases the firm's "leverage." It has the advantage that interest charges on borrowed funds are deductible from the firm's income before calculating its tax liability, but it has the disadvantage that interest obligations could become onerous in bad times. If bad times render a firm unable to service its debts, it may have to declare bankruptcy—an action that can reduce its fund-raising ability for a very long time. Issuing stocks has disadvantages, too, in that issuing stocks requires the sacrifice of ownership to additional stockholders. By issuing new stocks a firm increases the quantity of outstanding shares of ownership, which can reduce the earnings payable to individual stockholders and, in turn, the value investors place on the firm's stocks.

For a firm with more bonds outstanding than stocks, earnings after interest expense are paid to a relatively smaller group of stockholders. The result could be a relatively high average return and a high stock value. Need I caution, however, that the stock's high return is offset by its relatively high risk? Since larger numbers of bondholders have first claim on earnings, if the firm's earnings are low, the average stockholder may receive no return at all, in which case the stock's value could plummet. In general, the volatility of returns on stocks of a highly leveraged firm makes these stocks riskier than the stocks of a less leveraged firm.

Seeking the Lowest-Cost Financial Structure

To identify the optimal combination of stocks and bonds, Merton Miller collected data linking firms' financial structures with their cost of capital: the necessary compensation the firms had to pay buyers of their stocks and bonds. Miller expected to find a relationship between firms' financial structure and their cost of capital, but he was surprised to find no relationship at all. According to Miller's data, it simply does not matter what combination of stocks and bonds a firm uses to obtain investment funds; the value financial markets place on a firm (and, therefore, its cost of capital) is not correlated in any way with the firm's financing decision.

Franco Modigliani approached the financing question from yet another angle. Modigliani's main interest is business cycles, particularly cycles caused by fluctuations in business investments in plant and equipment. His research into investment behavior during a business cycle confirms the irrelevance of financial structure for determining a firm's value, and he explains his findings with a simple analogy. If a single wealthy investor were to purchase all of a firm's outstanding stocks and bonds, he says, the particular combination owned would have no bearing on the firm's true value and, therefore, no bearing on its cost of investment funds. The same result must hold if many ordinary investors purchase the firm's many outstanding financial instruments.

Modigliani arrived at the eminently sensible conclusion that a firm's value and its cost of capital are determined not by how the firm acquires funds but how it spends the funds it acquires. If a firm's managers want to increase their firm's value in the eyes of potential investors, they must use their investment funds to finance worthy projects, projects whose earnings exceed the cost of financing for the firm as a whole. When all the firm's investment projects are taken as a whole, the result is a particular level of earning power, a particular level of net revenue for paying contractual interest expense and dividends. It is a firm's earning power, along with its earnings volatility, that determines its value and its cost of capital. Investors will place the same valuation on firms with equal earning power and equal volatility, says Modigliani, regardless of the combination of stocks and bonds the firms use to obtain financial capital.[5]

The Factor of Arbitrage

According to Modigliani and Miller, investors just don't care what combination of stocks and bonds a firm uses to finance its investment projects. If investors don't like a firm's choice of stocks and bonds, they can structure their own investment with the combination they prefer. Then, by purchasing their preferred combinations of stocks and bonds, investors help push the prices of those assets toward the price that correctly reflects the firm's expected return and risk.

The reason is the factor of arbitrage. *Arbitrage* is the simultaneous purchase and sale of similar items whose prices are temporarily different. Temporary price differences arise from the fact that markets are not perfect—abnormal circumstances in one market pushing a security's price above or below its price in another. Arbitrageurs simultaneously buy in the low-price market and sell in the high-price market. Through their buying and selling they push the divergent prices closer together. Arbitrage is also known as the *law of one price*, since arbitrage prevents prolonged price differences for items that are fundamentally the same.

Consider a firm that is financed in part by issuing bonds and in part by issuing stock. The firm's particular combination of stocks and bonds yields a particular return and risk, a level that may or may not be acceptable to a potential investor. However, to the extent that the investor prefers a higher level of risk and a higher expected return, he can borrow and design his own personal combination of bonds and stocks. (In effect, the investor issues his own personal bond to finance additional purchases of the firm's stock.) By creating their own "leverage," investors achieve a personal financial structure that may be different from that of the firm but more in tune with their personal preferences.

Then arbitrage ensures that the firm's securities are correctly priced, that they truly reflect the firm's value. If a firm's stock price should fall temporarily below its true value in terms of the firm's expected net revenue and risk, the effect is to increase the firm's cost of capital. But such a condition could not last long because of arbitrage. Investors would borrow funds to purchase more of the firm's stock at its (temporarily) low price, increasing demand for that stock and increasing its price until price reflects the firm's true value.

Interestingly, Modigliani and Miller assert that a firm's value is independent of whether it actually pays dividends to stockholders. This conclusion seems to contradict earlier assertions regarding the determinants of corporate value: expected return and risk. But their point is that the firm's value is the same whether earnings are distributed currently as dividends or retained in the firm for purchasing growth-promoting investments. Supposedly, retained earnings are used to finance projects that increase the firm's ability to pay dividends in the future, with the effect of increasing the firm's value to its stockholders and its stock's price.

The Qualifications

All of the above ignores the effect of taxes. Corporate income taxes do affect a firm's financing decision because interest paid on bonds can be deducted from a firm's income before calculating tax due. Dividends paid to stockholders are not deductible for the firm and thus are fully taxed at the corporate level. They are also subject to personal income taxes at the rate paid by the stockholder, making issuing stock generally more costly to the firm than issuing bonds. In fact, a firm can afford to pay higher interest on bonds (sell bonds for lower prices) if issuing bonds saves the firm more in taxes than it costs in interest.

Leveraged Buyouts

The 1980s experienced a wave of borrowing to purchase all of particular firms' outstanding stocks. Buyers were primarily groups of wealthy investors and often managers of the target firm itself. Borrowing to purchase all of a firm's stock is called a leveraged buyout, or LBO. LBOs introduced into the financial language an entirely new vocabulary, much more colorful than financial economists' usual references to betas, covariances, and arbitrage. For example, a *raider* is an investor in pursuit of a buyout prospect; a *greenmailer* is a raider who threatens to buy the firm unless current owners pay a high price to ward him off; a *poison pill* is a condition inserted in a firm's rules that is unattractive to raiders and is activated when ownership changes hands; a *white knight* is an investor who rescues a target firm from purchase by a raider.

Purchase of an entire firm's stock is subject to the requirement that before a raider acquires more than a certain percentage (currently 5 percent) he must announce his intentions to purchase a controlling amount. Supposedly the firm's current owners can then mount a defense against an unattractive buyout. When it becomes generally known that a well-financed raider is pursuing a certain stock, the stock's price tends to rise. Having advance information about a particular raider's intentions thus provides an advantage to knowledgeable investors, who can buy the stock at its current price and resell to the raider for a gain. The use of "inside information" for this purpose is illegal, however, because it works to the disadvantage of ordinary stockholders. Lacking inside information, ordinary investors might be discouraged from buying any stocks at all, which would reduce the efficiency of the nation's financial markets. A number of wealthy investors were found guilty of using inside information for stock purchases in the 1980s and were sent to jail for the offense.

Many corporate raiders financed their purchases through issue of *junk bonds,* bonds sold at exceptionally low prices, thus promising exceptionally high rates of return. Buyouts of such well-known firms as Revlon, TWA, National Can, and RJR Nabisco were financed by junk bonds. In some cases, paying the hefty return on junk bonds was made possible by stripping the target firm of marketable assets or by closing plants, laying off workers, and reducing new capital investments. Competition between raiders for the same firm, or competition between a raider and the firm's managers, sometimes pushed the price so high that the possibility the acquisition would ever be profitable was virtually zero. Some buyers of junk bonds learned painfully the reason for the bonds' pejorative nickname.

Critics of the LBO movement describe the problem as "too much money chasing too few deals" and worry that it interferes with rational corporate governance. Nobel laureate Merton Miller is more positive, however, regarding LBOs as bona fide ways to shift risk from declining enterprises to risk-tolerant investors, investors who are willing to wait for their reward until such enterprises can be modernized, streamlined, and generally equipped to prosper in a competitive global economy. The generally increased profitability of U.S. corporations in the 1990s probably confirms Miller's expectations.

Chapter 30

INCORPORATING TIME IN THE FINANCIAL DECISION

The capital asset pricing model discussed in Chapter 28 was a milestone in financial analysis, but it had one serious flaw: CAP-M includes only instantaneous valuations and does not consider opportunities for financial gain that overlap time periods. As the global economy grows and as the pace of change accelerates, however, financial decisions must change as well, to take advantage of return and risk associated with the passage of time.

As far back as Aristotle, investors were exploring financial opportunities associated with the passage of time. Financial historians tell the tale of the Greek philosopher Thales, who is said to have taken advantage of uncertainty regarding the magnitude of the coming olive harvest in his region. The size of the harvest would affect the demand for olive presses and the potential rental income payable to owners of the region's limited supply of presses. Thales paid a small fee to owners of olive presses for the right to rent the presses when the harvest came in. In this way he guaranteed for himself control over the available supply of presses—and the opportunity to earn a substantial income—without obligating himself actually to rent the presses if the harvest were to be relatively meager. So was born the "option."

Options and Futures

Options were beneficial both to option buyers (Thales) and option sellers (owners of olive presses). Options buyers are relieved of risk at a relatively low cost; sellers receive a return for their asset even if circumstances turn otherwise unprofitable (if the harvest were to be so small that demand for presses turned out to be less than normal).

Ordinary men and women acquire options when we purchase a fire insurance policy. If our house burns down, we exercise the option guaranteed in the policy and receive the contractual payment. (We, in effect, sell the charred remains to the insurance company at a predetermined price.) If the house doesn't burn down, we enjoy the comfort of knowing that our potential loss is limited to the amount of our insurance premium.

Options differ from the more familiar and more ubiquitous "futures." Futures have also been around for hundreds of years, primarily in markets for agricultural commodities and minerals. Such basic commodities experience frequent shifts in demand and supply, so that their prices tend to fluctuate widely. For centuries, commodity buyers and sellers have used futures to protect against the risk of rising prices (a concern of buyers) and falling prices (a concern of sellers).

A *futures contract* establishes in the present a price for future delivery that is acceptable to both buyer and seller. Typically a future supplier of, say, corn wants to establish a price of, say, $2.50 per bushel three months in the future when the corn is ready for market. For a nominal fee, the farmer sells a futures contract to a potential buyer, who is willing to promise today to pay $2.50 for corn on delivery. At harvest time, unexpected changes in supply or demand may have pushed the market price above or below $2.50. If the market price is above $2.50, the futures contract becomes more valuable, since it entitles its holder to obtain corn at a price that is below the current market price. The holder can either exercise the contract (buy the corn for $2.50) or sell it back to the farmer for a higher price than the initial purchase price. Supposedly, the holder of a futures contract is indifferent between the choices: the first enabling him to buy a high-priced commodity at a low price; the second, allowing him to sell a contract he bought at a low price for a higher price. The farmer is willing to pay a higher price to repurchase the futures contract because his corn, the commodity that underlies the contract, can now be sold at a higher market price.[6]

Notice that neither the buyer nor the seller of corn futures experiences a significant gain or loss because of an unexpected change in the market price of corn. Both sacrifice the possibility of a significant gain for protection against a significant loss.

Options grew out of the use of futures. Futures contracts are obligations to buy or to sell and must be satisfied either by exchanging the underlying commodity or by exchanging the contract, thus canceling out the obligation. Options are not obligatory but "optional." They convey rights that the holder may exercise or not according to his or her choice. The commodities most subject to options contracts are corporate stocks, foreign currencies, mortgages, and other interest-earning assets.

Futures and options may be bought and sold either by actual traders of the underlying commodities or by professional risk-takers. When traders of the underlying commodities buy or sell such contracts, they are called *hedgers*. Hedgers differ from professional risk-takers, who are called *speculators*. Speculators buy and sell contracts, having no interest in the underlying commodities but expecting that small increases in the value of some contracts will exceed small decreases in the value of others. They hope that their willingness to assume others' risk of loss will reward them with positive returns. Speculators perform a valuable market function. Their willingness to assume risks makes it possible for traders who are more risk-averse to avoid risk, while accepting a lower return.

Options are of two types. Options like Thales' that entitle the holder to purchase a particular asset at a certain time in the future are called *call options*. Other options entitle the holder to sell an asset and are called *put options* (your fire insurance policy). Normally, prospective buyers of, say, a stock or foreign currency whose price is expected to rise purchase call options; then they enjoy unlimited upside potential for gain at a relatively low options price. Prospective sellers of, say, a mortgage whose price is expected to fall (generally because of a likely increase in interest rates) purchase put options; for a small options price they lock in the value of an asset whose market price may fall.

Executive Stock Options

Some firms reward their high-performing executives with bonuses paid in the form of stock options, which in 1998 constituted more than half of executive compensation in 100 of the nation's top companies. Stock options guarantee the right to purchase stock from the firm at a certain price during a certain future period. If the firm's value increases, its stocks and stock options become more valuable, too—supposedly creating incentives for the firm's executives to improve the firm's performance. Stock options are especially popular for start-up companies that can't pay high executive salaries but can offer the prospect of gains through rising stock values. Since options have come into widespread use, corporate profits have indeed increased, and stock prices have risen by as much as four times their initial values. Still, there is little evidence of a connection between firms' performance and executive compensation—some executives doubtless prospering more because of lucky increases in all stock prices than because of their managerial expertise.

In 1998, companies listed on the NASDAQ 100 index had outstanding four billion call options worth more than $200 billion. Outstanding options now amount to about 13 percent of corporations' net worth. Holders of those options have been willing to continue to hold as long as stock prices are rising. By continuing to hold, they anticipate growing gaps between the stock price guaranteed in the option and the stocks' resale value and, therefore, greater gains from exercising the option in the future. Nevertheless, today's vast overhang of options has prompted fears that if stock prices should slide, option holders would exercise their options, buy shares cheaply from their companies, and attempt to resell quickly before market prices fall farther—which, of course, is what prices would do. To avoid a collapse in stock prices, regulators have begun to investigate ways to regulate firms' issue of stock options.

Pricing Options

A problem with options is determining their correct price. Options prices were determined basically by guesswork until the early 1970s and the advent of two brilliant innovators in finance, both at that time younger than 30 years and both initially trained in mathematics. Fischer Black[7] and Myron Scholes became interested in financial economics as an application of their mathematical skills. Their research paper describing a formula for pricing options languished for three years before it was accepted for publication in 1973—ironically, almost simultaneously with a similar paper by Robert Merton. (In fact, it was Merton who exerted the pressure that resulted in its publication. Merton had once been an assistant to Paul Samuelson, who proclaimed him the Isaac Newton in his field, heady praise for a "mere" financial economist.) Scholes and Merton were awarded the Nobel Prize in 1997 for devising the formula for determining the worth of an option.

The appearance of the Black-Scholes-Merton options pricing formula was particularly propitious for two reasons. First, it occurred just a month after the Chicago Board Options Exchange (CBOE) was established. And second, it occurred when pocket calculators were first coming into general use. Before pocket calculators, financial analysis was constrained to the simplest calculations, so that many applications of financial theory were beyond the capability of traders in real markets. With the Black-Scholes-Merton formula programmed into their pocket calculators, however, options traders could accomplish significantly more profitable trades.

Options provide holders of financial assets a kind of insurance against changes in their asset's market price. That insurance protection comes at a cost to the seller (or "writer") of the option. While the buyer of an option acquires unlimited potential for gain just for paying the price of the option, the seller (or writer) of the option must be prepared to satisfy the holder's unlimited potential for gain. The seller's willingness to assume that obligation is contingent on receiving a "fair" price for the option. A fair options price is the *efficient price,* the one that justly compensates the seller for the risk assumed.

The concept of an efficient price is based on the same principles that govern the Arrow-Debreu general equilibrium model: that is, that buyers and sellers interact to equalize pain (value paid) with gain (value received). Thus, general equilibrium in the market for options is no different from equilibrium in markets for autos, houses, and pizzas. The efficient price equalizes the buyer's expectation of gain with the sacrifice endured by the seller.

Scholes has acknowledged that the inspiration for the options-pricing formula came from the formula used in physics to describe the transfer of heat from one material (a hot engine) to a cooler one (water circulating around it). In the process the two materials approach the same temperature—just as the prices of a stock and the options written on it adjust to provide the same rate of return.

The Black-Scholes-Merton formula breaks down the efficient option price into four factors describing the option's relative pain and gain.

- *The time during which the option is usable.* The longer the holder of an option is entitled to exercise it, the longer the writer of an option is constrained in making investment decisions and the higher is the necessary compensation.
- *The interest rate available on alternative investments.* During the time the writer is constrained in making investment decisions, the writer forgoes interest earnings on alternative investments. Therefore, the writer must receive a price at least sufficient to offset the forgone return on an asset that is temporarily unusable.
- *The option's "exercise" or "strike" price.* The *exercise price* is the price at which the holder of a put option has the right to sell (or the holder of a call option, to buy) the underlying asset. The higher the exercise price for a put option, the higher its price; the higher the exercise price for a call option, the lower its price.
- *The current price and expected future volatility of the underlying asset.* The higher the price and the higher the volatility of the underlying asset, the higher the price an option buyer must pay for insurance against a price change.

You are probably thinking, "Shouldn't the options pricing formula also include the expected rate of return on the underlying asset—the stock or international currency described in the contract?" Good question—but, as it turns out, irrelevant. Black and Scholes were surprised to find in constructing their option-pricing model that the expected rate of return on the underlying asset plays no part in determining the efficient price of an option.

Robert Merton joined Black and Scholes to demonstrate their formula for determining the efficient option price. They began by pairing a particular commodity with some number of options, such that the gain or loss on the commodity would be precisely offset by the loss or gain on the options. A single share of stock, for example, might be paired with three put options (price as yet undetermined) guaranteeing the right to sell the stock at a certain exercise price. The advantage of precisely paired holdings of stocks and options is that their owners are completely protected against the risk of changing stock prices. With complete protection against risk, holders of such stock-options pairs are holding a risk-free asset and are entitled to the risk-free rate of return—no more, no less. The options price is the price that provides that return. Thus, the options price is the one that fairly compensates the seller for accepting the obligation in the options contract. Any divergence in price invites arbitrageurs to push the options price up or down until price yields the risk-free rate on the stock-options combination.

Arbitrageurs can easily program their pocket calculators with the Black-Scholes-Merton formula to quickly note such price differences. If the market price of a stock falls, for example, the market price of put options on that stock should rise by just enough to retain the risk-free rate of return on the stock-options pair. If the options' price rises by more than enough to offset the stock's price decline, the Black-Scholes-Merton formula directs arbitrageurs to buy the stock and sell puts, raising the price of the former and reducing the price of the latter until the gain is again precisely equal to the loss. Ultimately the return on the stock-options pair must be just sufficient to compensate for holding a risk-free asset.

Options serve a valuable function in financial markets, acting in a way similar to the way insurance policies reduce other kinds of risks. By reducing the risks of holding securities, options increase the prices investors are willing to pay to buy them and reduce the rate of return issuing firms have to pay to sell them. When businesses, governments, and financial institutions can issue stocks and bonds at lower interest and dividend cost, they can acquire more funds for making growth-promoting investments.

The Crisis at Long Term Capital Management

The revolution in options trading produced a revolution in financial markets: the development of financial assets "derived from" real assets, hence the name, *derivatives*. In 1994 Scholes and Merton became partners in a major options trading firm established by other professors of finance and some of their former students, who had also worked as traders at Salomon Brothers, Inc. The firm, Long Term Capital Management, or LTCM, is described as a hedge fund,[8] which invites very wealthy, risk-tolerant investors to buy shares in a fund promising high returns. High returns were thought to be virtually guaranteed because the firm's portfolio investments were to be based not on the fallible prognostications of stock pickers but on serious number crunching by skilled users of the Black-Scholes-Merton options pricing formula. The minimum required investment was $10 million.

LTCM was wildly successful at first, investing $6 billion with annual rates of return in excess of 40 percent. A billion dollars in profits flowed to LTCM investors, including Scholes and Merton. Some of LTCM's investors bought fine homes, wine cellars, even shares in an Irish golf course. The firm was so successful that in 1997 it paid back half of its capital, claiming that it had exhausted all available sources of profit. Who could have predicted events of 1998 that obliterated the fortunes of LTCM's investors? First, in mid-year the Russian government allowed its currency's value to fall by half and then defaulted on its bonds. And second, panicky investors around the world began selling their holdings of—now more risky—stocks and bonds in order to purchase risk-free U.S. government securities. Many portfolio investors had imitated LTCM in its choice of investments, and when the copycats began selling their investments at once, prices dropped like a stone. By August of 1998 LTCM's fund had lost half its value. Further selling would have created a crisis throughout financial markets.

To avert disaster, LTCM looked for a major investor to purchase its assets and hold them until financial markets stabilized. Wealthy financiers Warren Buffett and George Soros were possibilities. But nothing seemed to work out, and finally the New York Federal Reserve used its influence to persuade a consortium of 14 banks and investment companies to pay $3.6 billion into the fund to secure its assets.

The apparent failure of the professional "number crunchers" generated some glee among financial commentators, but the fault was not with the economists' numbers or their pricing formula. A large part of the blame went to the firm's investors and managers, who had borrowed significantly in excess of their paid-in capital. When their debt obligations came due, they were forced to sell off securities even when market prices were below the securities' true values.

Fischer Black had anticipated just this possibility back in 1989. The Black-Scholes-Merton formula and its estimates of market volatility, he said, are always based on information currently at hand. The market as a whole may have information users of the formula don't have—occasionally worse, but often better. Generally, differences between market price and the formula-determined price exist for good reason, which suggests a degree of caution when using borrowed money to make large investments.

Chapter 31

GLOBALIZING RESOURCE ALLOCATION

Investors around the world learned a lot about financial markets in 1998. That year introduced global investors to the possibility of contagion, the idea that distress in a remote part of the world—even one whose significance in global financial markets seems rather trivial—could spread like a disease to erstwhile healthy markets. Whoever heard of a ringgit anyway? Or of short straddles[9] on the Nikkei, for goodness sakes? How could such insignificant concepts threaten the stability of global financial markets?

I have said that financial markets are critical to a market economy, acting as a sort of nerve center that collects a nation's savings and allocates them toward growth-promoting investments. Just as nerves link a burned finger to a whole complex of muscles, financial markets link flows of savings to real production. To the extent that saving and investment overlap more nations of the world, financial linkages are both more complicated and more efficient. As nations participate in the productive activity of other nations—as they extend their consumer markets over international markets, and as they participate in the saving and investing decisions of people in other nations—all the world's workers enjoy more opportunities for improved living standards. An integrated global economy produces greater benefits at lower costs than do self-sufficient economies acting alone.

Absolute and Comparative Advantage

This was the conclusion of the classical economists who, following Adam Smith, pressed governments to remove restraints on the free flow of products, resources, and savings among nations. And it remains the conclusion of the great body of economists today. (This is one thing on which economists agree!) Economists' support for free trade rests on the principle of comparative advantage, first articulated by the eighteenth-century economist David Ricardo. Ricardo contrasted comparative advantage with absolute advantage. Absolute advantage describes a nation that can produce all products at lower resource costs than other nations. It might seem that such a nation should devote its resources to produce all the things its people want, becoming self-sufficient and avoiding trade with other, higher-cost nations. David Ricardo pointed out the contrary—that even a nation with absolute advantage can produce certain products "comparatively" more cheaply than other products. When a nation can produce one product comparatively more cheaply than other products, it should concentrate its resources on producing that product and trade with other nations for products for which the first nation's relative cost advantage is less.

Explaining Trade Flows

Theories of international trade involve all aspects of economics: first microeconomics, which examines the benefits and costs from spending decisions in particular markets; second, macroeconomics, which examines total spending and the consequences of total spending for employment and price stability; and finally, financial economics, which examines the process of saving and growth-promoting investing.

Bertil Ohlin and James Meade were awarded the Nobel Prize in 1977 for their contributions to the theory of international trade and investment flows. Ohlin was born in Sweden and, he says, demonstrated a childhood affinity for economics by calculating the costs of the cakes his mother baked. His first formal achievement in economics was to calculate the optimal time to cut trees in a Swedish forest so as to maximize profit from sales of lumber. Trees should be allowed to continue growing, he said, as long as their value as timber is increasing faster than the value of an equivalent financial asset. (Ohlin was another distinguished scholar who faced the humiliation of rejection by Keynes' *Economic Journal.*) Ultimately, Ohlin entered Swedish politics, serving in the national Parliament, or Riksdag, and as leader of Sweden's Liberal Party.

Ohlin's major accomplishment in economics was to extend the ideas of his mentor Eli Heckscher to assert the Heckscher-Ohlin theory of trade. The basis of the Heckscher-Ohlin theory is consistent with Ricardo's pronouncements centuries before: that nations tend to specialize in products whose production requires the resources they have in greater abundance and, therefore, can be obtained at lower cost than in other nations. Conversely, nations import products whose production requires resources they lack (or have in less abundance), so that the necessary resources cost more. The effect is the same as if a nation could export its abundant resources and import resources it lacks; but since resources are more difficult to transport than products, exporting and importing its products is more efficient.

If a nation's borders were closed to trade, its abundant resources would command lower prices, and scarce resources higher prices, than if its borders were freely open to trade. Resource prices in different nations would differ sharply, sending confusing signals about global supply and demand and diminishing the efficiency of global resource allocation. The effect of specialization for export, however, is to push particular resource prices toward the same level. By increasing demand for resources the exporting nation has in abundance, producing for export increases those resource prices and rewards their suppliers more generously. When Argentina uses its abundant grazing land to specialize in raising livestock for export, for instance, its abundant land comes to earn nearly the same rent as land in land-poor Chile. Likewise, with international trade, lower demand for a nation's scarcer resources tends to push their price down to the world price. Economists describe the effect on resource prices of nations' openness to trade as *factor-price equalization.*

When a nation specializes for export, suppliers of its plentiful resources receive more generous rewards, and suppliers of its less-abundant resources less generous rewards, than without trade. It is easy to see that the first group gains from trade. At first glance, the second appears to lose. However, the second group's apparent loss from trade conceals the fact that, with trade, both groups benefit from the opportunity to purchase products produced by the lowest-cost producers worldwide.

A Paradox

Specialization according to Ricardo's comparative advantage would seem to dictate production of capital-intensive manufactured goods in the world's wealthiest industrialized nations and production of labor-intensive raw materials in the least industrialized. Because the former nations are heavily concentrated in the northern hemisphere and the latter in the southern, trade theory suggests that most trade would occur between the nations of the north and those of the south: northern nations exporting capital-intensive manufactured goods to nations of the south in return for southern nations' labor-intensive raw materials. Alas, this is not what actually happens. In fact, most trade occurs between nations that are similar in resource endowments and technological development—north to north and south to south—a disturbing development for believers in the Heckscher-Ohlin theory of trade.

The apparent failure of real economies to behave according to the Heckscher-Ohlin trade theory was first documented by Wassily Leontief, the originator of input-output analysis. His findings have been described as the *Leontief paradox* and refer to the fact that actual trade patterns appear to contradict the Ricardian principle of specialization according to comparative advantage. The United States, for example, has a significantly higher capital endowment relative to labor than most other nations. According to Heckscher-Ohlin, the relative abundance of capital resources should dictate specialization in and export of capital-intensive products, with imports consisting largely of labor-intensive products. Leontief used his input-output table to measure the resource content of U.S. exports and imports, expecting to confirm the Heckscher-Ohlin relationship. Instead, he found disturbing inconsistencies between economists' generally accepted conclusions and the actual content of U.S. trade. Contrary to his Heckscher-Ohlin expectations, Leontief found the United States exporting relatively land- and labor-intensive products (wholesale services, motor vehicles, textile mill products, coal, and special industrial machinery) and importing significant amounts of capital-intensive products (paper and pulp, crude petroleum and natural gas, and primary copper).

What a blow to the theorists! Could elegant theory be rescued from inconvenient fact? Or more fundamentally, what should be blamed for the inconsistency—theory or fact?

The first step toward a practical answer was to examine critically the assumptions from which the Heckscher-Ohlin conclusions emerged. Most obviously, Leontief examined the resources themselves—the labor, land, and capital available for producing U.S. exports and imports. He concluded, not surprisingly, that resources are not globally homogeneous—an acre of land, a dozen laborers, and a machine in the U.S. heartland being quite different from an acre of land, a dozen laborers, and a machine in the Southern Hemisphere. More specifically, U.S. land and labor embody elements of capital (including implementation of scientific techniques by highly skilled U.S. workers and farmers) that are less characteristic of the land and labor of the Southern Hemisphere. Differences in the capital content of resources explain in part the tendency of the United States to specialize in and export products using significant amounts of land and labor versus (conventionally measured) capital resources.

With correct information about the capital content of our labor resources, U.S. exports of labor-intensive products are not surprising.

Accounting for International Flows of Wealth

However a nation's exports and imports are determined, the actual quantities must satisfy a fundamental rule. (Economists like to have concepts named for themselves, so I will immodestly name this fundamental rule Marilu's rule.) Marilu's rule of trade is quite simple, asserting that whatever things one nation buys from another must ultimately be compensated by a return flow of desired things[10]—not necessarily today or even tomorrow, but ultimately. Ultimate compensation is the only reason any nation (or any person, for that matter) would give up the here and now.

The first critical measure for determining ultimate compensation is the nation's *balance of trade:* the value of the nation's exports minus the value of its imports. The balance of trade is positive when revenue from exports exceeds payments for imports and negative when the reverse happens, yielding, respectively, a surplus and a deficit in the nation's trade account. Since no nation will export to another nation without receiving payment (no more than an individual will sell to another without payment), any temporary deficit from trade must be compensated by sales of short- or long-term investments, including bank accounts, stocks and bonds, and ownership of factories, hotels, office parks, and the like. Hence, Marilu's rule.

Essentially, a nation that imports more than it exports compensates for its excess of out-payments by issuing claims against its own assets. It is as if the nation were to pay for its excessive imports by exporting a portion of its own productive capacity. Exporting assets to foreigners has both an advantage, in the nation's current ability to import more products than it exports, and a disadvantage, in its obligation to pay an acceptable rate of return to the foreign owners of domestic assets. A continuing obligation! One that lasts forever![11] Only if the current advantage exceeds the continuing disadvantage does export of a nation's assets yield net benefits.

Fortunately for the United States, exporting assets has generally yielded net benefits, particularly in our early history, when U.S. imports regularly exceeded exports—and by large amounts. In the 1800s, for instance, foreign suppliers of U.S. imports used their receipts to purchase bonds issued by the new U.S. railroads, thus contributing to the development of the United States' enormous productive potential. Investments financed by foreign investors ultimately earned more than enough revenue to pay an acceptable return to their foreign owners and at the same time generate profits for even greater domestic investments.

Even so, a nation may be better served by exporting more than it imports. Receiving from abroad revenues in excess of its payments for imports, a nation can use its excess funds to acquire claims against the productive capacity of other nations—much as Japan does today. Imports less than exports reflect the Japanese people's willingness to forgo consuming a portion of current income—to save for the sake of increased investments. A nation that saves and invests abroad enjoys increased ownership of the world's capital resources, along with whatever earnings those assets produce. The result for surplus nations like Japan is a kind of "virtuous cycle" in which investment earnings increase the saving nation's income and increase its opportunities to consume, to save, and to purchase still more investments.

The International Monetary System

Payments for traded goods and investments are made possible through the international monetary system. That system has two functions: one, to provide liquidity for making transactions and, two, to establish the means for adjusting nations' out-payments to their in-payments—for enforcing Marilu's rule. Providing liquidity for making transactions requires that one nation's currency be readily converted into currencies spendable in other countries: dollars into deutschmarks, rubles into ringgits, zlotys into—whatever. Thus, accomplishing the first function requires international cooperation to ensure the availability of all these national currencies. Accomplishing the second function is more difficult and contentious. Balancing out-payments with in-payments may require changes in domestic spending, changes intended to affect a nation's ability to import more (or less) than it exports. Both functions require decisions that can have painful consequences.

A degree of balance in trade is essential if a nation is to avoid sustained increases in its call for other nations' currencies, or vice versa, which can be almost as bad. Imbalances in exports and imports can so disrupt trade as to stifle opportunities for economic growth. Regrettably, when trade imbalances appear, governments are strongly inclined to avoid difficult and contentious decisions, preferring instead to place direct controls on international investments, regardless of the underlying trade flows. It probably goes without saying that controls established by governments are seldom the most efficient way to determine investment flows. Another frequent attempt to correct trade imbalances is government control of exports and/or imports. But, again, such controls as trade licenses, subsidies, and tariffs interfere with the free exercise of comparative advantage and, therefore, impair the efficiency of trade.

Many economists contend that the best remedy for imbalance of international payments is the use of monetary and fiscal policies to change a nation's total spending or to enforce changes in wages and prices that make its exports more competitive. Typically, a nation with excessive imports relative to exports (and, therefore, a deficit in its payments) would be advised to institute contractionary monetary and fiscal policies to reduce domestic spending. By reducing spending for all products—foreign as well as domestic—contractionary policies reduce the excess of imports and reduce the nation's call for other nations' currencies. Such policies are not popular, however, and domestic policymakers are generally reluctant to institute them.

To make the problem even worse, contractionary policies to reduce imports in a deficit country are not always offset by expansionary policies to increase imports in a surplus country. Countries with balance of payments surpluses could easily correct trade imbalances by instituting expansionary monetary and fiscal policies. Expansionary policies would increase total spending, increase a surplus nation's tendency to import, and increase out-payments by enough to offset its high in-payments. Surplus nations are not compelled to initiate such policies, however, since in contrast to the limits on out-payments any nation can make, there is no practical limit to the amount of in-payments a nation can receive. (Mercantilism lives!)

All these factors increase the likelihood that monetary and fiscal policies to balance international exchange might be biased toward contraction, thus slowing the volume of trade throughout the world economy. A slowdown in international trade is especially damaging for the world's less developed countries (LDCs), which urgently need increased spending worldwide so that they can sell their products and develop their productive capacity. While mature nations are encouraging LDCs to grow and develop, it makes no sense for them to refuse to buy the products the LDCs are capable of producing.

A final approach to balancing international exchange is to change a nation's currency's value, the exchange rate that links one nation's currency with another's: to allow a currency's value to increase (appreciate) or decrease (depreciate). In 1998 $1 exchanged for roughly 1.5 German marks, 150 Japanese yen, or 0.6 British pounds. For the United States to balance its payments (offset its trade deficit) through a change in our currency's value, the dollar would have to depreciate: $1 would have to exchange for only, say, 1.2 marks, 115 yen, and 0.5 pounds. The lower value would make it more costly for holders of dollars to purchase imported cameras, Toyotas, and fine porcelain, while enabling holders of marks, yen, and pounds to purchase U.S. dollars—and, therefore, U.S. exports—more cheaply.

A problem with currency depreciation is that there are certain products that most nations must import, in spite of the lower value of their domestic currency. When domestic production requires, for example, chromium and tin for basic manufacturing or silicon chips and precision instruments for high-tech manufacturing, a lower currency value increases the cost of acquiring these necessary imports. The result is higher costs of domestic production, which may make the nation's manufactured goods even less competitive in export markets. Moreover, a nation's willingness to allow its currency to depreciate makes all its financial assets riskier and raises the rates of return domestic firms must pay to attract international investors. Last but not least, currency depreciation diminishes the purchasing power of all incomes denominated in the domestic currency. All these changes arbitrarily reduce living standards for the domestic population, causing hardship and impairing the nation's ability to save for investing in new productive capacity.

The Postwar International Economy

Bertil Ohlin's co-Prize winner in 1977 was James Meade, who was a friend and disciple of John M. Keynes in Britain in the 1930s. Like Keynes, Meade was appalled by what he called "poverty in the midst of plenty." He was "inspired" by Keynes, he said, to develop a "hopeful answer" to "stupid and wicked" policies that he believed tolerated unemployment. He later claimed that Britain could have changed the course of world history if her policymakers had only implemented Keynesian policies for achieving full employment and supported the League of Nations for preserving peace.[12]

At the outbreak of World War II, Meade was in Geneva working in the Economic Section of the League of Nations. When the German army invaded France, he and his young family joined a horde of refugees in a perilous journey across southern France to sanctuary in Britain. As an adviser to the British government during the war, he was assigned the task of selecting the most vital parts of the German economy for ultimate destruction by the Royal Air Force. After the war he participated in the establishment in Britain of a "womb-to-tomb welfare state." He has also been described as an architect of the General Agreement on Tariffs and Trade (GATT), which after World War II helped member nations negotiate agreements to reduce restrictions on trade. The GATT continued to function until the mid-1990s, when it was replaced by the World Trade Organization (WTO).

Meade was especially interested in the consequences of international trade for domestic living standards. He is the first economist to classify the objectives of economic policy as to achieve what he dubbed *external balance* and *internal balance*. External balance refers to equality of international payments: out-payments for imports and purchases of long-term investments abroad being equal to in-payments for exports and sales of long-term investments to foreigners. Internal balance refers to domestic economic conditions, specifically, full employment and price stability. Meade believed in his colleague A. W. Phillips' downward-sloping curve, however, and realized that absolutely full employment might be inconsistent with absolutely stable prices. Therefore, he asserted as a policy goal three targets:

- Maximum possible employment
- Acceptable rates of inflation
- Balance of international payments

Following Tinbergen's rule,[13] Meade's three targets would require three types of economic policy. The first, maximum possible employment, would require monetary and fiscal policies—adjusting money growth, taxes, and government spending to ensure a full-employment level of domestic spending. The second, an acceptable rate of inflation, would require controls that fix money wage rates at a level consistent with workers' productivity. Guaranteeing workers money wages that increase only with increases in real output would ensure against wage demands in excess of real output and help hold down prices. Finally, the third target of economic policy, balance of international payments, would require changes in currency exchange rates—a deficit nation experiencing sufficient currency depreciation to make its exports more competitive, and vice versa. Along with currency depreciation, a deficit nation might increase its short-term interest rates to encourage an inflow of short-term investments just sufficient to balance excessive out-payments and keep the currency's value from falling too far. The United States experienced both these adjustments in 1999, in part to help correct record trade deficits.

Meade broke with prewar economists in his opposition to the use of monetary policies to achieve external balance. Monetary policy should be decided solely on the basis of domestic needs, he argues, expanding or contracting the domestic money supply to achieve an acceptable rate of unemployment and inflation regardless of the consequences for the balance of international payments.

Correcting payments imbalances generally requires international cooperation. Absent that cooperation, surplus nations can take actions that neutralize those of deficit nations. For this reason, Meade favors permanent global agreements to cooperate toward long-term balance. Such a generalized agreement is embodied in the International Monetary Fund (IMF), which draws on currencies from 182 member nations to provide short-term loans so that deficit nations can satisfy temporary payments obligations. As trade increases and more nations experience exchange imbalance, Meade recommends expanding the IMF and extending its responsibilities.

Occasional Conflicts Between Domestic and International Policy Goals

Following up on Meade's explanations of international economic relationships is Robert Mundell, awarded the Nobel Prize in 1999 to become the last Nobel economist of the twentieth century. Mundell is a true internationalist: born in Canada, educated at MIT and the London School of Economics, teaching at the University of Chicago and Columbia University, and working much of each year to restore his Renaissance-era castle in Italy. (His colleagues point out that the Nobel award will help him buy a lot of paint and plaster.)

Mundell places himself at the intersection of three theoretical camps: the Keynesian camp, the monetarist camp, and the Ricardian camp. Each camp contributes something of value to economic analysis and policymaking, he says. The Keynesian camp contributes the multiplier effect of tax cuts for ending recession; the monetarist camp, monetary stability for encouraging growth-promoting investments; and the Ricardian camp, the importance of free trade and investment flows for maximizing social welfare. In the tradition of his colleagues at the University of Chicago, Mundell favors minimizing the role of government, generally through lower taxes and restraints on government spending. But he departs from the Chicago school of economists in his opposition to a fixed money supply rule (favored by Friedman) and in his support for fixed currency exchange rates. Variations in money growth are occasionally necessary, he says, to balance a nation's total spending with its ability to export. And fixed currency values are necessary to sustain confidence in the value of assets and, therefore, continued willingness to invest beyond national borders. When international investors are more certain about future exchange rates, they can better concentrate on opportunities to improve productivity—building plants of optimum size and allocating resources efficiently throughout the world economy— rather than speculating on currency values.

Mundell is best known for his analysis of international investment flows and their links with a nation's internal monetary and fiscal policies. Typically, expansionary policy to reduce domestic unemployment worsens a nation's balance-of-trade deficit; contractionary policy to reduce inflation yields a balance-of-trade surplus. Either result violates Marilu's rule and calls into question a nation's resolve to keep its currency's value stable.

Until the 1930s, the gold standard regulated nations' money supplies, holding spending fairly constant so that currency values did remain roughly stable. Then after World War II representatives of trading nations met at Bretton Woods, New Hampshire, to establish a new international monetary system they hoped would achieve a comparable level of stability. Under the Bretton Woods agreement, the United States would provide dollars for conducting world trade and as reserve assets on which other nations would base their domestic money supplies. Participants in Bretton Woods would exchange their currencies for dollars at a certain agreed-on rate, thus ensuring a constant value. Further, participants in Bretton Woods expected that the United States would manage its money supply prudently so as to maintain the dollar's value and minimize the threat of global inflation. Alas, it wasn't long before increased government spending in the United States—for the Vietnam War and President Johnson's Great Society programs—prompted excess money growth, with accumulating dollar reserves in other nations, unwelcome money growth worldwide, and upward pressures on world prices.

The United States could have corrected world financial imbalances, either by adopting contractionary monetary and fiscal policies or by announcing lower values for the U.S. dollar. Although the first was preferred by the world community, it was politically unacceptable in the United States. The second was impossible—impossible, at least, as long as other nations continued to base their currencies' values on the dollar's value. For other nations, to allow the dollar's value to fall relative to their own currencies was equivalent to allowing their currencies' values to rise, which would be detrimental to their trade prospects. Not, after all, a desirable solution to the problem of payments imbalances.

The eventual collapse of the Bretton Woods agreement in 1973 had two outcomes. First, attempts to maintain fixed currency values were abandoned, and world currency values were allowed to float. With floating, a currency that is in high demand for purchasing that nation's exports (and, therefore, yielding a balance-of-trade surplus) floats up. Its higher prices reduce that nation's ability to export and push its international payments toward balance, and vice versa, of course. Free-market economists like Milton Friedman generally favor floating exchange rates because floating rates require minimum government involvement in currency markets

The second outcome of the collapse of Bretton Woods was a growing market in international currencies, first named the *Eurodollar market* because of the preponderance of dollars, but eventually named the *Eurocurrency market,* in which many international currencies are bought and sold, loaned and borrowed, subject to the same supply and demand forces that determine prices and quantities exchanged in markets for other things. The effect is a hodgepodge of currency values and interest rates, with vast opportunities for financial return and risk.

The Eurocurrency market is significant for domestic policymaking because it provides a source of liquidity outside the control of a nation's central banks. It makes possible arbitrary increases or decreases in global spending power—with massive potential for global inflation or recession. And it makes possible such international flows of investment funds as to undermine any single nation's ability to manage its domestic economy. In fact, with the free flow of investments among nations, one nation's domestic economic policy can lose its effectiveness entirely. Consider the typical reason for domestic economic policy—recession accompanied by high unemployment. If policymakers adopt expansionary monetary and fiscal policy to increase employment, the usual effect is to increase the threat of inflation, which reduces the real purchasing power of investments denominated in that currency. International investors are likely to withdraw their funds, and the outflow of the nation's money offsets whatever gains in employment are associated with the expansionary policy.

The fact that expansionary monetary and fiscal policies have the same effects on international investment flows suggests a way to achieve internal and external balance and at the same time maintain fixed exchange rates. It is to adopt opposite versions of the two policies. To reduce unemployment, for example, a nation might combine expansionary fiscal policy with contractionary monetary policy. The effect of both is to increase interest rates so that short-term investment funds flow in to offset the likely increase in the nation's trade deficit. Because total demand and supply of the nation's currency do not change, currency values would not change either.

This conclusion is called the Mundell-Fleming hypothesis because it was first articulated by the British economist Marcus Fleming, who died in 1976. If exchange rates are allowed to float, on the other hand, the Mundell-Fleming hypothesis recommends correcting unemployment through expansionary monetary policy. More money helps provide more jobs. At the same time, more money causes interest rates to fall and investment funds to flow out. But with floating exchange rates, outflows of investment funds cause currency values to fall, encouraging greater exports and creating jobs in export industries. Thus expansionary monetary policy has a double-barreled effect on employment, with significant advantages for both internal and external balance.

A Revolutionary Proposal

Mundell suggests that the ideal source of liquidity for the world economy would be a world central bank with power to create a single universal currency based in part on gold and in part on the bank's holding of certain national currencies. A world central bank could increase world liquidity at a rate consistent with growth in the world's productive capacity. Moreover, a world central bank would be less subject to error than many independent central banks. Much as the Federal Reserve Bank acts to offset surpluses and shortages of money across the United States, a world central bank could offset errors of money growth across nations. That ideal may be far in the future, of course. In the meantime, says Mundell, a useful alternative is regional combinations of nations with a common currency and common monetary policy. The European Union is just such an outcome.

Indeed, the European Union may be an example of what Mundell calls an *optimal currency area,* a region or group of nations in which it is practical to have a common currency. A common currency is practical if resources (especially labor) can move freely across jurisdictional boundaries. Unless labor can move freely among jurisdictions, rates of unemployment can differ widely. In order to provide jobs for their workers, some jurisdictions would allow their currencies to depreciate so as to stimulate demand for exports and give a boost to export industries. A common currency, however, would not be subject to differential depreciation and, therefore, would require free mobility of unemployed workers across jurisdictional boundaries.

Another advantage of an optimal currency area is that its prices remain relatively stable, since shocks to supply or demand in one part of the area are likely to be offset by opposite shocks in other areas. Moreover, in its larger market, the fraction of total output that is traded outside the area is smaller, so that changes in a currency's external value have less effect on domestic prices. One way to judge whether a region constitutes an optimal currency area is to determine whether regional integration increases welfare. By that definition the United States constitutes an optimal currency area. The single U.S. currency makes it easy to produce and sell to a larger market, with all the benefits of economies of scale that are now expected for the European Union.

Emerging Markets and Global Financial Crises

The 1998 crisis in world financial markets arose out of all the microeconomic, macroeconomic, and financial-market consequences of increased integration of the world's economies. First, improvements in the technology of communication and transportation have opened more nations to global economic activity, particularly the nations of Southeast Asia, whose people have traditionally valued education, job skills, and achievement. As they export more of their products and as their business profits increase, Southeast Asian nations have become the fortunate focus of more of the world's savings. Dollars, deutschmarks, and yen have flowed into domestic investments and into local banks where they were converted into local currencies and loaned to local businesses. International investors expected large returns from their investments in the "emerging markets" of Southeast Asia.

At first those expectations were fulfilled, so that still more of the world's savings arrived for investing locally. No economy can absorb unlimited quantities of investment funds, however, no economy having unlimited opportunities for their productive use. Lending itself is not a problem, of course, borrowers being easy to find whatever the locale. In many Southeast Asian countries borrowers were increasingly the friends or relatives of bank executives, not necessarily the most qualified users of investment funds.

When, inevitably, returns on investments in emerging markets stopped rising and turned down, international investors began to sell their investments and savers began to withdraw their bank deposits. Local banks were forced to call their loans to local businesses, businesses had to sell other assets, and economic activity was generally forced to slow. When the banks used local currency to purchase the dollars, deutschmarks, and yen necessary for paying off their international depositors, the effect was to push down the value of the former and push up the value of the latter. Lower values for investments denominated in local currencies further reduced the returns to international investors and accelerated the exodus of funds from these nations' economies.

The collapse in value of Southeast Asian investment properties diminished the value of portfolios, including their securities, often prompting sales of other securities that were used as collateral to secure outstanding loans. The "flight to quality"—meaning cash, insured savings accounts, and U.S. government securities—threatened massive sell-offs and precipitous price reductions worldwide. Indeed, no financial market was immune from the contagion, all being linked through holdings of securities and derivative instruments exchanged throughout the world's financial network. Fortunately, total collapse was avoided. Some businesses and financial institutions did fail, but IMF loans helped nations stem the decline in their currencies' value and halt the outflow of investment funds.

Chapter 32

COMBINING PUBLIC INVESTMENT WITH PRIVATE INVESTMENT TO PROMOTE GROWTH

We drive our private vehicles along public highways or ride public transportation to jobs in private firms or public institutions. We have dinner in private restaurants before attending classes in public colleges or universities. We visit private dental offices and public hospitals. In all such activities, so intricately linked are our associations with private and public institutions that it is impossible to be sure which activities contribute what amounts to our total welfare.

One thing we can be sure of, however, is the importance of both sorts of investments for providing the mix of benefits we savor every day: private investments in factories, office parks, research and development, transportation, and communication facilities; and public investments in physical infrastructure, such as highways, bridges, and port facilities, and human infrastructure, such as public research and development, education, health care, and improved nutrition for the nation's (current and future) workers. Unless a nation increases both sorts of investment at least as fast as its population, domestic living standards must inevitably fall. In that event, the nation can expect rising social conflict and perhaps even political upheaval.

Pointing out this unpleasant fact was the reason economics was nicknamed the "dismal science." No wonder economists are accepted only grudgingly as advisers to government policymakers.

The Efficient Private and Public Balance

How is society to balance the allocation of resources for public and private investments: for satisfying the private tastes of individuals, for providing public services to be enjoyed by the community as a whole, for bequeathing capital resources to future generations? In short, how much is it right to take away from Peter to provide services for Paul? Not an easy question to answer.

And we can't count on private markets to answer it. Although markets can answer most questions efficiently, some of the answers provided by private markets offend our sense of equity, or fairness. Which raises another question: If markets cannot ensure the "first-best solution" to society's allocative questions, is there perhaps a "second-best solution," one that relies on nonmarket criteria to answer such questions?

For better or worse, the primary institution for applying nonmarket criteria to investment decisions is government, through its tax and spending policies. Government's primary function involves collecting taxes and making expenditures, either for building infrastructure investments or for providing cash and noncash benefits to defined groups within the population. If private markets answer society's allocative questions imperfectly, we might call on government for answers that we regard as more equitable.

Deciding to allocate a portion of current income to investment implies a sacrifice, willingly entered into by private savers and somewhat less willingly by the taxpayers who make government saving possible. Still, it is only through the consensus of the taxpaying public that government can collect tax revenues in excess of current budgetary requirements and make the public investments that can enhance the nation's future productive capacity. The sacrifices associated with saving require that investments—whether public or private—earn returns at least sufficient to compensate for the current sacrifice.

Private investments yield a return to individual investors, in the form of interest, dividends, or capital gains on owned assets. Government investments yield a return to society as a whole, in the form of increased productivity and increased ability to pay taxes. To the extent that greater returns can be achieved through private rather than public investments, economic efficiency requires that savings be allocated by individual investors toward private investments. When public investments yield greater gains than the yield on private investments, efficiency requires allocation toward building infrastructure for the use of society as a whole.

Calculating the yield on public and private investments requires information on benefits and costs, information that is not easy to obtain. Markets depend on prices to convey this kind of information— as buyers willingly reveal the net benefits they expect to enjoy from various kinds of products. For government to decide the efficient level of taxes and public investments would require similar willingness on the part of users of government services. Similar willingness is not to be expected, however, when a person's revelation of the benefits he enjoys from public investments affects his susceptibility to taxation. Who among us would tell a government bureaucrat how much we would value a new high school gymnasium if our revelation allows the bureaucrat to increase our taxes to pay for it? To complicate matters, not all of the benefits and costs from investments are immediate and apparent, some expected in the (occasionally distant) future and some so widely dispersed that they are impossible to measure.

For all these reasons, calculating the yield on private and public investments is problematic, so that the allocative decision is frequently made on political grounds, where it is subject to interest-group pressure. Given such pressure, taxpayers may be assessed more or less taxes for more or less public investment than is economically efficient, as James Buchanan so emphatically predicts.

Information About Benefits and Costs

Without valid information from the citizens who are affected by its tax and investment decisions, government cannot be certain that its public investments actually increase social welfare. Citizens affected by government's tax and investment policies are likely to employ any legal means to avoid sharing with government crucial information about benefits and costs. They become free riders, enjoying the benefits of public investments while disavowing any obligation to pay taxes to finance them.

All of this has created the need for a new branch of economics: the economics of information, especially asymmetric information (information held by one party and desperately needed by another). This is the specialization of Nobel economists James Mirrlees and William Vickrey, joint Nobel Prize recipients in 1996 for their insights into how people with different information respond differently to economic incentives.

Mirrlees and Vickrey worked on opposite sides of the Atlantic to explore methods for extracting information from people reluctant to reveal it—not through such malevolent methods as those used in spy novels but through more benign incentives. They believed that, with correct information, government could structure tax and spending policies that ensure the efficient level of public investment.

In keeping with his interest in asymmetrical information, James Mirrlees is a very private person, not given to public revelations of personal characteristics. One known characteristic, however, is his fascination with whodunits, a fascination shared by many economists. Perhaps the vicarious satisfaction we enjoy from playing the clever detective is compensation for what some people might regard as the dreariness of our professional lives!

Taxation also fascinates Mirrlees, and particularly the use of taxes to allocate efficiently the costs of public investments. Since taxes affect prices, they affect the signals given and received by buyers and sellers and, therefore, the efficiency with which markets decide production. To make efficient tax and spending decisions, policymakers need correct information regarding: how an excise tax on, say, airline tickets or telephone service affects our decision to purchase those services; or how an income tax affects our decision to supply work effort. Inefficient taxes make for incorrect price signals, which distort market behavior, cause production to deviate from most efficient resource allocation, and reduce social welfare.

Visualize the market for airline travel or telephone service before government levies an excise tax. Typically these products sell for prices that are less than the benefits to be enjoyed by many of their consumers. The reason is that all buyers pay the same price, the price that just equals the satisfaction gained by the last—marginal—consumer. But by Bernoulli's law of diminishing marginal utility, which was studied in Chapter 5, the last—marginal—unit of the product provides less satisfaction than all previous units. When all consumers pay the same price, the consumers of all but the last unit enjoy satisfaction greater than price paid. The result is a net gain in welfare for the society as a whole, a gain known in economic theory as *consumers' surplus*. The larger the quantity consumed and the lower the price paid, other things being equal, the greater is the total gain and the larger the consumers' surplus.

The surplus enjoyed by consumers is mirrored by a surplus enjoyed by producers, and the logic is similar. Most products sell for a price that is greater than the price some producers would have been willing to accept. Here the reason is that price is determined by the added cost of producing the last—marginal—unit. But because marginal costs tend to increase with increased quantities produced, the last—marginal—unit of the product costs more to produce than all previous units. When all units receive the same price, producers enjoy revenue greater than their marginal cost for all but the last unit. The result for these producers is a net gain in profit, known in economic theory as *producers' surplus*. This time, the larger the quantity produced and the higher the price received, other things being equal, the greater is the total gain to producers and the larger the producers' surplus. When consumers' surplus is added to producers' surplus, the sum is the total social welfare enjoyed from producing the untaxed product. (Eureka! This is a way to measure society's net benefits from airline travel, telephone service, and anything else that is exchanged in markets.) Moreover, the gain in social welfare determined in perfectly free markets is the greatest possible gain from producing and consuming this product.

An excise tax changes all this. Placing an excise tax on a product requires the producer, first, to add the tax to the selling price and, second, to transfer a portion of producers' surplus to the tax collector. The higher selling price forces consumers to reduce their purchases. With higher prices and smaller quantities, consumers suffer a loss of consumers' surplus. With lower producers' and consumers' surplus, the effect of an excise tax is to reduce social welfare, indicative of an inefficient tax.

The loss in social welfare from an excise tax is mitigated by the possibility that government uses the tax revenue in a way that adds to social welfare. (Ensuring that tax revenues are spent for programs that increase social welfare is a topic taken up by William Vickrey. Stay tuned.)

If excise taxes are inefficient, can government collect needed revenue more efficiently through income taxation and, in particular, the progressive income tax? Initially, Mirrlees' answer was Yes. He believed that progressive income taxes increase social welfare by putting more of the burden of financing public programs on taxpayers with higher incomes. After paying their income taxes, high-income workers can purchase smaller quantities of goods and services, and low-income workers larger quantities, than they could with other types of taxes. Mirrlees believed in Bernoulli's principle of diminishing marginal utility, that the welfare we gain from our purchases diminishes with increases in quantity, so he expected progressive income taxation to increase society's total welfare and, therefore, economic efficiency.

When he examined more closely the effects of progressive income taxes, however, Mirrlees was forced to another conclusion. After building a complex model of a nation's incentive structure, he was forced to conclude that imposing progressive tax rates on the nation's most productive workers significantly reduces their incentives to produce—reduces incentives so much as to reduce society's total output. Furthermore, the loss of output from high-income workers is greater than the gain in welfare experienced by low-income workers—a troubling conclusion for Mirrlees and for other supporters of progressive taxation.

The negative incentive effect of progressive taxation has been disputed by another liberal economist, James Tobin. Tobin agrees that progressive taxation reduces work incentives. But, he says, whatever negative incentive occurs is a one-shot effect, after which the loss of work incentives at the high end of the income spectrum is insignificant and is more than offset by an increase in work incentives at the low end.

Looking for a Better Way

Judging that both excise and income taxes reduce society's total welfare led some economists to recommend replacing such taxes with a single lump-sum tax,[14] one that takes from taxpayers as a whole the total amount government would have collected in an excise or income tax but does not affect either prices or work incentives.

A lump-sum tax is different from the increasingly popular flat tax. The latter applies the same tax rate to all taxable income and may, therefore, have less of a disincentive effect on high-income workers than progressive tax rates. In contrast, a lump-sum tax is simply a stated amount paid by all taxpayers, not based on their income, wealth, or spending. The fact that a lump-sum tax is the same for all citizens, regardless of their behavior, is a real advantage in terms of preserving economic incentives. A lump-sum tax does not change behavior in such a way as to diminish economic efficiency.

The next question should be: How does a lump-sum tax affect tax equity? Unfortunately, requiring all taxpayers to pay the same tax means that low-income taxpayers pay a greater percentage of income and suffer a greater sacrifice relative to the sacrifice of high-income taxpayers—a result that may offend our sense of equity. Taxes that take a higher percentage of income from low-income taxpayers are described as regressive, as opposed to income taxes that in the United States are mildly progressive. Most excise taxes are also regressive because purchases of taxed items represent a larger fraction of income for low-income buyers: gasoline, liquor, and cigarettes, being the typical examples, not because low-income consumers purchase more of these products but because their purchases are greater relative to their total income. Lump-sum taxes are definitely regressive. Whether low-income buyers should assume a greater relative burden of financing public programs is a question for ethicists, but one that many economists would answer negatively.

And here we come to an unhappy but inescapable conclusion. It is that all taxes involve a Catch-22. Either we tax everyone the same, which is efficient but probably not equitable. Or we tax incomes progressively, which may be equitable but not efficient. Or we tax product markets regressively, which is probably neither efficient nor equitable.

Taxing What We "Do" or Taxing What We "Are"

There might be a way to avoid the Catch-22 of taxes that either distort consumer choices or impair work incentives. But that method requires government to obtain information that is virtually impossible to obtain.

The only way to resolve the conflict between efficiency and equity in taxation is to tax people differently not on the basis of what they "do" (what they buy or what they earn) but on the basis of what they "are." Instead of taxing people progressively on the income they earn, the more efficient method of taxation is to tax people on the income they are capable of earning. Based on their fundamental capacity to earn more income, a nation's more productive people might be assessed higher tax rates than its less productive people. Taxing everyone to the limit of his productive capabilities encourages everyone to produce the maximum quantities he is capable of producing and is, therefore, efficient. It is also equitable, if we define equity in terms of a taxpayer's ability to pay taxes.

Taxing everyone according to his ability to earn income leaves everyone with disposable income consistent with his ability to produce income and pay taxes. Then, when consumers use their disposable incomes to purchase goods and services, they reveal information about the true benefits society as a whole enjoys from various types of production. With this information, government is better able to allocate available resources toward the most efficient combination of private and public investments.

The chances of instituting such a tax are slim to none. In fact, governments are compelled to levy taxes on the basis of what people do, mainly because information about people's behavior is observable. It is easy to observe what people buy and what they earn. In contrast, information about people's fundamental characteristics (what they are) must come from the people themselves, and people are not generous in revealing information that causes them to be taxed. (Actually, it is easier for most people to claim less than their true ability than to claim more.) Thus, the problem remains. Allocating society's resources efficiently to public or private investments requires information: first, about people's preferences for particular goods and services; and, second, about their capacity to produce them. Unfortunately, valid information about either is almost impossible to obtain.

Cost-Benefit Analysis

Mirrlees' studies took him beyond the types of taxes for financing public investments to evaluating public investments themselves through cost-benefit analysis (CBA). Some people call CBA "applied welfare economics" because it applies basic optimization principles to real investment decisions.

Whether consciously or not, consumers use CBA with every purchase, and businesses more consciously with every investment. In both cases, we start with a fixed budget to be allocated to one or another product. We sum up the benefits of both products (as nearly as we can identify them) and discount them; we do the same thing with costs. We choose the product with the greatest benefits relative to costs—with the proviso that benefits must be greater than costs, for a benefit-cost ratio greater than one. Similarly, government policymakers use CBA to decide between, say, education or incarceration to treat drug abuse; buses or subways for mass transit; public research institutes or business tax credits to encourage R&D.

Mirrlees applied CBA to public investments in LDCs, an application that is particularly difficult because LDC budgets are severely constrained, costs are horrendous, and benefits are not always immediately apparent. Reaching a positive investment decision in an LDC may require a leap of faith uncharacteristic of cautious investors— whether private or government. Valid CBA in an LDC requires full information regarding the benefits to be enjoyed from an added unit of public investment—benefits occupying a long and hazy chain of responses to new market conditions: the career opportunities provided to poor children, the skills gained by unskilled workers, the enhanced vision opened to budding entrepreneurs. Whatever benefits an LDC enjoys from increased production in the public sector must not be at the expense of more beneficial products not produced in the private sector.

Failure to conduct valid CBA has resulted in faulty investment decisions in many LDCs, wasted resources, and stalled economic growth. "Project appraisal is an essential part of avoiding these mistakes in the future," says Mirrlees.[15]

The Cost of Congestion

Even before winning his Nobel Prize in 1996, William Vickrey was well known in the United States for his work in the economics of information. He was said to have had a restless intellect, often attending academic seminars in which he rested with eyes closed, apparently oblivious to the topic at hand until abruptly he came to life with a question more astute and challenging than the questions raised by his more obviously alert colleagues. Sad to say, Vickrey died three days after the announcement of his Nobel Prize, before he had the chance to accept it.

Vickrey is most closely associated with pricing, especially the pricing of public goods and services that are not usually exchanged in product markets. The most obvious example of a public service is travel on public highways. If government is to provide efficient investments in public highways, it must be able to evaluate the benefits society enjoys from highway use. (According to standard optimization theory, investments in highways should proceed only up to the point that the added benefits just compensate for the added costs. Try telling that to any state highway department!) Making efficient investments in public highways is complicated because it is difficult to require drivers to reveal the benefits they enjoy from highway use—and to assume the cost thereof.

Public investments are different from private because the goods and services they provide are nonexclusive and nonrivalrous. Investments in clean air and well-defended national borders are nonexclusive, for example, because providing them to some consumers is impossible without providing them to all. Consumers who do not pay the price cannot be excluded from the benefits of clean air and defense. Such products are also nonrivalrous because more consumers can enjoy them without diminishing the enjoyment of other users. All this is in contrast with perfectly exclusive and rivalrous products, enjoyed only (exclusively) by owners whose enjoyment would be sorely diminished if others were allowed to use them (rivalrously).

Exclusivity and rivalry are important concepts in economics because buyers are inclined to pay the costs only of products whose benefits only they enjoy, exclusively and rivalrously. This means that information regarding the benefits of nonexclusive and nonrivalrous products is typically not revealed through ordinary market behavior. If such products are provided at all, they are normally provided by government, but government lacks the benefit-cost information for providing them efficiently. The magnitude of the investment required of government depends on the magnitude of the free-rider problem—more users refusing to pay necessarily increasing government's obligation to pay.

To be correct, of course, most products are neither perfectly exclusive and rivalrous nor absolutely nonexclusive and nonrivalrous but rather occupy a spectrum extending between the two extremes. Highways are only partially nonrivalrous, for example, which isn't news to millions of frustrated commuters. Highway use by too many drivers creates congestion, and congestion diminishes the benefits enjoyed by other drivers—not infrequently yielding negative net benefits.

Congestion occurs only when all highway users are charged the same price, however. When all drivers pay the same price, rush-hour drivers are permitted to impose the costs of their added congestion on other drivers without themselves paying an equivalent cost. Under such circumstances, the only solution to highway congestion in peak driving times is to expand highway capacity far beyond that required for use in nonpeak times.

Not surprisingly, William Vickrey disagreed with that solution. Vickrey was the first economist formally to examine the issue of congestion, in the context of government provision of nonexclusive, nonrivalrous products. Probably his most important contribution to collective decision making is to analyze the consequences of peak-load pricing for congestible public services, like highways and, increasingly, airports. He points first to privately produced goods and services, products whose prices differ so as to ration limited quantities to users who value them most highly. Tickets for the more popular evening performances of Broadway plays are priced higher than matinees. Long-distance calls and electric power cost more during periods of peak usage. And on and on. Vickrey saw the objective of pricing for public services as similar to these examples—that is, to ration the limited quantities available at peak-load periods to those users who value them most.

With peak-load pricing, users of a public service who add to the costs of congestion pay a price that increases with increases in the costs they impose on other users. Peak-period drivers can justify paying the peak-load price only if they receive greater benefits from driving at peak-load times. Drivers that expect lesser benefits can avoid the peak-load price by choosing other times to travel. Thus, peak-load pricing helps reduce congestion at peak times and reduces the costs congestion imposes on highway users. Moreover, just as is true in markets for private goods and services, different people's willingness to pay different prices for public services reveals valuable information about their personal benefits and costs, information that enables government policymakers to make more efficient decisions regarding public investments.

Congested Singapore has instituted a peak-load pricing system in which drivers purchase stickers entitling them to use certain public highways at certain times. In the United States, Houston and San Diego are testing similar systems in which drivers pay for the privilege of driving in high-occupancy-toll (HOT) lanes. Electronic readers suspended above the highway verify drivers' display of the appropriate driving permit. The objective of all such programs is to smooth out the use of public highways and avoid the need to build more of them.

Vickrey regards actual pricing for public services as inefficient, particularly services that are provided by large, "lumpy" investment expenditures—highway systems, bridges, major waterways, and airport runways being prime examples. The reason is political constraints, which generally require that government charge prices for these services that recapture the project's full costs of construction. The effect of full-cost pricing is to price the service too high at first, until construction costs are covered, and then to price too low, increasing congestion. Vickrey recommends pricing according to marginal costs: the added maintenance and congestion costs an additional driver imposes on the system. Both maintenance and congestion costs are likely to be low at first, which should call for lower prices and greater use of the service, and high later, which should call for higher prices as the project ages and becomes more congested.

To many government policymakers, this method of pricing doesn't seem logical, with the result that the prices of public services are often set incorrectly and public investments are used inefficiently. The airlines have found Vickrey's pricing system eminently logical, however. By pricing air travel according to marginal costs, the airlines improve efficiency in the use of their large investments in passenger aircraft.

Air travelers are frequently bewildered at the wide variety of fares available on the same flight, carrying the same passengers to the same city at the same time. Vickrey explains the bewildering array of air fares this way. The efficient way to price air travel is to set price according to the number of seats remaining to be sold and the time remaining before the flight. The efficient price at any point in time is the price that, if maintained until departure time, would result in all seats being sold. Plenty of seats and not much time should call for low prices; the reverse, high prices. This system is equivalent to marginal-cost pricing, since the sale of a single airline seat must raise the price of remaining seats by whatever amount is necessary to reduce demand by one seat.

Auctions

Increasing economic efficiency was Vickrey's motivation for another significant contribution to the economics of information. Economic efficiency requires that goods and services be distributed among users on the basis of individual benefits and costs, toward the objective of maximum net benefits for society as a whole. But many of our institutions are structured so as to conceal information about our personal benefits and costs and impair the efficiency of allocation. In such cases, we waste valuable energy sizing up the market and developing a strategy for serving our personal self-interest while avoiding revealing personal information.

Surprisingly, an institution that tends to obscure true valuations is the auction. In a typical auction, individuals estimate the benefits they would enjoy from the auctioned item and submit sealed bids. In general, bids are lower than bidders' true valuations so as to avoid the "winner's curse": the fact that the winner of a typical auction necessarily pays more for the commodity, artifact, or collectible than every other bidder believes it is worth. To avoid the winner's curse, a potential buyer might bid only, say, $750 for a vase she actually values as much as $1000. Suppose another potential buyer evaluates the vase at $800 and bids $775. By misrepresenting her personal evaluation of the vase, the first bidder allows it to go to the $775 bidder, who actually places a lesser personal valuation on the item. The result for society is the inefficient allocation of a scarce asset.

In fact, all bidders in a typical auction face a trade-off between bidding low to avoid the winner's curse and bidding high to increase the probability of winning. A more efficient auction would allocate items in such a way as to maximize net benefits—with items going to bidders who truly value them most.

But achieving this goal requires correct information from bidders. Vickrey proposes to glean such information through a "second-price auction." In a second-price auction the high bidder wins the item but pays the second-highest bid. The effect is to encourage all bidders to offer a price that truly reflects their personal evaluation of the item. In the preceding example, the bids for the vase would be $1000 and $800, with the $1000 bidder winning the item and paying $800. The advantage is that the item goes to the bidder who values it most highly, and the seller receives the price he would have received in an ordinary auction if the winning bidder had not entered.

With the development of electronic communications, formal auctions on the Internet are becoming common means of exchange for businesses and ordinary consumers. The Internet is especially popular for business-to-business sales of commodities, used business equipment, and special expertise. Through eBay and Amazon.com, ordinary consumers exchange such diverse items as vintage Barbies, archeological relics, and secondhand surfboards. Internet auctions are efficient because they allow large numbers of bidders to bid openly and, therefore, come close to revealing the auctioned items' true value. As a result, the winner's curse is not as great as in auctions with more limited participation. There is one potential problem with Internet auctions, however. Because bidding is transparent, some bidders may use revealed information to collude, holding their bids below their true valuation and paying less to the seller.

PART 8
SOCIETY'S INSTITUTIONS: THEIR ORIGINS AND POTENTIAL FOR CHANGE

John Nash • John Harsanyi •
Reinhard Selten • Douglass North •
Robert Fogel

It's impossible to understand the workings of an economic system without understanding the institutions that support it. Institutions are more than the mere bricks and mortar of school buildings, churches, courthouses. They include all those patterns of behavior that have evolved over time to satisfy our societies' objectives—in somewhat the same way that plant and animal species have evolved particular living arrangements to suit their particular physical environments. In both cases, the behavior patterns that endure are the ones that adapt most successfully to the challenges of the environment.

Patterns of behavior exist because people interact with other people. Alone, Robinson Crusoe needed fewer institutions to ensure his survival than does an apartment dweller in a crowded city. When people interact, they must decide how to behave in all of life's many encounters. Making new decisions for every new encounter is time-consuming and prone to costly mistakes. Life is simpler when we establish rules of thumb for behaving similarly in similar circumstances. Relieved from the need to compare and choose among trivial alternatives, we can pay attention to the more complex decisions that significantly affect our lives. Think how distracting it would be to have to decide on our way to work every morning which side of the street to drive on. An established society with more firmly established institutions has greater potential for economic growth and development and, therefore, greater scope for improving the living standards of its people.

Chapter 33

PEOPLE'S INTERACTIONS ARE LIKE GAMES

The remarkable thing about institutions is that they achieve two opposite effects at the very same time. First, they free individuals from the onerous task of making trivial decisions, thus allowing them to focus on the larger choices that significantly affect their self-interest. And second, they bind up individual self-interest with the interests of the group, thus advancing the prospects of the larger society. The most fundamental institution of market economies is the institution of private property.

Almost from the beginning of human history private property has been intimately linked with an explosion of economic growth and prosperity. During what is sometimes called the world's first economic revolution, primitive hunters and gatherers settled down to practice agriculture. In that long ago time there was plenty of land relative to population, so there was no need for exclusive property rights. As populations grew, however, land became relatively scarce, and primitive people were driven to establish rights and responsibilities over particular tracts of land. With the assurance of rights to property came opportunities to specialize and trade, which activated the spur of competition, stimulated the development of technical knowledge, and began the world's historical upward trend in worker productivity. In fact, many of our family names originated in our ancestors' specializations as farmer, tailor, carter, or smith.

While strengthening individual incentives to achieve, specialization and trade also bound the welfare of those early humans more closely with the welfare of the community. At first groups of families and then entire tribes established communal systems for storing food in times of plenty and distributing it in times of famine. They constructed communitywide irrigation systems and forged arrangements for the equitable distribution of fresh water, in all such ways increasing economic efficiency and improving the lives of group members. Specialization and trade did create some problems, nevertheless. By separating the functions of producers from consumers, specialization and trade opened opportunities for people to shirk their responsibilities—to free ride. Greater opportunities to free ride eventually called for more complex institutions to guide or restrain people's behavior relative to others in their group.

As all sorts of institutions evolved, primitive societies grew and developed into the forms familiar today. Remembering Robert Solow's growth theory, we might conclude that economic growth would eventually stabilize, as mature nations settled down to grow at a steady rate determined by population growth and proportionate growth in capital resources. Under those conditions, we might expect income per capita to remain the same, as would average living standards. (Remember we are dealing with the "dismal science" here.) Fortunately, the dismal conclusions of neoclassical growth theory have not been borne out by actual growth experience. In many nations of the world, limitations on per capita growth have been offset by advances in technical information so that labor and capital resources, working together, have become more and more productive. The happy result for their people has been fairly steady increases in living standards, with even greater expectations for increases in the future.

In the meantime, other nations have slipped farther and farther behind, so that their people suffer even lower standards of living than their ancestors endured a century ago. We might wonder: Why? Why, if people behave rationally and if rational behavior leads to efficient uses of available resources, do some nations prosper and others stagnate?

Our answer would have to include consideration of nations' differing institutions, differences in the ways their people use information to guide their interactions with other people.

Information and Institutions

Population growth, the increasing separation of functions, and, in consequence, the greater interdependence among people make all social interactions more complicated. With interdependence, people's behavior comes to be guided by the expected behavior of other people. But frequent changes in information lead people to change their behavior, such that the ultimate result of any social interaction becomes harder and harder to predict.

This tendency for new information to cause changes in behavior makes interactive behavior infinitely regressive, looping back and forth and subject to change at every turn. What will she do? What should I do if she does this? What will she do then?

The complexity of interactive behavior is sometimes illustrated by one of the great Sherlock Holmes stories, the one about the detective's flight to elude his nemesis, the evil Professor Moriarty. As Holmes explains to Dr. Watson, the two protagonists occupy the same intellectual plane, so that even the cleverest tactics devised by one are quickly anticipated and countered by the other. Will the clever Holmes take the Continental Express to Paris, or will he divert through Belgium and Luxembourg to Switzerland? Will the equally clever Moriarty correctly anticipate Holmes' destination as the falls of Reichenbach? Will Holmes' solicitous companion, Dr. Watson, be deceived by a bogus message and leave the detective alone on a ledge overlooking the falls? True to Holmes' worst fears, Moriarty correctly anticipates all his behaviors and confronts the detective in his most vulnerable circumstance, with the result that the two protagonists plunge together, "reeling over, locked in each others' arms" into the "dreadful cauldron of swirling water and seething foam" at the base of the falls. The only evidence of the tragedy is Holmes' distinctive alpenstock (walking stick) propped against a rock, along with his silver cigarette case and a note guiding police to evidence for bringing Moriarty's evil gang to justice.[1]

(Not to worry. Holmes was found later to have survived the episode, his creator's response to apparently irresistible pressure from avid fans.)

Questions involving patterns of interactive behavior opened an entirely new realm of economic theory called *game theory*. The name sounds trivial but the applications are far from trivial, including such human interactions as are involved in military[2] and business strategies, monetary and fiscal policies, international trade negotiations, political campaigns, and even the evolution of plant and animal species.

Of particular interest to economists, game theory helps explain how one person's behavior can be consciously designed to influence the behavior of another: in short, how we create the incentives that encourage people to behave in certain ways. A proper incentive system is an essential institution in a market economy, which depends for efficiency on the decisions of many independently motivated people, interacting as buyers and sellers, savers and investors, borrowers and lenders. Since a free society cannot compel us to behave efficiently, it must create the incentives that promise rewards—or punishments—from our behavioral choices.

Playing the Game

The name *game theory* is another example of economists' use of metaphors to describe economic behavior. Such metaphors help simplify the complexities of real life and make them more easily comprehensible. Indeed, economists probably use the phrase "it is as if" almost as often as they say "second derivative." Game theory is a huge metaphor that conjures up the poker player's tendency to bet on a poor hand, the quarterback's tendency to feint a pass and then run with the ball, the batter's tendency to bunt to the infield. Game theory may even explain the strategies we use in that most important game of all, the "game of love."

Game theory begins with the introduction of players, strategies, moves, and payoffs. The game in question is not a game of chance where, for example, tossing pennies or dice determines winners and losers. The game is one of strategy, where players use available information to choose their moves, either for a onetime play of the game or for a sequence of plays. In addition to asking "What should I do?," game theory forces players to ask themselves what the other player might do—and how the other player might be influenced to behave in such a way as to increase the resultant payoff, either for one or both players.

There are two extreme types of situations in which game theory is not helpful for analyzing behavior. At one extreme, only one player is involved—again, Robinson Crusoe, alone on a deserted island. Until Friday appeared, the shipwrecked sailor did not have to consider the behavior of other players when making his own decisions. No human interaction—no game theory. At the other extreme, so many players are involved that no one player's behavior has any perceptible effect on the outcome. This is the condition economists describe as perfect competition.

Most real-life situations can be described by neither extreme but rather occur in a midrange where there are few enough players that decisions made by one significantly affect the outcome experienced by the others. Consider the situation facing an industry including a few large firms. In such an environment, a decision by one firm to build a new plant and increase output has a significant effect on the profit potential of the other firms. Or consider the international arena, in which a decision by one nation to impose trade sanctions or tariffs has a significant effect on the trade prospects of its trading partners. Within a single nation, a decision by an independent monetary authority to increase or decrease the rate of money growth has a significant effect on the ability of governmental departments to fund their spending programs. In all these cases, decisions by one player affect the payoffs enjoyed by the other players.

Game theory came to be recognized as a scientific discipline through the work of John von Neumann, a brilliant mathematician, and Oskar Morgenstern, an economist, who together authored *The Theory of Games and Economic Behavior* in 1944. Von Neuman was initially drawn to game theory because of his fondness for poker, although he was said to be an indifferent player. The advent of this game theory book has been compared (with apologies for hyperbole) to the revolution in astronomy that followed Isaac Newton's theoretical exposition of the structure of the universe. To be truthful, relatively few people have probably read the book, reaching perhaps as far as page 100 out of 600, before its dense mathematics deterred further progress (I'm speaking from personal experience here). The fiftieth anniversary of its publication was celebrated by awarding the Nobel Prize in Economic Sciences to the three modern scholars whose work advanced and made applicable the concepts introduced by von Neumann and Morgenstern. It was John Nash, John Harsanyi, and Reinhard Selten, the 1994 recipients of the Nobel Prize in Economic Sciences, who successfully applied game theory to economics.

Maximin Strategies in Zero-Sum Games

The simplest von Neumann game is described as a two-person, zero-sum game with perfect information. In a zero-sum game, what one player wins the other loses, making a zero-sum game one of pure conflict. When a game is zero-sum, there is no incentive for the players to cooperate toward a mutually beneficial outcome.

Since it is impossible for both players to "win" a zero-sum game, there is no winning strategy. There is an optimal strategy, however, a strategy that rational players will soon discover. The optimal strategy has no winner or loser but, within the rules embodied in the game, gives equitable advantage to both players.

Von Neumann named the optimal strategy in zero-sum games the *maximin strategy*. A maximin strategy requires first that both parties have full information about gains and losses from all combinations of strategies. With this information, the players choose strategies that maximize their smallest possible gain (maximin) or minimize their largest possible loss (minimax). You might say they try to make the best of their most pessimistic expectations about the strategic choice of the other player. For example, suppose playing strategy A gives the first player a score of 5 or 7, depending on the second player's choice of strategies A or B, respectively. The first player's worst possible outcome from playing strategy A is 5, which occurs when the second player also plays strategy A. Now suppose playing strategy B gives the first player either 3 or 2, again depending on the second player's choice of strategy A or B.[3] This time the first player's worst possible outcome is 2, when the second player also plays strategy B. Comparing worst outcomes, the first player chooses the "best-worst strategy" and plays strategy A.

The choices in such a game are typically displayed in a simple box diagram like the one following, where the rows and columns indicate, respectively, the strategies followed by the first and second players. The numbers in the boxes are the payoffs for the first player.

First Player's Payoffs
Strategy of
second player

		A	B
Strategy of	A	5	7
first player	B	3	2

A payoff table for the second player would be identical to the above except that all the values would be preceded by minus signs. In a zero-sum game, the second player's payoffs are the negatives of the first's, which is what makes the game zero-sum.

The first player's absolutely best outcome would follow from playing strategy A, with the second player playing strategy B, a combination that yields the maximum payoff of 7. That combination will not happen, of course, since it is the second player's absolutely worst outcome (-7). Rather, the second player is more likely to choose a strategy that yields the best possible outcome under the worst possible choice by the first player.

When both players maximize their worst possible outcomes, they arrive at an acceptable balance between their respective interests. Comparing the first player's worst possible outcomes, 5 (from playing A) and 2 (from playing B), identifies the first player's maximin strategy as A. Playing strategy A yields a payoff of at least 5, which we have called the first player's best-worst result. For the second player, the possible outcomes from playing strategy A are -5 and -3, which are the negatives of the first player's potential payoffs. The second player's possible outcomes from strategy B are -7 and -2. Now comparing worst outcomes for the second player, -5 (from playing A) and -7 (from playing B), we identify the second player's best-worst outcome as -5, which occurs with strategy A. Thus, comparing prospective losses identifies strategy A as the second player's minimax strategy.

With both players following a maximin (minimax) strategy, the first player plays A and the second player also A, yielding the best-worst result for both players. Neither player wins and neither loses. Both have to accept a result that is less than their preferred result—which sounds a little like life itself.

When a maximin strategy yields the same strategy for both players, a zero-sum game has a unique solution. Such a game is said to be strictly determined, with a unique equilibrium in pure strategies. This means that there is one strategy that dominates every time the game is played. Both players continue to play strategy A, and the second player continues to pay 5 to the first player. (This is the best the players can do within the rules embodied in this game. The players may hope for an invitation to play future games that have more favorable prospects.) The value of a zero-sum game is defined as the amount collected (paid) by the respective players, in this case, 5.

In zero-sum games, a single strategy that yields the best-worst outcome for both players is said to have a "saddle point," indicating the point in a saddle where one curve reaches a maximum and the other reaches a minimum. (The outcome is not as good as it might be for one player nor as bad as it might be for the other.) By guaranteeing the best-worst result for both players, the maximin strategy reduces the risk of play for both players and encourages them to play again—a significant incentive in an economic system that depends on continuing interactions between buyers and sellers, savers and investors—and a significant advantage in an economic system that seeks to avoid exploitation of one player by another.

A recent example of maximin strategies occurred when the U.S. government auctioned portions of the radio spectrum to telecommunications companies. The objective was to allocate broadcasting licenses equitably, giving all interested firms an opportunity to bid on valuable properties but allowing no single firm to dominate the distribution. Up for grabs were licenses in as many as 51 broadcast zones. To ensure against local monopolies, no firm was allowed to acquire more than one license in a single zone. Licenses in adjoining zones were permitted, however, providing the advantage of scale economies for the winning bidder. There were 112 rounds of bidding, in which the telecommunications companies revealed their willingness to give up certain stand-alone locations in exchange for locations adjoining their existing locations. As firms learned the strategies of other firms, they were able to put together efficient packages of bids and, ultimately, to establish a distribution of spectrum rights that may not be exactly what the bidding firms prefer but settles the issue fairly to all contenders. Incidentally, by auctioning licenses to the telecommunications companies (instead of giving them away) the U.S. government collected almost $8 billion. The value of the game to the broadcasters is evidenced by the fact that they paid as much as $32 per person in the relevant markets for the right to serve them.

Whether the item being auctioned is a portion of the radio spectrum, rare Beanie Babies, or Elvis memorabilia, bidders understand they cannot dominate the distribution. Still, each player can come away with a sense of fairness in the game's outcome—which is the principle that underlies the maximin strategy.

Some philosophers have recommended a maximin strategy for distributing a nation's income. A maximin strategy for distributing income would maximize the minimum level of income for all households: that is, guarantee every household the largest income possible given the nation's total income and population. With such a distribution, there would be no "losers"—but no clear "winners" either.[4]

Economists' chief objection to a maximin strategy for income distribution, of course, is the damage it would do to economic incentives. Implementing a maximin strategy for income distribution would require steeply progressive income tax rates, with significant income redistribution from the nation's most productive workers to the least productive. Some amount of income redistribution is acceptable to most of us as a way to reduce social conflict and to provide every citizen the means to develop his or her abilities to the fullest. But beyond some level of relative equality, further redistribution would probably reduce people's incentives to achieve, and our market system depends on such incentives. This result reflects the familiar trade-off between equality and efficiency, in which efforts to distribute more equally the economic "pie" generally result in a smaller pie.

The United States tolerates a more unequal distribution of income than other industrialized countries—but much less than is typical of less developed countries. Since World War II the top 20 percent of U.S. families have consistently received almost 50 percent of the nation's income. At the other end of the income spectrum, the percentage of U.S. families in poverty reached a low of 11 percent in the early 1970s but has since increased to more than 13 percent. (The income that defines poverty for an urban family of four is currently about $16,400.) The U.S. population is fairly mobile among income classes, however, so that this year's poor families may be next year's middle-class; and middle-class families, next year's wealthy.

Mixed Strategies When Games Are Not Strictly Determined

In our zero-sum example, maximin strategies for the two players coincide, with both players playing A. In many pure conflict games, maximin strategies do not coincide, so that the game is not strictly determined, and there is no pure strategy (no single strategy that is optimal for both players). As an example, consider another game in which the first player's payoff from strategy A is 10 or 3, depending on the second player's choice of A or B, respectively. The first player's payoff from strategy B is 4 or 15, again depending on the second player's choice of A or B. Comparing minimum payoffs, the maximin strategy for the first player is B (providing the largest minimum payoff of 4). But the best-worst strategy for the second player is A (which provides a maximum loss of 10 versus 15 with strategy B). With different optimal strategies—B for the first player and A for the second—there is no single strategy that dominates the game and therefore no pure strategy.

First Player's Payoffs

| | | Strategy of second player | |
		A	B
Strategy of	A	10	3
first player	B	4	15

Second Player's Payoffs

| | | Strategy of second player | |
		A	B
Strategy of	A	-10	-3
first player	B	-4	-15

In the absence of a pure strategy, the players' optimal course of action is a mixed strategy: playing one strategy in some plays of the game and the other in the remaining plays. Such a game can have an almost infinite array of outcomes, of course. Still, it is possible for the players to determine a mixed strategy that yields the optimal outcome for both when averaged over many plays of the game. In fact, there is a rule that determines the fraction of the time each strategy should be followed. If both players follow the rule, the result is the maximum gain (or minimum loss) on the average over many plays of the game.

The fraction of time a particular strategy should be played is determined by a simple ratio. The ratio has as its denominator the sum of the differences between the best and worst outcomes for the respective strategies. In the example, the denominator of the ratio for the first player is determined by $(10 - 3) + (15 - 4) = 18$. For a particular strategy, the numerator of the ratio is the difference between the best and the worst outcomes from playing the other (!) strategy. For the first player the numerator associated with strategy A is $15 - 4 = 11$, read from the second row in the table. Thus, the fraction becomes $11/18 = 0.61 = 61$ percent, which defines the percent of the time the first player should play strategy A. The fraction $(10 - 3)/18 = 7/18 = 0.39 = 39$ percent defines the percent of the time the first player should play strategy B. Notice that the strategy that yields the smaller difference between best and worst is played more often than the other, a natural consequence of its lower risk.

We defined the value of a strictly determined zero-sum game as the amount that is transferred using a single optimal strategy. The value of a zero-sum game that is not strictly determined is more difficult to calculate, since different amounts are transferred in different plays of the game. In a game of mixed strategies, the value of the game is calculated using another ratio with the same denominator as the ratio above: in our example, 18. The numerator is the product of the best outcomes from alternative strategies minus the product of the worst: $(10 \times 15) - (3 \times 4) = 150 - 12 = 138$. Thus the ratio that defines the value of this game is $138/18 = 7.67$. This result says that in the long run after many plays of the game, by playing strategy A 61 percent of the time and strategy B 39 percent of the time, the first player will collect an average of 7.67 over all the times the game is played.

Perhaps the most familiar example of a zero-sum game with mixed strategies is the game of "matching pennies." This game has two players, each of whom must display a penny with "heads" or "tails" showing.[5] If the pennies match, the first player takes both pennies. If they don't match, the second player takes the pennies. The problem facing both players is to choose a strategy that maximizes the chance of taking the pennies. No pure strategy exists in this case, since what is best for one player is always worst for the other, Following the procedure above for determining the best mixed strategy yields a 50 percent rule for playing heads and 50 percent for playing tails. Both players should play heads or tails 50 percent of the time, and both should select their moves at random so that the opposing player cannot anticipate and take advantage of advance knowledge. The value of this game is zero, as you might have expected.

There are recorded examples of military uses of mixed strategies in games that are not strictly determined. A military commander was once said to face the choice every day of attacking outright an opposing convoy or simply harassing it from cover. Likewise, the leader of the convoy could choose to defend against a full-blown attack or against nuisance potshots. The commander routinely made his choice by concealing a blade of grass in one fist and inviting an aide to choose a fist. The randomness of the commander's strategy made it impossible for the leader of the convoy correctly to predict and defend against it. In fact, sometimes the players' strategies coincided and sometimes not, with outcomes that favored one or the other depending on objective circumstances in the environment.

Imagine a business firm following a random strategy for deciding where to spend its advertising dollars. Lacking information about a rival firm's strategy, the firm might randomly choose markets for advertising campaigns—capturing some markets entirely, losing others abjectly, and sometimes going head-to-head against competition. Over the long run the firm's advertising campaigns would achieve a gain somewhere between its highest and lowest expectations.

Non-Zero-Sum Games

In a zero-sum von Neumann game, what one player wins the other loses. There is no single outcome that is best for both players and, therefore, no opportunity for cooperation toward a mutually beneficial outcome. Not many social situations can be described this way, most having some degree of overlap in the interests of the players. Even war has no clear winners and losers, since both sides have a degree of interest in both outcomes. John Nash's contribution to game theory was to analyze non-zero-sum games: games in which both players could gain or lose.

Born in West Virginia, John Nash was the son of well-educated parents who provided significant direction to his intellectual development. In fact, he was said to have read the entire *Compton's Pictured Encyclopedia* as a child and whistled Bach melodies as he played with his toys. Early on, he displayed a natural aptitude for mathematics, and at age 20 while attending Princeton, he was proclaimed a mathematical genius. He was awarded his Ph.D. degree on his twenty-second birthday. His 27-page dissertation (double-spaced!) made a fundamental contribution to game theory and was the basis for his Nobel Prize. At age 23 Nash began his teaching career at MIT, where he became friends with Nobel economists Paul Samuelson and Robert Solow and became interested in applications of game theory to economics. He was described by colleagues as having a "keen, beautifully logical mind." Tragically, Nash fell victim to mental disease before reaching age 30 and for the next 25 years lived outside the scholarly community. He was slowly emerging from paranoid schizophrenia when his loyal colleagues insisted that he be considered for the Nobel Prize.

The classic example of a non-zero-sum game is the "prisoner's dilemma." Nash showed how non-zero-sum games like the prisoner's dilemma could have predictable, stable solutions and how this game is applicable to many kinds of social interactions.

The game has two players, both being held for questioning in connection with a burglary. The players are questioned separately and offered two options. The first option is to confess; if both players confess, both will be sentenced to a two-year prison term for the crime. The second option is to refuse to confess; if both players refuse to confess, there is not enough evidence to convict them for more than possessing stolen goods, which would mean six-month sentences for both. Of the two options, both players would surely prefer the outcome from refusing to confess. However, there is a third possibility, which they fully understand and which can significantly affect their choice of strategy. The third possibility occurs if only one player confesses and implicates the other, in which case the confessor will be set free (as a reward for assisting the authorities) and the other will receive a five-year sentence (the added years as a penalty for obstructing justice). Understanding the third possibility reduces the attractiveness of refusing to confess, along with the attractiveness of a six-month sentence. In fact, the possibility of being set free is so compelling that both players attempt to achieve this outcome. Both confess, and instead of being set free, both suffer a two-year sentence.

The prisoner's dilemma is described as a static, noncooperative game with complete information. It is static and noncooperative because it is played only one time, with decisions made simultaneously so that the players cannot learn from experience and cooperate to their mutual benefit. It is a game of complete information because both players know the consequences of all the available strategies. What the players don't know is the strategy that will be chosen by the other player. Therefore, both players must choose strategies that deliver the best outcomes to themselves, regardless of the choice made by the other.

And this is what they do. Note that if the second player chooses a "confess" strategy, the best choice for the first is also to confess, so as to serve only two versus five years. If the second player chooses a "not-confess" strategy, the best choice for the first is still to confess and be set free, rather than to serve the six-month sentence for the lesser crime. The surprising result is this: Even if the first player knows in advance the second player's decision, his own choice is still to confess. You might think that agreeing beforehand not to confess would yield a better outcome than the one I have described. Unfortunately, any agreement arrived at before playing the game is not self-enforcing unless the agreement yields the same outcome as the one that would have occurred without agreement. If it does not, both parties have incentives to cheat so as to secure an advantage for themselves.

Some Implications of the Prisoner's Dilemma

Specialists in game theory usually describe the options in the prisoner's dilemma game as, one, to cooperate (refuse to confess) or, two, to defect (confess). To cooperate means that both players consider the interests of the other player when deciding their strategies; to defect means that they behave according to pure self-interest. The arrangement of payoffs in the prisoner's dilemma drives both players to defect (to pursue individual self-interest) and suffer consequences more damaging than if they were to cooperate.

If the players could learn from their interaction and develop enough trust to cooperate in repeated plays of the game, they might arrive at a cooperative strategy that yields a better outcome for both. Both would refuse to confess, and six-month sentences from refusing to confess would be more tolerable than two-year sentences from confessing. Unfortunately for the players, under the simplest conditions in which this game is played, the best outcome will not occur.

There is another irony associated with the prisoner's dilemma that relates to neoclassical economic theory. Remember the neoclassical economists' most fundamental principle: that individual pursuit of self-interest increases the welfare of society as a whole. Contrary to neoclassical theory, if society is structured according to the rules of the prisoner's dilemma—if the prisoners' defections have negative-sum consequences—individuals' pursuit of self-interest will yield lower social welfare than if people could arrange ways to cooperate.

Sad to say, real life is full of situations where the players choose behavior with results detrimental to society as a whole—not to mention their own long-range interests. The U.S. Congress engages in a prisoner's dilemma game when its appropriations committees independently approve budget-busting programs, even though cooperation to restrain government spending might ultimately be more efficient. Perhaps closer to home are independent behaviors that damage the environment, behaviors that cause suffering to all the players but that no one player has the incentive to change. (How many drivers would install antipollution devices in their automobiles if environmental regulations did not require them? Most of us would defect.)

The tendency toward self-interested behavior (to defect) is the reason economists believe that international commodity cartels are generally short-lived. Even the notorious Organization of Petroleum Exporting Countries (OPEC) has trouble restraining its members' tendencies to increase output and push down the world price of oil.

The prisoner's dilemma illustrates in an especially lurid way the frequent divergence between individual rationality and collective rationality, thus exposing the contradiction between what is best for the individual and what is best for the society as a whole. One final application of the prisoner's dilemma illustrates this point with perhaps a more pathetic example. It is the situation biologist Garrett

Hardin describes as the "tragedy of the commons." The situation: shepherds use a common field for grazing goats. The problem: more goats grazing the field damage its value for all future uses. The incentive: graze as many goats as possible as quickly as possible. The final result: the field is quickly rendered unusable and the society loses a valuable resource. Ipso facto. End of story.

As individuals, the shepherds may understand the tragic consequence of their behavior. Even so, each realizes that if only one shepherd increases his herd, he profits from the grazing privilege. The adverse impact on the field is of less concern to the shepherd who grazes more goats, since the cost of the damage he causes will be shared among all the other shepherds. (The first shepherd will have imposed a negative externality on all the others.) In fact, the likely consequence of using any resource in common (the seas, the air, the highways) is that any single user can achieve disproportionate benefits while passing on the costs to the other users. Knowing this, all the shepherds have an incentive to increase their herds (to defect), to the lasting detriment of the resource on which their livelihood depends.

(A pertinent qualification: When shepherds own their fields, they are less likely to ruin them through overgrazing, making the institution of private property absolutely essential for conserving natural resources.)

Many human interactions are like non-zero-sum games, often yielding poorer payoffs than might be achieved through cooperation and enforceable agreements. During the Cold War, the U.S.-Soviet nuclear arms race imposed significant costs on both nations while increasing their security not a whit—a typical prisoner's dilemma result. Indeed, many of the early game theorists worked in U.S. nuclear research laboratories during the Cold War and ultimately at the RAND Corporation, where they studied the international implications of proliferating nuclear armaments. Von Neumann himself was particularly concerned about the "mutually self-excitatory process" put in place by acquisition of weapons of mass destruction. All the RAND scientists worried about nations' participation in a game that could end by destroying the world, ironically the same concern that led Alfred Nobel to initiate the prizes that bear his name.

Chapter 34
SOME GAMES ARE IMPROVED BY BARGAINING

S ome people think economists have a talent for taking the simplest ideas and making them extraordinarily complicated. In some of its applications, game theory seems as complicated as astrophysics, evidenced by Figure 6, which shows part of a page chosen at random from von Neumann's *The Theory of Games and Economic Behavior*. One is tempted to say, "Hey, Guys! Enough already. These are games we're talking about. Games!!"

Of course, economists would respond by pointing out that the goal of the complexity is simplification: to classify, generalize, and identify the commonalities in what appears to be random behavior so as to better understand how human societies organize themselves.

John Nash helped simplify explanations of human behavior by developing the concept of equilibrium in non-zero-sum games, the idea that there is a strategy that is optimal for both players regardless of their expectations of the other's strategy. Not all non-zero-sum games have a single Nash equilibrium, however, one that leads to a unique (frequently adverse) outcome. In fact, the "battle-of-the-sexes game" has two equally likely Nash equilibria.

The battle-of-the-sexes game describes a situation in which a man and a woman want to meet for an evening together, but each

17.8. Analysis of General Strict Determinateness

17.8.1. We shall now reformulate the contents of 14.5.—as mentioned at the end of 17.4.—with particular consideration of the fact established in 17.6. that every zero-sum two-person game Γ is generally strictly determined. Owing to this result we may define:

$$v' = \operatorname*{Max}_{\vec{\xi}} \operatorname*{Min}_{\vec{\eta}} K(\vec{\xi}, \vec{\eta}) = \operatorname*{Min}_{\vec{\eta}} \operatorname*{Max}_{\vec{\xi}} K(\vec{\xi}, \vec{\eta})$$

$$= \operatorname*{Sa}_{\vec{\xi}|\vec{\eta}} K(\vec{\xi}, \vec{\eta}).$$

(Cf. also (13:C*) in 13.5.2. and the end of 13.4.3.)

Let us form two sets $\bar{A}$, $\bar{B}$—subsets of S_{β_1}, S_{β_2}, respectively—in analogy to the definition of the sets A, B in (14:D:a), (14:D:b) of 14.5.1. These are the sets $A^{\bullet}$, $B^{\bullet}$ of 13.5.1. (the ϕ corresponding to our K). We define:

(17:B:a) $\bar{A}$ is the set of those $\vec{\xi}$ (in S_{β_1}) for which $\operatorname*{Min}_{\vec{\eta}} K(\vec{\xi}, \vec{\eta})$ assumes its maximum value, i.e. for which

$$\operatorname*{Min}_{\vec{\eta}} K(\vec{\xi}, \vec{\eta}) = \operatorname*{Max}_{\vec{\xi}} \operatorname*{Min}_{\vec{\eta}} K(\vec{\xi}, \vec{\eta}) = v'.$$

(17:B:b) $\bar{B}$ is the set of those $\vec{\eta}$ (in S_{β_2}) for which $\operatorname*{Max}_{\vec{\xi}} K(\vec{\xi}, \vec{\eta})$ assumes its minimum value, i.e. for which

$$\operatorname*{Max}_{\vec{\xi}} K(\vec{\xi}, \vec{\eta}) = \operatorname*{Min}_{\vec{\eta}} \operatorname*{Max}_{\vec{\xi}} K(\vec{\xi}, \vec{\eta}) = v'.$$

Figure 6

enjoys a different sort of entertainment: one preferring the opera and one a prize fight. To avoid the taint of sexism, we will make no assumption as to which of the parties prefers which entertainment. We will assume only that the parties cannot communicate their intentions in advance, but that they prefer to arrive at the same event: opera/opera and fight/fight being preferable to opera/fight and fight/opera. Unless one of the two preferred outcomes is clearly superior, the optimal mixed strategy for both players is to attend the opera 50 percent of the time and the fight 50 percent. Unfortunately, if both players follow a 50–50 strategy, the least preferred result would occur a significant percentage of the time: one player showing up at the opera while the other sits alone at the fight. (Do we have a plot for a sit-com here?)

In the battle-of-the-sexes game, the only way to avoid the least favorable outcome is to communicate in advance and choose together one or the other entertainment, perhaps taking turns as most couples do. Cooperation is possible in a battle-of-the-sexes game because the cooperative outcome is always preferred to either noncooperative outcome.

A real-life application of the battle-of-the-sexes game is a nation's decision to drive on the right or the left side of the road, either decision obviously preferable to the third possibility: a mixed strategy, in which each player drives right 50 percent of the time and left 50 percent. Some nations coordinate behavior by driving on the right and others on the left, experiencing no ill effects from their decision since neither choice is inherently better than the other. Most likely, certain factors in the external environment propel a nation toward a particular alternative, which then becomes embedded in its laws and customs. Indeed, it is often said that the British drive on the left because the knights of old needed to expose their right, sword-wielding arms when confronting enemies approaching from the opposite direction.

Other battle-of-the-sexes games have yielded equilibria that have prevailed over decades, creating ripple effects that have entrenched one of the initial choices over the other. The choice of VHS over Beta for video recording is an example of a decision that might have gone either way but, once decided, effectively committed users of video equipment to continue with their initial choice. Economists refer to the *network effects* of such choices: the ties that develop, in this instance, between viewers and producers of VHS tapes. An initial chance decision, followed by the creation of networks, leads to a kind of "path dependency" that propels an entire economy along one course, whether or not that is the economically efficient choice.[6] Users of desktop computers recognize path dependency in their initial selection of IBM or Apple computing equipment, and users of manual typewriters in the choice of QWERTY or Dvorak keyboards.[7]

Benefits From Bargaining

Many social interactions are like battle-of-the-sexes games in that they allow the players to meet and bargain toward outcomes more preferable than the outcomes of random choice. Bargaining is the way players in a game convey information about their expected benefits and costs from alternative choices. Shared information can guide opposing players toward the most efficient strategies and the most beneficial outcomes.

Bargaining can be explicit, such as the bargaining done by a labor union and company management, or it can be implicit, in the same way that diners share space at a lunch counter (and birds along a power line?), leaving comfortable intervals between. An example of implicit bargaining is a game we all played as children, when sharing a treat with a playmate. The game involves two children sharing one cake, with one child given the opportunity to cut the cake and the other to choose first. The cutter can see ahead to the chooser's choice and is careful to cut the cake to yield the largest possible piece for herself after the chooser has chosen. The usual effect is to share the cake equally (or "go halvsies").

If game players are sufficiently rational, they can recognize the efficient solution and reach it as readily by implicit as by explicit bargaining. Indeed, even animals may have used a kind of implicit bargaining in their biological evolution. In evolutionary bargaining, the payoffs are the potential reproduction rates of individual members of a species, and the strategies are the different levels of combat among them. Combat between two fierce fighters is likely to impose greater costs on the species than combat between two timid fighters, since fierce combat reduces reproduction rates and may even threaten species survival. Many timid species have increased their reproduction rates relative to the fighters by evolving such nonlethal weapons as backward-bending horns and threatening snarls that discourage confrontations. While reducing lethal combat, such characteristics may have increased the survival prospects of the species as a whole. (What are the two Nash equilibria here?)

Military historian John Keegan has found the same inhibitions against fierce combat in early humans, who suppressed confrontations through ceremonial rituals rather than engaging in behavior detrimental to species survival.[8] Thus, the human species has progressed from war dances to tournaments, from chess to video games—with as yet no serious damage to our evolutionary prospects.

Explicit bargaining is more formal, exemplified by union-management arbitration for settling wage disputes. In final-offer arbitration both union and management propose a wage rate, and an arbitrator chooses the rate that will be implemented. Before the negotiations begin, the arbitrator might be expected to have some idea of the appropriate wage. Without disclosing the preliminary estimate of the ultimate settlement, the arbitrator reviews the two proposals, typically a high wage demand from the union and a low offer from management. Then the arbitrator calculates the average of the two and compares the average with the preliminary estimate. If the average is higher than the preliminary estimate, the arbitrator rejects the union's high wage demand and selects management's offer for implementation. If the average is lower than the estimate, the arbitrator rejects management's low offer and implements the union's demand. You might imagine the arbitrator moving along a spectrum from management's (low) offer to a point that is halfway to the union's (high) demand and implementing the wage that lies on the same side of the midpoint as the preliminary estimate.

Although neither player knows the arbitrator's preliminary estimate of the proper wage, each attempts to make its offer as close as possible to that amount, so as to increase the likelihood that its offer will be selected. Such a strategy subjects both players to a trade-off, of course, between the objective that its offer should be closer to the arbitrator's estimate and that it more nearly reflect the bargainer's true preferences (low for management and high for the union). An aggressively high wage demand from the union increases the average of the two wages and increases the likelihood that the average will exceed the arbitrator's preliminary estimate. In this case, management's low offer is more likely to be implemented. On the other hand, an aggressively low offer by management reduces the average and increases the likelihood that the average will fall short of the preliminary estimate. In this case, the union's high wage is more likely to be implemented. (Are you reminded of children dividing a cake?)

The U.S. government submitted to arbitration to determine the price to pay for the Zapruder film of the assassination of President John Kennedy. The government offered $1 million and the Zapruder family requested $30 million. The ultimate price was $16 million. Perhaps the arbitrator used a process similar to ours, choosing a price that roughly "splits the difference" between the two offers.

A more ubiquitous type of final-offer arbitration occurs when political candidates choose platforms in an election campaign (with voters playing the role of arbitrator). Expecting voters to choose the candidate whose platform is closer to their own preexisting beliefs, candidates propose platforms that maximize their assured support plus the average of their difference with the opponent's platform. This time, instead of imagining unions and management, imagine opposing political candidates moving from opposite ends of the political spectrum toward resting points somewhere near the middle. Each candidate enjoys the benefits conveyed (voters persuaded) up to the candidate's own resting point on the spectrum plus half of the benefits (voters) whose preferences lie between the two positions. Like labor and management, political candidates face a trade-off between taking an aggressive position near one end of the political spectrum and arriving at a point that is nearer the center of the voting population. The lamentable consequence of this behavior is a certain sameness among politicians—the successful ones, that is.

Repeated Games Offer More Opportunities for Cooperation

Some games occur over and over again, with the players choosing a succession of simultaneous moves. Each independent play of a repeated game may have the characteristics of a prisoner's dilemma, but with repetition the outcome can be quite different.

Consider repetitions of the prisoner's dilemma in which, in every successive play, both players are fully informed of the other's previous moves. Knowing an opponent's previous moves, what strategies will the players select? Experiments involving human subjects have discovered some remarkable patterns of behavior in repeated non-zero-sum games. In experiments involving a series of interactions, game players appear to arrive at a tentative agreement to cooperate, thus achieving a better outcome than if they followed the dominant one-play strategy (to defect).

It seems to work this way. At one play of the game a player chooses the cooperative strategy and waits to see if the other player cooperates too. If the other player defects on the next play, the first player reverts to noncooperation and the game continues with both players defecting at every play. But if the second player responds to the first's cooperation by cooperating, the game continues cooperatively and both players enjoy a better outcome than if they had defected. Israelis and Palestinians, Greeks and Turks, Northern Ireland's Catholics and Protestants, even North and South Koreans may be moving toward this level of cooperation, but it has required many repetitions of their non-zero-sum (indeed negative-sum) games.

The drift toward cooperation in non-zero-sum games is called *tit for tat*. In computerized experiments against other strategies, the tit-for-tat strategy has always received the highest total score. This is true even though a single payoff from defecting might be greater than the payoff from cooperating.

A drift toward cooperation is apparent in many frequently repeated social interactions. In fact, most of us adapt our own social behavior to the behavior adopted by other players. We speak pleasantly to the salesperson who speaks pleasantly to us—and, one is forced to admit, vice versa. Through repetition we learn what sorts of behavior yield optimal outcomes, and we base our subsequent behavior on previous experience. The rate at which we converge to cooperation depends on our trust in the consistency and rationality of the other player.

We should not wax too optimistic about society's drift toward cooperation, however. Tit for tat has a fundamental flaw in that cooperative behavior is not truly rational. What a devastating conclusion! The reason for such a devastating conclusion is that it is never rational (efficient) to cooperate the last time a game is played. The last time a game is played there is no advantage in demonstrating a willingness to cooperate in future plays (which explains why political lame ducks have so little clout). In a game's last play, the rational strategy for both players is to revert to purely self-interested behavior. Unfortunately, if both players understand that the other will defect the last time the game is played, there is no advantage in cooperating the next-to-last time it is played either. Which means that there is no advantage in cooperating the next-to-next-to-last time—or for that matter any time the game is played.

Although this kind of reasoning suggests that cooperation will never be achieved in repeated games, in real life it often is achieved. This is how civilizations develop. This is how societies create the institutions that enable people to interact positively with other people. We consider the likely reactions to our own behavior before we act. Instead of exploiting other people for the sake of a one-shot gain, we surrender our right to exploit others in return for others' commitment not to exploit us.

Probably the reason for the drift toward cooperation in repeated games is that the players do not know how many times the game will be played. (We might hope it will be played forever.) Not knowing when we are playing the game for the last time, we choose behavior that is consistent with unlimited future repetitions.

Dynamic Games Give More Opportunities for Using Information

A dynamic game is different from a repeated game in that it involves a sequence of moves in the same game, with perfect information regarding previous moves and with complete information regarding the payoff from any combination of future moves. At any move, a player's options include terminating the game.

The simplest dynamic game has three moves: a move by the first player, a move by the second, and a final move by the first player. (To reduce confusion, let's call the first player "she" and the second "he.") The Nash equilibrium in a dynamic game is best observed from the termination point, where the first player makes her best response to the second player's second move. For deciding his second move, the second player calculates his final payoff from the first player's best final move and then chooses between (1) continuing the game toward the end and accepting the final payoff, and (2) ending the game with his second move and receiving his indicated payoff at that stage of play.

Meanwhile, the first player is reasoning similarly. Proceeding backward in time, she calculates her options at the final play and imagines how the second player will choose his second move. Then she compares her payoff from responding to the second player's best second move with her payoff from terminating the game at the first play. She chooses the strategy that maximizes her payoff, even if that choice brings an abrupt end to the game, before the second player even has a chance to play.

To understand the situation, look at Figure 7 and imagine two cyclists traveling together along a road. There are three successive

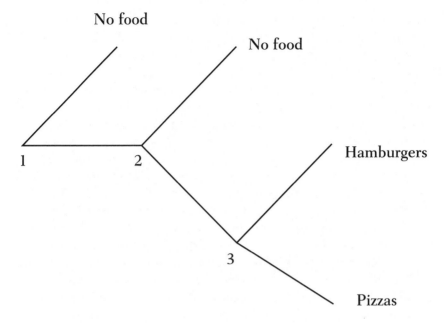

Figure 7

forks along the road, and the cyclists have agreed to take turns deciding which fork to take. Their optimal destination is either a ham-
burger joint or a pizza parlor, the first strongly preferred by the first
cyclist and the second by the second. The first cyclist chooses at the
first and third forks. Both players understand that at the third fork,
the first cyclist (if given a chance) will choose hamburgers. Therefore, at the second fork when it is the second cyclist's turn to choose,
the second cyclist will choose the route that leads away from hamburgers. Knowing the second cyclist's likely choice at the second fork
affects the first cyclist's decision at the first fork. In fact, expecting
that the ultimate outcome will not include hamburgers, the first
cyclist may choose a route that leads away from any sort of food at
all, thus ending the game with the worst possible outcome for both
players.

The important characteristic of dynamic games is that, prior to
their own turn to choose, both players anticipate the other's rational
calculation at his or her time to choose. It is as if both players lay out
an entire game and base all their moves on their expectations about
the other player's moves. The process is similar to what happens when

people write contracts. The first player writes a contract specifying a certain action and the distribution of benefits and costs from that action. The second player evaluates the distribution that will ultimately occur if he or she accepts the contract's terms and decides whether or not to agree to them. If the second player does agree, he or she signs the contract, and the first player implements the terms and carries out the indicated distribution. If the second player does not agree, he or she does not sign the contract, and the action is not carried out. (The game ends with the second play.) To avoid abrupt termination of the game, writers of contracts are motivated to structure contracts so that their final payoffs are acceptable to both parties.

An economic application of a dynamic game involves bank runs. Suppose a certain bank has only two depositors whose funds the bank has invested in a project that will pay a return only after an extended period of time. If both depositors leave their funds in the bank until the project is complete, the bank remains solvent, the bank's assets are safe, and the depositors are rewarded with interest income. On the other hand, if one depositor withdraws his or her deposit before the bank's investment has matured, that person receives the full amount, but the bank fails and the other depositor loses everything. Understanding this possibility, neither depositor wants to stand aside and wait for the other depositor to withdraw, both rushing to withdraw simultaneously. This behavior is similar to the behavior of international currency speculators who act in "herds," either holding a currency in anticipation of an increase in its value or dumping it abruptly in anticipation of its collapse.

In all these examples, the outcome of a dynamic game depends in large part on the conditions established by the first player—which suggests a moral to the story of dynamic games. When initiating a game, a clever player considers the choices offered the second player. In any sort of personal or business relationship or even an international relationship, including war, a clever player ensures the second player sufficiently favorable options so as not to foreclose favorable end results. By setting up conditions agreeable to the second player, the initiator of a game (contract, tariff negotiation, financial relationship, or whatever) can ensure that the game proceeds to a mutually beneficial conclusion—a fair distribution of hamburgers and pizzas rather than no benefits at all. The clever first player avoids forcing the second player into a corner so that his only options are capitulating to an unfavorable final outcome or avoiding the game altogether.

Failure to establish favorable initial conditions in dynamic games can set the stage for cumulative defections—a sort of reverse tit for tat in which everyone loses. Game theorists at RAND Corporation sometimes played out these consequences in a game they called the *dollar auction*. In a dollar-auction game, players are invited to bid any amount for the right to receive $1. The winning bidder pays her bid, but the second highest bidder is also required to pay her bid. Start with a bid of $.05, which would award the bidder a profit of $.95. That is, of course, unless someone else enters the bidding at $.10, for a personal profit of $.90 and, for the first bidder, a loss of her $.05 bid. To avoid her loss, the first bidder could bid again, say, $.15 for a personal profit of $.85 and a loss of $.10 for the other bidder—who is motivated to bid again to avoid her own loss. And you can see what is beginning to happen.

In fact, once the bidding starts in a dollar-auction game, the incentives are to continue bidding, to such an extent that the winning bidder frequently pays substantially more than $1 for the $1 prize, while the losing bidder pays the second-highest bid and receives nothing in return. (It is reported that some of the RAND marriages were seriously strained by the dollar-auction game.) Both bidders persist in their losing strategies, in the hope that they can recoup their losses and "it all won't have been in vain."

Of course, it is in vain and they both lose, the nuclear arms race being a good example of a reverse tit-for-tat game. It is to ward off similar futile efforts to avoid cumulating losses that nations establish institutions to constrain defections and promote positive outcomes from dynamic games.

Chapter 35

GAMES WITHOUT FULL INFORMATION REQUIRE USE OF PROBABILITIES

John C. Harsanyi and Reinhard Selten shared the 1994 Nobel Prize with John Nash for their later refinements of game theory.

Born in Hungary, John Harsanyi escaped deportation to a Nazi concentration camp in World War II, receiving sanctuary in a Jesuit monastery. After the war he returned to communist Hungary as a professor of philosophy, but his outspoken anti-Marxist views led to his ostracism from his university. Again he escaped from his homeland, fleeing through a marshy area that was poorly guarded by the communist police. He traveled to Australia where he worked in a factory until he could obtain a teaching position at the University of Sydney. Although he was trained as a mathematician, in Australia Harsanyi was introduced to economics and impressed by its "mathematical elegance." Eventually he moved to the University of California as a professor specializing in mathematical economics and, ultimately, games with incomplete information.

In John Nash's games, the players have complete information about all possible outcomes, an assumption not always borne out in real life. In real life, games are often played out in a kind of fog that obscures such things as opposing players' resources and strategies, their expectations, and their expectations about the other players' expectations. In real life, the prospective buyer of a used car has incomplete information about the car's repair history; the prospective employer of a new worker has incomplete information about the worker's skills and work ethic; a prospective suitor, about a potential mate's good and bad habits.

Lacking complete information, rational game players use the laws of probability to help them choose among available alternatives: used cars, new workers, and even mates. Based on information learned in previous plays of life's games, they can estimate the probability distributions of gains and losses associated with particular strategic choices. Then, using probabilities, players can choose strategies that best protect their own interests against a range of circumstances, in somewhat the same way that investors choose securities on the basis of historical information about return and risk.

Bargaining Games

If game players are permitted to communicate before playing the game, they can bargain—the first proposing a solution and the second accepting or proposing a counteroffer. Typically, the first player suggests a position somewhere between her or his best and worst outcomes, with the closeness to best or worst depending on that person's "risk limit," the tolerable risk that the proposal will not be accepted. The higher a player's risk limit, the closer is the offer to the preferred outcome.

A player's risk limit depends on two factors: the attractiveness of the other player's expected counteroffer and the attractiveness of the default payoff, the payoff to be awarded if no agreement is reached. The poorer the opposing player's likely counteroffer, the higher the probability of rejection a player will tolerate and the closer is his or her offer to the best outcome. (The player believes it is better to reach no agreement at all than to accept a counteroffer that is so far beneath the preferred outcome.) On the other hand, the poorer the default payoff, the lower is the maximum tolerable probability of rejection, and the farther is the offer from the best outcome. (No agreement at all might be even worse.)

Not surprisingly, a game player who is more tolerant of risk has the greater advantage in reaching the preferred outcome in a bargaining game. The more risk-averse player is the one who makes the next concession, since that player would lose more if no agreement is reached.

Ultimatum Games

Concern for reaching a preferred outcome leads to a natural expansion of bargaining games: that is, the threat of retaliation if the second player cannot be persuaded to accept the first player's offer. If the first player is in a position to make threats, a bargaining game can be converted to an ultimatum game. Whereas bargaining games yield outcomes somewhere between the players' best and worst outcomes, this is not the case in ultimatum games. With a credible threat, the first player may be able to guarantee his or her preferred outcome. To strengthen credibility (to prove the threater is not bluffing), a threater might arrange to become physically incapable of failing to implement the threat. The usual example of a credible threat is the practice among advancing armies of burning their bridges behind them, thus foreclosing the possibility of retreat. A less orthodox example might be the practice of using horseback-mounted police to quell urban riots.

A threat reduces the value of the default payoff and increases the cost of failing to reach agreement—since the retaliatory actions the threater would take in the absence of an agreement would surely damage the threatee. At the beginning of an ultimatum game, both players announce their retaliatory strategies. Each player seeks a retaliatory strategy that minimizes his or her own conflict costs and maximizes the conflict costs imposed on the opposite player (where conflict costs are the differences between a positive payoff and the default payoff in the event of failure to reach agreement). The assurance of retaliation reduces the default payoff, reduces players' tolerance for risk, and encourages them to make the concessions necessary for a satisfactory end to the game.

Threats strengthen the position of the threater and increase the cost of conflict for the threatee. But threats are also costly to the threater, who must take steps to carry out the threat—which probably explains why President Clinton declined to threaten the use of ground troops in the Serbia-Kosovo conflict. A threat is credible only if carrying it out increases the costs of conflict for the threatee in a greater proportion than it increases the cost of conflict for the threater. A nontrivial cost of threats is the reputation a threatee earns for having given in to threats, a reputation that weakens his bargaining power in future games. For this reason, true ultimatum games are rare. If a threat is serious enough to affect the game's outcome, it may be difficult to convince the opposing player that it is sincere. (Would you really strangle the trash collectors if they disturb another sleepy Saturday morning?)

Without a real commitment to carrying out a threat, the threater loses credibility. Suppose a blackmailer threatens to inflict damage on a rich man amounting to $1000. Conceivably the possibility of suffering damage of $1000 would force the rich man to pay as much as $999 to the blackmailer. But suppose the rich man stands firm and refuses to pay. Who is the threater now? In effect, the rich man has imposed a reciprocal threat on the blackmailer, who must decide whether to carry out his threat knowing that he will receive nothing whatever he decides. The threat of receiving nothing could force the blackmailer to accept anything greater than $1 from the rich man. Without an irrevocable commitment actually to inflict the $1000 damage, the blackmailer cannot be assured the maximum payment, and the ultimatum game is reduced to a simple bargaining game.

Harsanyi suggests a more constructive way than threats to increase players' bargaining power, namely, coalitions. Most game players belong to one or more overlapping coalitions, he says, increasing their bargaining power with every coalition they join. The strength of a coalition depends on its members' ability to convince other players of their common interests. Coalitions are especially common for promoting political strategies in the interests of particular groups of voters: racial and ethnic minorities, industrial or occupational groups, and followers of a particular philosophy or ideology. When many interest groups form coalitions to promote their interests, the result is what political scientists call a *pluralistic society.* For a sense of the value to society of coalitions, Harsanyi compares the richly diverse set of coalitions that govern the U.S. democracy with the more homogeneous society that governs Islamic nations.

Building Credibility in Repeated Games

Threats and credibility in repeated games are the particular interest of Reinhard Selten, who has been the only German yet to win the Nobel

Prize for Economic Sciences. Selten was born in a part of Germany that was fiercely contested during World War II and is now part of Poland. Many of his relatives died in the Holocaust, and he himself escaped from Germany on one of the last trains to take refugees out. As a child, Selten says he spent three and a half hours every day walking to and from school, time he spent thinking about geometry and algebra (obviously before the advent of the Sony Walkman).

Selten first encountered game theory in an article in *Fortune* magazine, read when he was in high school. To Selten game theory seemed to explain the logic underlying animal and plant evolution. Remembering Herbert Simon's "bounded rationality," Selten visualizes groups of animals and plants adopting strategic behaviors to protect against mutant invaders. They join in tribes or herds, select defensible locations, and occasionally even sacrifice their individual interests to ensure survival of the group as a whole. (Think of the "wounded" bird that leads a predator away from her defenseless young.) Selten goes so far as to suggest that welfare-maximizing rationality is even more easily observed in plant and animal communities than it is in human society, evidence of the theory's power for identifying strategic equilibria even when there is no possibility of conscious or overt thought.

Selten studied games with many possible equilibria, especially games that incorporate threats. He likens repeated social interactions to games in which interacting players build trust and ultimately reach a Nash equilibrium. To illustrate the process, he created subgames, or episodes in a long series of games that together constitute what he calls a *super game*.

Selten also agrees with Herbert Simon about the importance of empirical data to test new theory. Therefore, he conducted experiments in which he discovered a critical difference between what theory predicts about a super game and what really happens. To explain the difference, he suggests an analogy involving a hypothetical chain store. The store has branches in 20 towns and faces the possibility that local entrepreneurs will establish a competing store in any of the towns. Competition, if it appears, will emerge sequentially in towns 1, 2, 3, . . . 20, as potential rivals accumulate sufficient capital to set up shop. If competition appears, the chain store has two possible responses: first, do nothing and suffer lower sales in that town; or, second, cut prices in that town and drive the rival out of business. The immediate cost of the first strategy is the chain store's lower sales in the town where it must share its market. Initially, the cost of the second strategy is greater, since lower prices for the chain store's sales reduce its profit on every item it sells. Still, unless the chain store chooses the second strategy—unless it carries out its threat to extinguish the first spark of competition—other potential rivals will be encouraged to establish competing stores in the other towns. The ultimate consequence of unrestrained competition would be even greater reductions in the chain store's profits.

The chain-store analogy is like a three-stage game in which the chain store looks ahead to the third-stage consequences of second-stage response to successful entry in the first stage. By retaliating against its very first competitor, the chain store strengthens the credibility of its threat to retaliate against other competitors. By retaliating, the chain store effectively ends the game at the first play—or at any subsequent play in which a competitor enters the market.

But this is where theory runs into some inconvenient realities.

Suppose the chain store adopts the optimal strategy and retaliates against competitors in towns 1 through 19. Its managers understand that if entrepreneurs in the twentieth town in the sequence (the last to accumulate sufficient capital) establish a competing store, it is no longer necessary to exercise its threat to retaliate. A threat is useful only for affecting future behavior, and there is no future beyond the twentieth town.

Are we satisfied, then, that the store would drive out competition in 19 towns and accept it in the twentieth? Not likely. If potential competitors understand that the chain store would not carry out its threat in the twentieth town, in effect, the nineteenth town becomes the last in the sequence. If it is unnecessary to carry out the threat in the last town, the threat loses its credibility in the nineteenth—and, by the same reasoning, in the eighteenth and in any of the other towns. In fact, by this reasoning, the chain store would never cut its prices to drive out a competitor and would, therefore, resign itself to the diminished profits from competition.

You've probably noticed some similarity here to our objections to tit-for-tat strategies in repeated games. Remember that tit for tat allows a tentative move toward cooperation in one play of the game, to be followed by more cooperation in every play—right up to the last time the game is played. The objection to tit for tat comes from players' understanding that the rational strategy the last time the game is played is to defect. With this knowledge, players in tit for tat defect in the next-to-last and next-to-next-to-last—and every time the game is played. The players never cooperate to reach the game's optimal solution. The perverse result in the chain-store analogy is similar. In the chain-store analogy, the reluctance to carry out threats extends from the twentieth town backward to the first, such that the chain store might never take action to deter competition.

And here again, game theory loses its ability to predict real behavior. The facts, according to Selten, indicate that this theoretical version of repeated games does not comport with real life. Experiments with real people provide evidence for what Selten calls the *chain-store paradox*. Although it is logically correct for the chain store not to take action to drive competing stores out of business, in fact the chain store's managers understand the consequences of failing to do so. Therefore, the chain store does take action to demonstrate its resolve to deter further competition. Game theory cannot predict the precise point at which the chain store will cut its prices and destroy a rival—with that point depending on such ill-defined and unanalyzable factors as intuition or luck.

Instead of tit for tat, it is more likely that managers of the chain store will subjectively determine the maximum number of towns in which a competing store will be permitted to survive. Then, at some point before the last time the game is played, the chain store acts aggressively to drive a competitor out of business. The time before the chain store takes such action depends on the expected payoff and the perceived social relationship with the other players. If past history suggests a friendly relationship, competition is likely to be permitted for more repetitions of the game than if the relationship is unfriendly, since a friendly relationship confers benefits over and above the game's profit payoff. A friendly relationship also suggests trust, which prolongs the period of cooperation. Nevertheless, the longer the period of cooperation, the harsher are the ultimate consequences of a "betrayal of trust." Defection is punished severely through harsh anticompetitive actions against an unfriendly upstart.

Perhaps this explains Microsoft's alleged attempts to drive Netscape out of business and Israel's reluctance to abandon contested settlements to Palestinians. In both games, the dominant player understands the strategic disadvantage of appearing weak in the face of a competitive challenge.

In Selten's chain-store games, the player that responds immediately to competition establishes a reputation as a stalwart defender of his position—even if he never again plans to implement that strategy. In the same way, a monetary authority that pushes up interest rates to reduce inflationary pressures enhances its credibility as an inflation fighter—as U.S. Federal Reserve Chairman Paul Volcker demonstrated in the 1980s. With its enhanced credibility, a monetary authority can accomplish its anti-inflation objective even if it never again plans to implement the contractionary policy.

From Game Theory to Institutions and, Finally, the Common Good

I have admitted that the term *game theory* sounds trivial. To counter that impression, I have suggested nontrivial applications, including market competition, union-management bargaining, political campaign strategies, warfare, and—least trivial of all—our evolution and survival as species. Beyond these specific applications, game theory has even broader philosophical implications. In fact, game theory helps explain how societies develop a sense of morality: how people's rational interactions with other people come to affect their most fundamental sense of right and wrong.

John Hàrsanyi is particularly interested in how rational people form groups, learn collectively about probabilistic behavior, and use the information they learn for taking ethical positions or making moral judgments.

The role of a moral code is to relieve the tension between what is good for the individual and what is good for society as a whole: the interest of the individual prisoner facing the game's dilemma, as opposed to the interests of both prisoners taken together. In neoclassical economic theory, there is no conflict between the two, individual pursuit of self-interest being the only way to understand and explain human behavior. As rational individuals pursue maximum welfare for themselves, they are lead inexorably to the most efficient resource allocation for the economic system as a whole—all this expressed most figuratively in Adam Smith's "invisible hand," another of economists' famous metaphors. The immensely satisfying conclusion: there is no conflict between individual rationality and the common good.

One problem with neoclassical theory is that its immensely satisfying conclusion requires complete information about all the individual benefits and costs of alternative behaviors, some of which we have noted are impossible to understand or to measure. Another problem is the requirement that individual behaviors and outcomes not be influenced by chance or by the behavior of other players with divergent interests. Neither of these requirements is satisfied in a social environment. Game theory provides a way to close the gap between individual self-interest and the broader social welfare.

Indeed, game theory provides a rigorous rationale for Kant's categorical imperative: act in the way you wish others to act. Kant's categorical imperative is the rule-for-living proposed by the German philosopher Immanuel Kant in the eighteenth century. Although Kant's imperative may sound like pure altruism, it is actually a rational approach to behavioral choice in human society.

The bottom line: An economic system cannot operate effectively unless the people have some moral sense of commitment to the group as a whole.

Chapter 36

HOW INSTITUTIONS HAVE EVOLVED

Perhaps the most ubiquitous institution in any society, primitive or advanced, is the market. Markets are like games, in that they have players, strategies, and outcomes. Market outcomes are generally non-zero-sum (indeed positive-sum), yielding welfare gains to all the players. The market game is repeated over and over again, providing opportunities for cooperation among the players and giving rise to trust.

Trust is essential to market transactions, since most exchanges require us to give up something prior to receiving something in return. In a market economy, business firms interact with other firms, firms that supply needed resources as well as firms that buy their products. Perhaps in the earliest stages of a market economy, firms might behave like the burglary suspects in the prisoner's dilemma, with naked self-interest the dominant strategy. The longer firms interact, however, the greater is the possibility that the players will develop trust—that they will arrive at tit-for-tat strategies that yield mutually beneficial outcomes.

The Nobel economist who most successfully describes the historical evolution of society's institutions is Douglass North. North and Robert Fogel were awarded the Nobel Prize in 1993 for their applications of economic theory to economic history.

North had a privileged childhood, benefiting from an intellectu-
ally curious mother and a superior education. During World War II
he joined the merchant marine, occupying the long hours at sea
reading. Partly as a result of that experience, he developed a strong
desire to understand what makes society work and how to improve it,
the cherished goals of economists throughout history. Indeed, North
aspired to emulate the great Austrian economist Joseph Schumpeter
in building an analytical framework to explain how an economic system grows and develops. On a purely personal level, North is said to
enjoy his work so much that he returns 40 percent of his salary to his
university.

North's primary professional interest is how population growth
brings change, how growing populations interact to share information, how the institutions people create affect incentives, and how
expectations of future outcomes affect current behavior. He found
neoclassical theory inadequate for explaining these things. In fact,
he found neoclassical theory inadequate for explaining anything
other than fully informed, self-interested behavior.

By limiting its focus to strictly self-interested behavior, North
argues, neoclassical economic theory leaves little room for cooperation, still less for altruism. There is little room for shared information
or for people to come together and agree on such shared concerns as
public investments in human and physical capital, conservation of
natural resources, and relief of congestion. By putting so much
emphasis on individual self-interest, neoclassical theory ignores the
power of institutions to guide collective behavior.

A society's most obvious institutions are its legal, financial, and
political rules and regulations. Laws decide what is permissible,
banks and other financial institutions encourage saving and investing,
and democratically determined regulations ensure consistency in
business practices. More powerful than these formal institutions,
however, are a society's informal rules of behavior—the moral code or
ethical base that underlies all our social interactions. Informal rules
embody information learned from past experience to regularize and
constrain future behavior, thus stabilizing social relationships. Even
when a society's formal institutions change, its informal rules endure,
thus ensuring a degree of continuity in an infinitely repeated game.

Another word for informal rules of behavior is *ideology*. In
North's words, "ideologies are intellectual efforts to rationalize the
behavior of individuals and groups." They are a form of cultural

learning, arising out of cumulative experience and shared explanations for observed phenomena. Most behavior occurs in a climate of imperfect information, he says. But ideologies guide behavior when the informational basis for behavior is weak. Ideologies are like rules of thumb (the formal term is "heuristic") that tell us what to do when we don't fully understand why we're doing it. More fundamentally, our ideological base determines our view of legitimacy, and our view of legitimacy leads us to behave in certain ways. North coined the phrase "God lowers enforcement costs" to describe the stabilizing effects on society of a generally agreed-on ideology.

The Parallel Evolution of Governmental and Market Institutions

Western nations have created two types of institutions: one, the institutions of democracy, including a democratic government's role in a market economy; the other, the institutions of the market, including the role of markets for strengthening government. In Western historical development, the two types of institutions have evolved together, fueling the strengths and shoring up the weaknesses of each other.

Governmental institutions evolve out of population growth and the tendency in growing populations for relationships to become impersonal and occasionally confrontational. Yes, population growth brings marvelous advantages, in particular, specialization and the economies of scale that lead to growth in production and the material benefits of civilization. But specialization and economies of scale necessarily aggravate the separation between producers and consumers. Increased separation between producers and consumers increases Ronald Coase's transactions costs, breeds uncertainty in human relationships, and creates opportunities for free riding. If a society is to enjoy the maximum benefits from population growth and suffer the minimum costs, it must find some way to regularize and enforce acceptable kinds of behavior. It must, in a word, establish an efficient government.

Population growth generally brings territorial expansion, which increases a government's ability to collect tax revenue. Tax revenue is essential if a government is to defend its expanding borders and protect its growing population. Within a government's expanding jurisdiction, citizens accept an obligation to pay taxes in exchange for government's guarantee of protection, against aggressors both from within and without the nation's borders. For efficient tax collection, the tax source must be measurable. Therefore, a government must adopt procedures to identify wealth, primarily by identifying and enforcing property rights. By establishing well-defined property rights, a government helps reduce the risks and uncertainties of doing business. Well-defined property rights promote technological innovation, thus pushing economic growth beyond Robert Solow's steady state and increasing per capita income. Through its protection of property rights, government becomes both the enforcer of private contracts and the extractor of income from private production.

As it expands its jurisdiction, government enhances the source of civilized society, the economies that result from increased specialization and large-scale production. The product that benefits most from expanding jurisdictions is information, since (remembering Herbert Simon) association with larger numbers of people yields more and more varied information at lower costs. Increased agglomeration of economic activity in cities and towns reduces the costs of transferring information and increases productivity, not only through shared information about advances in science and technology but also through the "learning by doing" associated with producing for larger markets.

Nothing good comes without costs, however. When a government's jurisdiction expands, its need for tax revenue increases, forcing government to expand its borders still further. Wider borders, in turn, increase necessary spending for defense, requiring still more tax revenues in a kind of vicious cycle. A government's revenue requirements prompt a scramble for new tax sources—one requirement feeding into the other and swelling the need for both. Protection of property rights creates another kind of vicious cycle. While secure property rights increase production incentives and promote technological progress, they also permit growth of a property-owning class whose power ultimately challenges government's power. As a government pressures its property-owning class for more tax revenue, those taxpayers tend to shift their allegiance to rival power sources that promise lower taxes. To retain the support of its most powerful constituencies, government must bribe them with lower taxes, financing its bribes from higher taxes collected from its least influential constituencies. Increasing the tax liabilities of these latter groups reduces their economic incentives and reduces the economic growth on which increased tax revenues depend. In the end, a government's struggle to maintain its control may come at the expense of economic efficiency and political stability.

As the conflict between taxpayers and government worsens, pressures build for a change of government. The players defect.

North's second type of institution typically develops in parallel with government and includes the institutions of a market economy. With the development of settled agriculture millennia ago came complex economic institutions for identifying and protecting property rights. As civilizations grew, division of labor and specialization increased, along with economies of scale from serving larger populations. All these preconditions provided the basis for efficient markets and for the growth of manufacturing. But growing manufacturing firms suffer from another vicious cycle similar to that of expanding governments. To reduce their transactions costs, manufacturing firms are driven to integrate more and more stages of production under a single management. The problem is that, ultimately, increased economic integration aggravates the separation between the managers who make a firm's decisions and the workers who carry them out. The perverse result is to increase transactions costs and reduce economic efficiency.[9]

For an integrated manufacturing firm, transactions costs include the costs of measuring resource inputs, monitoring worker performance, and controlling product quality all along the chain of production. The longer the chain required for producing a product, the greater is the separation between contributors to production. Transfers from one stage of production to another become more and more impersonal; loyalties and basic commitments break down; opportunities increase for shirking (Ronald Coase's principal-agent problem) and opportunism (cheating). To reduce shirking and opportunism requires precise measurement, monitoring, and control; but measurement, monitoring, and control also have costs. Measuring inputs, controlling outputs, and monitoring performance require contractual or organizational integration, both of which require even greater specialization along the chain of producers and bring on even higher transactions costs.

To reduce all these transactions costs requires standardization and regulation, both of which require enforcement. Enforcement is carried out at various levels: first, at the level of simple retaliation for improper behavior (a dressing down by the foreman); second, at a higher level that involves internally enforced rules of conduct (a disciplinary hearing); third, at a still higher level of social sanctions (separation from the institution); or, fourth, the highest level of all, a coercive third party. That coercive third party is, of course, government. Through its ultimate enforcement powers, government can help reduce the costs of transactions and ensure that individuals carry out their responsibilities toward the firm or toward the larger economy.

North sees society today as more dependent on its governmental and market institutions than ever before. With population growth and increased economic interdependence, societies need more institutional constraints to protect ordinary men and women from economic instability and inequity. What some economists have called the "commoditization of land, labor, and money" has weakened the old social fabric, the informal rules of behavior that guided the world's people in more primitive times. Today's increased separation of producers from consumers—in effect, the loosening of direct economic bonds—has increased the need for an ideological superstructure to legitimize the rules underlying society's games.

Building New Institutions in Russia

The world is now witnessing the painful consequences of the lack of adequate institutions for a nation's ability to function efficiently. The breakup of the Soviet Union and the collapse of communism left Russia in a sort of limbo—having rejected central control of economic activity but lacking the institutions essential for operating a market economy. In Western nations, building market institutions required generations, even centuries, of repeated interactions, during which game players developed trust in the consistent behavior of other players. Today's Russia cannot afford extended years of institution building. With its large population and claim to world leadership, Russia is seeking short cuts.

Some advisers to Russia's government recommended "shock therapy" to replace abruptly the nation's obsolete institutions with institutions more appropriate to a market economy. The first step in shock therapy was to offer for sale to private investors enterprises that were formerly owned and operated by the state. The result in most cases has been disaster. First, the shortage of personal savings shut ordinary men and women out of the market and placed the most profitable enterprises in the hands of a few groups of wealthy (and often corrupt) investors. Second, lacking experience in independent decision making, managers of newly privatized enterprises made costly mistakes that reduced output and severely constrained income growth. Even IMF assistance amounting to more than $20 billion[10] has failed to create market activity sufficient to give value to the Russian ruble and may even have worsened corruption. Third, released from the protective arm of the state, private enterprises have been forced to cut costs and eliminate waste, effected mainly by laying off workers. The result for the Russian people has been growing economic inequality, falling production, and rising unemployment, causing some to question their decision to convert to a market economy.

The problem with shock therapy is that it allows insufficient time to build the institutions that provide essential support for free markets:

- Legal institutions, including business and professional licensing requirements, laws protecting property and enforcing contracts, and laws governing debt restructuring and asset distributions in bankruptcy
- Social and political institutions, including ideological support for individual achievement and social status for achievers
- Financial institutions to facilitate all the complicated interactions that must develop between small suppliers of materials and parts and large industrial users

Without these sorts of institutions, the outcome of new business interactions is uncertain, and few people are willing to take the risks.

The function of legal, political, and financial institutions is to "institutionalize" or make routine that most necessary ingredient of market economies: trust. Institutionalized trust does not spring up overnight. Failure to establish trust subjects Russia to the risk of disillusion and ultimate collapse—an outcome the rest of the world has a clear interest in avoiding.

Chapter 37

CHANGING ONE "PECULIAR" INSTITUTION

Douglass North's critique of neoclassical theory did not endear him to his colleagues, many of whom consider North and his co–Nobel Prize winner Robert Fogel the equivalent in the academic community of "bomb throwers" in less placid communities. While applying economic theory to historical puzzles, both North and Fogel arrived at conclusions diametrically opposed to those sanctioned by neoclassical economic theory.

Robert Fogel shares North's interest in how institutions evolve. While classified as an economic historian, Fogel differs from other historians in a fundamental way. Many historians avoid the use of economic theory when describing historical events. Because events occur at different times, they say, under widely differing conditions and affected by widely differing circumstances, it is impossible to explain historical fact through economic theory. On the contrary, history should be presented, as correctly as possible, as a series of pure facts, while avoiding any sort of theoretical explanation of how certain historical facts are related to other facts.

Fogel is not satisfied with pure facts. No account of so-called facts is possible without theory, he says. History is not revealed to the historian neatly, in a coherent system of related information. Not at all. Rather, history is a tangle of conflicting, inconsistent, complicated, poorly defined pieces of data that must be sorted, sifted, and rearranged until a coherent idea emerges. The way historians select and link facts depends on their conception of the relationships among them. And those conceptions differ among historians. Thus, the choice in economic history is not between theory and no-theory but between openly acknowledged theory and casual and unsystematic theory.

Nevertheless, Fogel criticizes too much theory just as severely as too little. He would limit the use of theory to explaining specific problems at particular points in time, not for making grandiose generalizations to be applied for all time. If historical analysis is to be credible, he says, it must be supported by empirical evidence. And its conclusions should refer only to the specific historical event under examination.

With respect to two highly controversial issues, Fogel uses econometric analysis to arrive at conclusions contrary to the generally accepted conclusions of other historians. One, assessing the importance of railroads in U.S. economic development, we have already considered. Another, dealing with slavery in the pre–Civil War South, describes how institutions evolve in response to both the economic and the ethical requirements of their time.

The Economics of Slavery in the American South

The question regarding slavery is important because slavery provided the justification for a long and bloody civil war. According to some historians, the American Civil War was unjustified because slavery would have come to an end without it. The high cost of slave labor was rendering it unprofitable, those historians claim, relative to free farming. Therefore, the trend was for slavery gradually to die out. In this opinion, the war that freed the slaves amounted to unnecessary bloodshed to decide the fate of an institution that was already dying.

Fogel concludes otherwise, that slavery as an economic institution was never stronger than immediately before the Civil War and that it was becoming even more entrenched as an institution of southern agriculture. He bases his conclusion on data describing 40,000 slaves, along with mortality records that included 4 percent of all the slaves who ever lived in the United States. On the basis of data from plantation accounts, government records, and legal reports describing the plantations of 5000 farmers, Fogel concludes that slavery was highly profitable and efficient.

Fogel's first revelation has to do with the profitability of slaves as investments. If investments in slaves are to be undertaken, he says, the return on investments in slaves must be at least as great as the return on other sorts of investments. The rate of return on an investment is "capitalized" into the investment's price. (To capitalize the value of an investment is to calculate its present value by summing the net revenue it produces during its years of service, with future revenues discounted at the appropriate discount rate.) Sales contracts and probate records from the prewar South confirm the considerable value of slaves, a value not likely to be jeopardized, says Fogel, by mistreatment or neglect.

Another measure of the healthy return on investments in slaves is the rate of growth of the slave economy. During the two decades prior to the Civil War, annual economic growth in the slave-holding states was 1.3 percent per capita, a growth rate almost 2 percentage points faster than that of the non-slave-holding North.

Moreover, southern agriculture was demonstrably more profitable than northern. Before Fogel, the superior productivity of southern agriculture was thought to be caused by the mismeasurement of slave labor: the fact that slaves worked longer hours than free farmers, that slave women and children worked along with the men, and that the skills of slaves may have been more appropriate to agriculture than were the skills of free farm workers. Fogel's empirical data contradict the most significant of these assumptions. First, Fogel shows that slaves employed on large plantations actually worked fewer hours than free farmers. Indeed, the difference in the work of slaves and free farmers was not longer hours but the greater intensity of slaves' work, which was almost double that of free farmers. The greater intensity of slaves' work was made possible by granting slaves longer rest breaks and more Sundays off than were enjoyed by free farmers.

The South's faster economic growth was due not to larger quantities of labor and capital inputs, says Fogel, but rather to superior total factor productivity (using Robert Solow's terminology). Total factor productivity estimates the efficiency with which a given quantity of labor and capital resources is combined and depends on technological and organizational characteristics of production.

Fogel explains the superior total factor productivity of the slave economy as the result of critical differences in markets in the northern and southern states. First, he observes that income distribution in the South was highly unequal, which had the effect of limiting home markets for diversified farm products. The lack of home markets forced southern farmers to produce large crops that could be sold in bulk outside the South: in particular, cotton and sugar. Specialization in large cash crops yields economies of scale and requires less supervision than diversified farming. Slave labor was especially appropriate for specialized, large-scale farming, such that southern slaves produced on average nearly twice the output per hour of work as northern free farmers. Specialized farming enabled slaves to perform at an assembly-line pace, generally organized in "gangs" supervised by other slaves. Fogel concludes that the gang system was the primary reason for the superior total factor productivity of slavery in the South. And that the high cash value of the cotton and sugar produced by slaves was responsible for the high market value of the slaves themselves.

Fogel's research has not been accepted uncritically in the economics profession or among the general public, some of whom assume that his favorable assessment of the productivity of slavery implies support for the institution. Not so. In spite of his findings regarding the high productivity of slavery in the South, nowhere does Fogel suggest that slavery's economic advantages justified the accompanying loss of slaves' freedom.

The chief implication of Fogel's study is the persistence of an institution whose continued existence is supported by favorable economic conditions. For slavery to die on its own would have required long years of change in economic conditions, changes that ultimately would have undermined slavery's profitability. In the event, slavery came to an end not because of its economic costs but because of its moral and social costs, which could not wait for the gradual unfolding of economic laws.

Fogel's bottom line: Slavery, as abhorrent an institution as could be imagined, was defeated not for economic reasons but for ethical reasons, in response to society's changing perception of legitimacy with respect to the (economically profitable) institution.

CONCLUSION

A good way to clear a room—or at least to stifle conversation—is to mention economics and economists. Too many people think of economists as bearded old men pictured in dusty library books shunned in our youth. Yes, a few of the Nobel economists sport beards, and a few probably fulfill our most negative expectations. But by and large they exemplify the characteristics of the population at large, only perhaps more so. Certainly they are more brilliant, each blessed with unique intellectual gifts and each having developed his gifts superbly.

(I use "his" here correctly, since there has as yet been no "her." The gossip within the profession is that a renowned female economist was once considered a shoo-in for the prize, but that her tendency to challenge established theory militated against her. The economist so rejected was Joan Robinson, whose pioneering efforts in the theory of imperfect competition are fundamental to the theory of industrial organization.)

The Nobel economists are described by their colleagues as self-effacing or arrogant, sociable or timid, generous or curmudgeonly. Their personal ideologies vary from fervently individualistic to benignly collectivist. Each stands above the crowd of other intelligent, prolific, sensitive economists because he created something entirely new. Each distilled the information from his experience to produce a new idea, a new focus for the attention of the economists that followed. Without invalidating the work of those that came before, each of these men casts new light on the important questions that confront ordinary men and women every day of their lives.

Which suggests another characteristic these men share in abundance: their deep and sincere concern about the welfare of ordinary people. In all their scholarly endeavors, the Nobel economists keep coming back to the fundamental question: How (and when) will this event, action, or policy affect real human beings? (Ironically, few economists use their analytical skills to pursue personal wealth. That's just not on their agenda. But it is a source of much of the disparaging humor about them—"If you're so smart, why aren't you rich?")

Most of the non-U.S. Nobelists live and work in northern Europe. And many of the U.S. Nobelists were European immigrants or born to immigrants—blue-collar workers, small business owners, a few professional people, generally not from society's privileged ranks. They demonstrated from early childhood a drive to excel and a consummate curiosity about their world, as reflected in their passion for reading and in their academic specializations in mathematics and physical science. Their interest in mathematics was not so much in mathematical processes, however, as in using mathematics for organizing and simplifying large amounts of complex information: information about the ways people behave, people's responsiveness to incentives and to changes in human conditions. Their interest in science derived from a fascination with laws explaining cause-and-effect relationships among natural phenomena. For specialists in mathematics and science, extending cause-effect laws for explaining physical phenomena to laws explaining human behavior seemed perfectly natural.

The Nobel economists' aptitude for mathematics and physical science instilled in these men an appreciation for logic versus unsubstantiated opinion. And it was a natural complement to their interest in the social sciences. They saw scientific analysis as every bit as vital to the social sciences as to the physical sciences. Without valid information and scientific analysis of social issues, societies are vulnerable to extreme and irrational doctrines. A society founded on irrational beliefs cannot establish the policies and foster the behaviors that best serve its people.

The Nobel economists benefited from a congenial intellectual environment in which "the companionship of scholars and the thrill of continuous learning" (Robert Fogel) diffused and expanded on their individual accomplishments. Their ideas meld or clash, in either case enriching our understanding of human behavior. Indeed, controversies are the best way to publicize and confirm ideas, much as confining a tiger and a panther in a single cage ultimately imparts a certain authority to the superior contender (George Stigler). An objective of this book has been, therefore, not so much to showcase these economists' singular contributions to economic thought as to tell the broader story of their connectedness. Each fills a niche in our continuing drive to understand and affect economic society—and occasionally to create new niches for future explorers to fill.

The Nobel Economists Are a Product of Their Era

Concern about the betterment of human society came naturally to men who reached intellectual maturity in mid-twentieth century.

The twentieth century began as the era of Queen Victoria was coming to an end. Historians describe the Victorian era as a time of optimism regarding the perfectibility of the human species and, ultimately, human society as well. Perhaps as an outgrowth of Darwinian biology, with its implied assurance that natural selection would guide physical and social evolution in beneficent ways, the Victorians expected human beings to become more and more rational, economic life more efficient, and social conditions more nearly ideal. Many such expectations were dashed with the wanton carnage of the First World War and the Depression a decade later. It was difficult to see rationality in the senseless destruction of human and material wealth or efficiency in the years of forced idleness for the world's farm families, assembly-line workers, and construction crews. World War II demolished whatever hopeful expectations may have remained about the perfectibility of society and liberalization of the human spirit.

Many of the Nobel economists experienced twentieth century traumas firsthand: childhood poverty and economic distress; the disruption of war and the terror of systematic persecution; the uncertain prospects and competitive challenges of the postwar years. Observing and participating in global collapse, they felt compelled to participate also in its revival. While some observers asked why and shook their heads in despair, these men actively probed for answers.

The social traumas that engaged these men forced the intellectual discipline then called *political economy* to confront an apparent inconsistency between established economic theory and economic reality. In established theory, the vision of universal happiness through individual pursuit of self-interest was increasingly challenged by the reality of economic paralysis and waste, monopoly, and raging inequality. Twentieth-century economists were forced to admit the possibility that free markets, left on their own, could end up very unfree.

Coincident with trauma in the social sciences, the physical sciences were also experiencing revelations that undermined scientists' confident explanations of the structure of matter. The revolution in quantum mechanics replaced scientists' secure beliefs regarding molecular structure with the "uncertainty principle," the discovery that the building blocks of matter are not situated in identifiable spaces but are constantly moving. Their locations at any point in time are not deterministic but stochastic—not known for certain but governed by the laws of probability. If the most basic behavior of matter is not fully understandable, then who can believe the old theories purporting to explain the behavior of living people and free societies?

It is not surprising that the confusion in beliefs regarding both our physical and social environments should erode support for traditional economic theory and policy. The nineteenth-century characterization of an economic system as a perfect structure—one whose pieces fit together harmoniously to create a totality that is aesthetically pleasing, efficient, and enduring—seemed an inappropriate metaphor for what was happening in the twentieth century. How appealing it had been to describe an economic system in which free people rationally compare the benefits and costs of alternative courses of action and, while seeking maximum personal welfare, also promote the greatest possible welfare for the society as a whole. How inconvenient it became for real events to chip away at the foundation of such a perfect structure.

The disruptions of the twentieth century opened minds to new ways of thinking about how societies organize themselves: how people working together make decisions about the use of their limited resources; how they establish institutions to regularize decisions found to produce beneficial results; how those institutions evolve with the changing requirements of their social and economic environment.

Of course, these are the issues addressed by the Nobel economists: How do societies bring order out of chaos? How do we organize society to secure the best possible results? (For that matter, how do we define "best"?) How do we reconcile innate human tendencies toward selfishness with an equivalent human yearning for harmony in our social relationships? How do we balance social control with freedom for individuals to exercise their creative initiative?

This is the remarkable objective of the Nobel economists: to explore the ways human societies ensure a level of individual freedom and initiative while restraining individualistic tendencies toward self-interested behavior. Never denying (in fact, celebrating) the inherently selfish nature of the human species, these economists look for the structures that curb and guide behavior toward accommodation—that ensure an acceptable balance between selfish behavior and conciliation.

So it was the exigencies of twentieth century life that forced economics to become practical—to get real! The exigencies of real life forced twentieth-century economists to focus on society's optimal course, how to define the optimum and how to achieve the possible—whether through individual or collective means, through free markets or through central guidance or control.

Modern Economic Thought

From the achievements of the Nobel economists emerges a coherent story of the progress of modern economic thought. Indeed, the story told recounts the scientific method, writ large, as the discipline has moved from theory to empirical analysis to testing and revision and, ultimately, to tentative guides for thinking about what makes our societies tick.

Through studying their work, I have discerned two trends that seem to define the course of economic sciences during the half-century in which these men worked. The first theme is the drive to make economics more scientific, to move from the deductive methods of traditional economic theory to the more inductive methods of the physical sciences. Thus, the first theme describes the progress of analytical methods in economics, initially glorifying the power of statistical tools, then counseling balance between economics as a "pure" science and as the study of the imperfect, not always scientifically analyzable, behavior of independently motivated people. The second theme is related to the first in the recognition that independently motivated people function within societies and that a society needs an institutional structure as a means of framing interpersonal relationships. Thus, the second theme describes the intellectual and legal struggle between an incentive system that depends on individual self-interest and a society built on the interdependencies of fundamentally independent people.

The First Theme:
Developing Economics as a Science

The challenges of the twentieth century called for a new way of thinking about social issues—a shift from deductive thinking to inductive thinking, from theory based on personal introspection to theory that emerges from empirical observation. Ronald Coase describes theory based on deductive thinking as "blackboard economics," renowned chiefly for the elegance and simplicity of its exposition. Inductive thinking is messier. It begins with apparently chaotic data and seeks the grid that, when placed on chaotic data, reveals its fundamental order. "The role of a science, in fact, is to simplify and to choose" (Maurice Allais). Organizing and analyzing apparently chaotic data became the first step in the process of establishing economics as a science, in unraveling the complex patterns of human responses to incentives.

Still, single-minded devotion to the science of economics can be almost as damaging as neglecting science altogether. Human relationships are not fully amenable to simplification, being describable through useful approximations rather than through precise truths. The real world is not "elegant," and much of human behavior is only distantly describable by the laws devised by economic science. "We cannot use the *in vacua* [italics in original] version of the law of falling bodies to predict the sinking of a heavy body in molasses" (Herbert Simon). Total immersion in abstract models risks neglect of the true substance of economic phenomena (John Hicks). Indeed, there is an inescapable tension between complex reality and scientific analysis that reduces the amount of information that can be jockeyed into the scientist's grid—subsumed, as it were, *in ceteris paribus*. Jettisoning all motivations other than those that are observable and measurable can suggest cause-effect relationships that are "not predictively useful and [have] dubious empirical support" (Amartya Sen). A too earnest attempt to be scientific can fatally reduce the dimensions within which an issue is examined (Milton Friedman). Human motivations are much richer than mere self-interest (Gary Becker). Better to think scientifically with a small "s," logically and with respect for fact but, like a vacuum cleaner, picking up bits of information that resist gridification (Robert Solow). Better to avoid the comfortable world of differential calculus; better not to be distracted from truth by mathematical "charlatanry" (Wassily Leontief).

Thus, economists must attack with scientific methods phenomena that are only partially amenable to scientific analysis. They must bring to their analysis all of their personal versatility and breadth of experience. "Nobody can be a great economist who is only an economist" (Friedrich von Hayek).

The Second Theme: The Individual in the Larger Society

Traditional economic theory was a reaction against the dreary pronouncements of the seventeenth-century philosopher Thomas Hobbes, that people's interests are always and everywhere in conflict. That in a world in which the "life of man [is] solitary, poor, nasty, brutish, and short" people are compelled to snatch what they can and protect what they have from the similar compulsions of their neighbors. Hobbes' view of society requires a government strong enough to suppress the civil disorder that inevitably results from constant conflict. The classical economists of the nineteenth century advanced the more attractive notion that people can actually live in harmony with nature and one another. In this more harmonious state, self-interested behavior actually benefits society, calling for minimum government to ensure the richest possible results from infinite types of human relationships.

Human beings are born helpless. By joining together in groups we are helped to enjoy more of the benefits rightfully pursued by group members. "Flocks are the product of selfishness, not groupiness" (Reinhard Selten). We are rewarded for our acceptance of society's strictures by receipt of society's altruism. "Altruism is an investment in trustworthiness" (Reinhard Selten). When we join together in society, we are in effect agreeing to allow ourselves to be forced to behave in certain ways (Paul Samuelson).

Governing a flock requires a delicate balance, however, between the interest of the individual and the interests of the whole. The noted economist Thomas Schelling graphically describes society's dilemma this way. Imagine a hot Sunday afternoon and a heavily traveled highway clogged with motorists returning to the city from a weekend on Cape Cod. A mattress has fallen off the top of a recreational van, blocking one lane of traffic and slowing all lanes. All the motorists would benefit if one civic-minded person would park his car on the shoulder and walk across the highway to push the obstruction away. The problem is that no single motorist has an incentive to do so. After spending useless time in the traffic jam, no "good Samaritan" is willing to pay the extra cost of delay to perform an act that benefits only other motorists.

Now imagine a helicopter hovering over the highway with a megaphone and proposing that the next one hundred motorists passing a putative "good Samaritan" flip a dime out the passenger-side window to compensate for his cost. This gives a potential road clearer a property right in the path he opens, a right that yields both an economic return on his personal investment and a benefit to the motorists behind him.

A good part of governing a society consists of institutional arrangements like this one. Our institutional arrangements define the processes through which we make our collective decisions (Kenneth Arrow and James Buchanan). They help bridge the gap between our perceived individual interests and the larger collective interest. Some of our institutional arrangements are market-oriented, some governmental, and some moral or ethical. However they are classified, their result is a kind of social contract that induces us to cooperate toward results that benefit the society at large while imposing the least cost on its individual members.

For the Future

Future Nobel economists are working today in realms suggested by the work of the economists profiled in this book. Probably the hottest area of economic research is the economics of information. The economics of information spans both of the themes I have identified in the work of past Nobelists:

- The first, for its scientific investigations into how economic agents acquire and use information, frequently from noninformative sources. Acquisition and application of information is essential for designing efficient solutions to practical problems.
- The second, because it demonstrates how information links self-interested individuals into efficient collective institutions. In fact, it is the "common denominators" that people extract from disparate information that promote the institutions that advance society's goals (Herbert Simon).

Understanding information can help avoid the sorts of "market failures" that arise from incomplete information. And it can help society deal with issues involving distribution, in particular, identifying the distribution of resources and products that yields maximum value.

A Final Word

There is, of course, much more to learn from the work of the Nobel economists, which has only been touched upon in these summaries. The aim of this book is not to provide a comprehensive account of their contributions but rather to choose from their work the parts that, woven together, tell the story of modern economic thought. I hope that readers will explore beyond the material in these pages to read their words directly—a few of which are identified in the section entitled "Further Reading."

Neither is this book intended to prescribe solutions to problems—personal, business, governmental. The intention is to let the story these economists tell suggest ways to look at problems—to help us evaluate the ways societies organize themselves to satisfy both individual drives and collective sentiments, to achieve both personal freedom and social order. Economics doesn't answer questions so much as add dimensions to our understanding of human behavior (Robert Fogel).

Discovering new ideas is not always a straightforward process. It is not as graceful as a skilled gymnast but more like stumbling about in a jungle of facts and ideas that seem to defy logic (George Stigler). Such difficulties do not relieve us of the task, however. The expansion of democracy worldwide and improvements in global communications and transportation require that societies resolve their dilemmas to the satisfaction of larger and more diverse populations. By unraveling the processes societies use to make their decisions, the Nobel economists help us move toward that resolution—and perhaps give us reason for renewed optimism at the beginning of the new millennium.

As is so often true, Robert Solow captures with brevity and wit the essence of economists' struggle to understand our human condition. Recalling the dismissive claim that one can teach a parrot economics simply by teaching it to say "supply" and "demand," Solow admits this is true. But he insists this is not the worst thing that could be said about a discipline. Indeed, says Solow, there really is no other game in town.

NOTES

Part 1

1. This is not to suggest that marginal decisions affect welfare only in the current period. It is increasingly evident that current decisions affect welfare in the future. For making such decisions, we evaluate a current decision on the basis of the benefits and costs incurred over a period (definite or infinite) in the future.

2. The distinction here is between positive economics, which provides as clear as possible a picture of the effects of alternative policy choices, and normative economics, which goes beyond the information-providing role to actually advocate particular policies.

3. Such behavior is called "predatory pricing" and was once a justification for breaking up large companies. Recent research has questioned the prevalence of predatory pricing, since a company that underprices its competitors must eventually offset its losses by raising price. Higher prices would then invite more competitors, so that the tendency toward predatory pricing is ultimately self-defeating.

4. Economic Report of the President, 1998.

5. Laissez-faire is the French expression for "let alone" and calls for government to let markets alone to function without government involvement.

6. H. von Hayek, *The Road to Surfdom,* University of Chicago Press, 1972, p. 24.

7. Ibid., p. 63.

8. Ibid., p. 139. The bailiff is the sheriff's assistant who administers bankruptcy proceedings.

9. Ibid., p. 157.

10. Ibid., p. 156.

11. Scientists who study the relationship between biological evolution and social structures.

12. In economic jargon, criminals compare at the margin the added benefits with the added cost and select the level of crime that equates the two measures.

13.   Not to mention the occasional attempt to defraud the scientific community in the manner of the Piltdown Man fiasco and the more recent skin grafts that simulated cloning in mice.

14.   Jonathan Williams, "A Life Spent on One Problem," *The New York Times,* November 26, 1978.

15.   Herbert A. Simon, "Altruism and Economics," *American Economic Review,* May 1993, 156–161.

Part 2

1.   Although Arrow did not claim originality in the voting paradox, his expression of it in his dissertation caused a fundamental shift in economic thinking.

2.   *Social Choice and Individual Values,* 2nd ed., Yale University Press, New Haven, 1951.

3.   J. A. Kregel (ed.), *Recollections of Eminent Economists,* vol. 2, New York University Press, New York, 1989.

4.   With Gordon Tulloch in *The Calculus of Consent,* University of Michigan Press, Ann Arbor, 1965.

5.   Buchanan supports inclusion of rigid rules governing property rights in the Constitution.

6.   One was Arthur Pigou, who lived in the early part of the twentieth century and is responsible for the pre-Coase policy recommendations for handling externalities.

7.   Note the structure of the word *transactions:* actions across. Thus, the word means actions across divisions. Actions across divisions are the core of a modern economy, where self-sufficiency has been replaced by cooperation among diverse entities.

8.   Edmund Clerihew Bentley, quoted in Amartya Sen, *On Ethics and Economics,* Basil Blackwell, Oxford, 1987.

9.   Stephen Leacock, *Hellements of Hickonomics,* Dodd, Mead and Co., 1936, quoted in *On Ethics and Economics.*

Part 3

1.   Mark Blaugh, *Great Economists Since Keynes,* Cambridge University Press, Cambridge, 1985.

2.   Ragnar Frisch, "From Utopian Theory to Practical Applications: The Case of Econometrics," *American Economic Review,* December 1981, 71, no. 6, 1–16.

3.   Ibid.

4.   Robert Fogel, "Economic Growth, Population Theory, and Physiology: The Bearing of Long-Term Processes on the Making of Economic Policy,"

in Torsten Perrson (ed.), *Nobel Lectures in Economic Sciences, 1991–1995,* World Scientific, New Jersey, 1997.

5.   Squares are used to avoid negatives. Otherwise, positive values for points lying above the regression line would be precisely offset by negative values of points below the line.

6.   Not for very long, of course. After having slaughtered their livestock, ranchers have no more to sell, so that prices tend to rise.

7.   To add credibility to the estimated relationships, econometricians calculate the standard errors associated with each cause-effect relationship. To add credibility to the form of the equation, they calculate correlation coefficients describing the entire structure. Calculating a new correlation coefficient as each causal variable is added helps identify the most nearly correct combination of variables.

8.   Tjalling C. Koopmans, "Economics Among the Sciences," *American Economic Review,* March 1979, 69, no. 1, 1–13.

9.   Blaugh. *Great Economists Since Keynes.*

10.   The true figure now is closer to 6 billion.

11.   Trygve Haavelmo, "The Probability Approach in Econometrics," supplement to *Econometrica,* 12th ed., quoted in Mary S. Morgan, *The History of Econometric Ideas,* Cambridge University Press, Cambridge, 1992, p. 250.

12.   Alan B. Krueger at Princeton and the National Bureau of Economic Research.

13.   Joseph G. Altonji at Northwestern and the National Bureau of Economic Research.

14.   Alan Krueger, "Reassessing the View that American Schools Are Broken," *FRBNY Economic Policy Review,* March 1998. See also David Card and Alan B. Krueger, "Labor Market Effects of School Quality: Theory and Evidence," in *Does Money Matter?* Brookings, 1996.

Part 4

1.   Inflation rates in the thousands have been recorded, for example, in Russia, Israel, and Brazil.

2.   We temporarily ignore the involvement of government in those decisions.

3.   After allowed deductions and personal exemptions.

4.   The usual assumption is that the employers' portion is actually paid by the worker, since without the employers' obligation to pay the tax they could increase the worker's pay.

5.   Personal saving in the United States turned negative in 1999.

6. We leave taxes out of the picture for simplicity.

7. "Milton Friedman" in William Breit and Roger W. Spencer, *Lives of the Laureates*, MIT Press, Cambridge, Massachusetts, 1997, p. 3.

8. The simplest way the Fed can increase the level of lending is by buying from lending institutions some of their holdings of government securities. The Fed pays for the securities by increasing the reserve assets of lending institutions. It is the quantity of reserve assets owned that determines an institution's ability to issue new loans.

9. The reserve assets.

10. None of these is a true "innovation," all having appeared at earlier times in history, only to be restored to popularity in the 1970s.

11. John R. Hicks, "Preface—And a Manifesto," in Arrow and Scitovsky, *Readings in Welfare Economics*, Irwin, Homewood, Illinois, 1969.

12. Robert E. Lucas, *Studies in Business Cycle Theory*, MIT Press, Cambridge, Massachusetts, 1994, p. 9.

13. In addition to its implications for business cycle theory and policy, Lucas's theory of rational expectations also helps explain the failure of most forecasters to predict future prices accurately. When people's expectations are rational, they immediately incorporate in their decisions whatever available information might affect future prices. Behaving rationally, buyers and sellers estimate the probability of price-affecting events in the future and build the consequences into their current behavior. This is as true of workers as it is of businesses. Both groups include estimates of expected future events in their current wage-price calculations, with the result that wages and prices adjust immediately to future expectations.

14. Modigliani's lifetime-income concept is somewhat different from Friedman's permanent-income concept in that permanent income allows for bequests that support consumption after the saver's death.

15. Note that by reducing their spending in inflationary periods and increasing spending in recessions, consumers alternatively add to and draw down their accumulated wealth. A logical conclusion is that increases in saving occur only when economic activity is increasing. And here is the heart of Modigliani's argument: Changes in saving depend less on arbitrary decisions of savers (as suggested by Keynesian theory) than on changes in the growth rate of the economy.

16. James Tobin, "Inflation and Unemployment," *American Economic Review*, March 1972, vol. 62, no. 1, pp. 1–18.

17. As measured by the Consumer Price Index, inflation in seven industrialized countries averaged 9 percent per year in the mid-1970s.

Part 5

1. In addition to their usefulness for measuring economic activity, Stone's national income accounts were also used for evaluating other aspects of national life, such as population trends and environmental gains or losses.

2. Arrow and Debreu did not write the precise equations required to solve their general equilibrium model. They simply formulated the broad organizational framework for understanding how markets process information: how markets convert consumers' preferences and producers' profit motive into a particular allocation of resources for current production.

3. Maurice Allais, "The Passion for Research," in Michael Szenberg (ed.), *Eminent Economists: Their Life Philosophies*, Cambridge University Press, New York, 1993.

4. Ibid.

5. Ibid.

6. Wassily Leontief, "Theoretical Assumptions and Nonobserved Facts," *American Economic Review*, March 1971.

7. Wassily Leontief, "Input-Output Economics," *Scientific American*, October 1951.

8. "Exodus: 1974," *Forbes*, January 1, 1974.

9. Kuznets' original calculations included all production by U.S. nationals, whether conducted within U.S. territory or abroad. Other nations include production conducted within domestic territory, whether conducted by nationals or foreigners. The second calculation yields gross domestic product (or GDP). For ease of comparability among nations, the United States has recently adopted the second method of calculation, so that current figures refer to GDP.

10. Since the 1870s gross investment in the United States has exceeded one-fifth of GDP, but increasing depreciation expense has caused net investment to decline from 15 percent of GDP a century ago to about 7 percent in recent years. In part, the reason is the fact that producers' durable equipment constitutes an increased share of gross investment. As compared with investments in construction, producers' equipment requires more frequent replacement.

11. The main characteristic of indirect taxes is that they can be shifted between the buyer and the seller of the product, according to the urgency of the buyer's demand versus the seller's need to sell.

12. Simon Kuznets, "Modern Economic Growth: Findings and Reflections," in Assar Lindbeck (ed.), *Nobel Lectures in Economic Sciences, 1969–1980*, World Scientific, Singapore, 1992.

Part 6

1. "Department of Dubunkery," *The Economist,* January 18, 1997, vol. 342, no. 3000.

2. The U.S. capital/labor ratio differs among industries, being highest in nonmanufacturing industries like real estate, electric, gas, sanitary utilities, and railroads. Among manufacturing industries, the capital/labor ratio is highest in petroleum and coal and lowest in apparel.

3. Solow estimated the value of TFP over a recent period and found beginning in 1930 an increase in the growth rate of technological change to about 1.5 percent a year. Output per worker approximately doubled, with about one-eighth of the increase traceable to increased capital per worker and seven-eighths traceable to technical change.

4. Paul W. Bauer, "Are We in a Productivity Boom? Evidence from Multifactor Productivity Growth," FRB of Cleveland Economic Commentary, October 15, 1999.

5. Retirement benefits might fit into this category, although the promise of retirement benefits might encourage working people toward greater productivity so as to retain their jobs. This is an example of the difficulty of drawing precise lines between consumption and investment spending.

6. Exclusive of South Africa.

7. Theodore Schultz, "Investment in Human Capital," *American Economic Review,* March 1961. Presumably Schultz did not intentionally exclude women from his recommendation for investments in human capital.

8. Schultz's research concludes that 36 to 70 percent of the unexplained increase in national income is explained by returns to additional education.

9. For the uninitiated, a moon pie is a confection made from graham wafers, marshmallow filling, and a waxy chocolate coating—quite addictive, actually.

10. Schultz. "Investment in Human Capital."

11. Arthur Lewis, "The State of Development Theory," *American Economic Review,* March 1984, vol. 74, no. 1, pp. 1–10.

12. Sharp differences in domestic wage rates are a special problem in certain LDCs: those that depend on one industry that employs only a few people but produces a major export product. High wages in the dominant industry pull up average labor costs, which worsen tendencies toward unemployment in the rest of the economy and lead to political unrest and corruption. This effect is often called the "Dutch disease" because it happened in the Netherlands in the 1980s with the expansion of natural gas production in the North Sea. Growth in the dominant export industry stim-

ulated wage and price increases in other sectors of the Dutch economy, creating unemployment and inflation at the same time.

13. Lewis. "The Statement of Development Theory."

14. Robert Fogel, "Railroads and American Economic Growth," *Essays in Economic History,* Johns Hopkins Press, Baltimore, Maryland, 1964, pp. 235–236.

15. Certainly Italy and the United Kingdom would also be classified as mature nations, but with GDP per capita less than $20,000 they do not satisfy the criterion used in this list.

16. David S. Landes, *The Unbound Prometheus,* Cambridge University Press, London and New York, 1969.

Part 7

1. In Peter Bernstein's fine book *Against the Gods,* the author says that life allows us to draw a proverbial pebble from a proverbial jar, but it doesn't guarantee whether the pebble will be black or white.

2. Peter Bernstein, *Capital Ideas,* Free Press, p. 81.

3. Bernstein, *Capital Ideas,* p. 188.

4. Real domestic investment was 17 percent of real gross domestic product in 1997, as opposed to less then 15 percent in previous decades.

5. Bernstein, *Capital Ideas,* p. 170.

6. If the price of corn had fallen below $2.50, the holder of a futures contract would sell it back to the farmer at a lower price, experiencing a loss on the futures contract that offsets the ability to buy the corn more cheaply than expected. The farmer would gain something on the contract transaction to offset the loss on the sale of corn at the currently lower market price.

7. Black died in 1995 at age 57 before the Nobel Prize was awarded to Merton and Scholes.

8. As it turns out, LTCM acted more as a speculator than a hedger.

9. A short straddle is the sale of a call and a put on a particular asset with the same exercise price. The writer of the straddle risks unlimited loss if the price of the asset either rises or falls. The only gain is the price received for the options.

10. You may think this concept is so obvious as not to require articulation. However, in college classes I have often heard highly intelligent graduate students propose to remedy a domestic scarcity by "get[ing] it from abroad," with no consideration of how the acquisition is to be compensated.

11. Even if the nation with excessive imports eventually repurchases the investment, the purchase price will include the discounted value of expected future returns. In effect, the nation pays in a lump sum all the expected future returns on the investment made possible by capital inflows.

12. By changing world history, Meade probably meant avoiding World War II.

13. Tinbergen's rule states that for every policy objective there must be a separate enabling policy action.

14. A lump-sum tax is generally assumed to be positive but it could be negative. A negative lump-sum tax would be a transfer payment (or subsidy) intended to increase the equity of income distribution.

15. I. M. D. Little and J. A. Mirrlees, *Project Appraisal and Planning for Developing Countries*, Basic Books, New York, 1974.

Part 8

1. A. Conan Doyle, "The Final Problem."

2. Thomas Schelling applied game theory in his strategic theories regarding the value of brinksmanship in international relations.

3. You might think of strategies *A* and *B* as "high price" and "low price."

4. An advantage of a maximin strategy for income distribution is that it does not require a way actually to measure the satisfaction provided by income. Remember that in neoclassical economic theory the optimal distribution of income would maximize the nation's social welfare function, the combined welfare enjoyed by all its income recipients. But to maximize social welfare requires some standard measure for measuring and comparing individual's welfare, and we have no such measure. A maximin strategy requires only a measure of the "least bad" income possible for everyone and the assurance that everyone enjoys at least that income. Achieving the "least bad" income for everyone would require shifts of income to the nation's poorest households and assumes that such shifts provide enough added welfare to offset the loss of welfare to the richest households—even though the gains and losses in welfare cannot actually be measured.

5. Note that the pennies are "displayed" not "tossed."

6. This example has been used often by economists to illustrate network effects, initially with the belief that the choice could have gone either way—neither system being superior. More recent analysis asserts that VHS received the initial boost because it was the superior technology.

7. The same qualification expressed in note 6 applies here also.

8. John Keegan, *The History of Warfare*.

9. North disagrees with Ronald Coase that firms will create the most efficient structures. Insufficient information and incomplete feedback make the efficient structure unlikely, he says. Rather, it is more likely that firms will create the structures that serve groups with the greatest bargaining power.

10. Since 1992.

FURTHER READING

"The Alternative to Not Planning May Be Chaos: A Conversation With Wassily Leontief," *Business and Society Review*, Spring 1976.

Arrow, Kenneth J., "Criteria for Social Investment," in *Readings in Public Sector Economics*, Samuel H. Baker and Catherine S. Elliott, eds., D.C. Heath, Lexington, Mass., 1990.

———, "A Difficulty in the Concept of Social Welfare," in *Readings in Welfare Economics*, Kenneth Arrow and Tibor Scitovsky, eds., Richard W. Irwin, Homewood, Ill. 1969.

———, *Social Choice and Individual Values*, 2nd ed., Yale University Press, New Haven and London, 1951.

Aumann, Robert J., "Game Theory," *The New Palgrave: Game Theory*, John Eatwell, Murray Milgate, Peter Newman, eds., W.W. Norton, NY, 1987.

Barro, Robert J., and Xavier Sala-I-Martin, *Economic Growth*, McGraw-Hill, NY, 1995.

Becker, Gary, "Altruism, Egoism, and Genetic Fitness," *Journal of Economic Literature* 14, No. 3 (September 1976).

———, *The Economic Approach to Human Behavior*, University of Chicago Press, Chicago, 1976.

Bernstein, Peter L., *Against the Gods: The Remarkable Story of Risk*, John Wiley, NY, 1996.

———, *Capital Ideas*, The Free Press, NY, 1992.

Black, Fischer, "How We Came Up With the Option Formula," *Journal of Portfolio Managment* 15, Winter 1989.

——— and Myron Scholes, "The Pricing of Options and Corporate Liabilities," *Journal of Political Economy* 81, May–June 1973.

Blaug, Mark, *Great Economists Since Keynes*, Cambridge University Press, NY, 1988.

Breit, William and Roger Spence, eds., *Lives of the Laureates, Ten Nobel Economists*, MIT Press, Cambridge, Mass., 1990.

Buchanan, James M., "The Constitution of Economic Policy," *American Economic Review* 77, No. 3, June 1987.

————, *The Limits of Liberty*, University of Chicago Press, Chicago, 1975.

———— and Gordon Tullock, *The Calculus of Consent*, University of Michigan Press, Ann Arbor, 1962.

Chari, V.V., "Nobel Laureate Robert E. Lucas, Jr.: Architect of Modern Macroeconomics," *FRB of Minneapolis Quarterly Review*, Spring 1999.

Coase, Ronald, *The Firm, the Market, and the Law*, University of Chicago Press, Chicago, 1990.

————, "The Lighthouse in Economics," in *Readings in Public Sector Economics*, Samuel H. Baker and Catherine S. Elliott, eds., D.C. Heath, Lexington, Mass., 1990.

Debreu, Gerard, "The Mathematization of Economic Theory," *American Economic Review* 81, No. 1, March 1991.

Diamond, Peter, and James A. Mirrlees, "Optimal Taxation and Public Production I: Production Efficiency," *American Economic Review*, March 1971.

Eatwell, John, Murray Milgate, and Peter Newman, eds., *The New Palgrave Game Theory*, W. W. Norton, NY, 1987.

Evans, Michael K., *Macroeconomic Activity: Theory, Forecasting, and Control (An Econometric Approach)*, Harper and Row, NY, 1969.

Fogel, Robert William, "The Conquest of High Mortality and Hunger in Europe and America," in *Favorites of Fortune*, Patrice Higonnet et al., eds., Harvard University Press, Cambridge, 1991.

————, *Railroads in American Economic Growth*, Johns Hopkins Press, Baltimore, 1964.

———— and Stanley Engerman, *Time on the Cross*, Little, Brown, Boston, 1974.

Friedman, Milton, "The Role of Monetary Policy," *American Economic Review* 63, No. 1, March 1968, 1–17.

———— and Walter Heller, *Monetary vs. Fiscal Policy: A Dialogue*, W.W. Norton, NY, 1969.

Frisch, Ragnar, "Autonomy of Econometric Relations," in *The Foundations of Econometric Analysis*, David F. Hendry and Mary S. Morgan, eds., Cambridge University Press, NY, 1995.

Gordon, H. Scott, "The Economic Theory of a Common-Property Resource: The Fishery," *Journal of Political Economy* 62, 1954.

Gul, Faruk, "A Nobel Prize for Game Theorists: The Contributions of Harsanyi, Nash and Selten," *Journal of Economic Perspectives*, Summer 1997.

Haavelmo, Trygve, "Econometrics and the Welfare State," *American Economic Review*, December 1997.

———, "The Probability Approach in Econometrics," in *The Foundations of Econometric Analysis*, David F. Hendry and Mary S. Morgan, eds., Cambridge University Press, NY, 1995.

Hanushek, Eric A., "The Economics of Schooling: Production and Efficiency in Public Schools," *Journal of Economic Literature* 24, September 1986.

Hardin, Garrett, "The Tragedy of the Commons," in *Readings in Public Sector Economics*, Samuel H. Baker and Catherine S. Elliott, eds., D.C. Heath, Lexington, Mass., 1990.

Harsanyi, John C., *Essays on Ethics, Social Behavior and Scientific Explanation*, D. Reidel Pub. Co., Boston, 1976.

Hayek, Friedrick von, *Individualism and Economic Order*, University of Chicago Press, Chicago, 1948.

———, *The Road to Serfdom*, University of Chicago Press, Chicago, 1944.

Hester, Donald D., "Innovations and Monetary Control," *Brookings Papers on Economic Activity*, 1:1981.

Hicks, John R., "Mr. Keynes and the 'Classics': A Suggested Interpretation," *Econometrica* 5, April 1937.

Humphrey, Thomas M., *A History of the Phillips Curve*, FRB of Richmond, October 1986.

Kantorovich, Leonid V., "Mathematics in Economics: Achievements, Difficulties, Perspectives," *American Economic Review*, December 1989.

Kindleberger, Charles, *International Capital Movements*, Cambridge University Press, Cambridge, 1987.

Klamer, Arjo, "An Accountant Among Economists: Converstions With Sir John R. Hicks," *Journal of Economic Perspectives* 3, No. 4, Fall 1989.

Klein, Lawrence R., *An Introduction to Econometrics*, Prentice-Hall, Englewood Cliffs, NJ, 1962.

———, "New Developments in Project LINK," *American Economic Review*, May 1985.

Koopmans, Tjalling, "Efficient Allocation of Resources," *Econometrica*, October 1951.

Krainer, John, "The 1997 Nobel Prize in Economics," *FRBSF Economic Letter*, February 13, 1998.

Kregal, J.A., ed. *Recollections of Eminent Economists*, Vol. 2, New York University Press, NY, 1989.

Kuznets, Simon, *Capital in the American Economy: Its Formation and Financing*, Oxford University Press, London, 1961.

———, "Interpretation of National Income Accounts," *Contemporary Economics: Selected Readings*, 2nd ed., Reuben E. Slesinger, Asher Isaacs, and Mark Perlman, eds., Allyn & Bacon, Boston, 1967.

Leonard, Robert J., "From Parlor Games to Social Science: von Neumann, Morganstern, and the Creation of Game Theory, 1928–1944," *Journal of Economic Literature*, June 1995.

Leontief, Wassily, "Input-Output Economics," *Scientific American*, October 1951.

———, "The Structure of the U.S. Economy," *Scientific American*, April 1965.

Lewis, W. Arthur, "Economic Development with Unlimited Supplies of Labor," *Paradigms in Economic Development*, Rajani Kanth, ed., M.E. Sharpe, Armonk, NY, 1994.

———, *Theory of Economic Growth*, Harper and Row, NY, 1965.

Lindbeck, Assar, ed., *Nobel Lectures: Economic Sciences, 1969–1980*, World Scientific, Singapore, 1991.

Little, I.M.D. and J. A. Mirrlees, *Project Appraisal and Planning for Developing Countries*, Basic Books, NY, 1974.

Lucas, Robert E., Jr., "Expectations and the Neutrality of Money," *Journal of Economic Theory*, 1972.

———, "On the Mechanics of Economic Development," *Journal of Monetary Economics* 22, 1988.

Maler, K.-G. ed., *Nobel Lectures in Economic Science, 1981–1990*, World Scientific, Singapore, 1992.

McMillan, John, "Selling Spectrum Rights," *Journal of Economic Perspectives* 8, No. 3, Summer 1994.

Meade, J.E., "Exchange-Rate Policy," in *Readings in Money, National Income and Stabilization Policy*, Warren L. Smith and Ronald L. Teigen, eds., Richard D. Irwin, Homewood, Ill., 1970.

———, "The International Money Mechanism," *Readings in Macroeconomics*, M.G. Mueller, ed., Holt Rinehart & Winston, NY, 1966.

Merton, Robert C., "In Honor of Nobel Laureate Franco Modigliani," *Journal of Economic Perspectives* 6, No. 2, Fall 1987.

Miller, Merton H., "The Modigliani-Miller Proposition After Thirty Years," *Journal of Economic Perspectives* 1, No. 4, Fall 1988.

Mirrlees, James, "An Exploration in the Theory of Optimum Income Tax, *Review of Economic Studies* 38, 1971.

———, "Information and Incentives: The Economics of Carrots and Sticks," *The Economic Journal* 107, September 1997.

Modigliani, Franco, "Life Cycle," *American Economic Review*, March 1963.

———, "MM—Past, Present, Future," *Journal of Economic Perspectives* 2, No. 4, Fall 1988.

Morgan, Mary S., *The History of Econometric Ideas*, Cambridge University Press, NY, 1990.

Mueller, Dennis C., "Normative Public Choice: The Arrow Impossibility Theorem, in Public Choice Theory," David Greenaway et al., eds., *Companion to Contemporary Economic Thought*, Rutledge, London and NY, 1991.

Mundell, Robert A., "International Monetary Reform: The Optimal Mix in Big Countries," in *Macroeconomics, Prices and Quantities*, James Tobin, ed., Brookings, Washington, 1983.

Myrdal, Gunnar, *An American Dilemma: The Negro Problem and Modern Democracy*, Harper, NY, 1944.

Nasar, Sylvia, *A Beautiful Mind*, Simon & Schuster, NY, 1998.

Nash, John F., Jr., "The Bargaining Problem," in *Classics in Game Theory*, Harold W. Kuhn, ed., Princeton University Press, Princeton, 1997.

Neumann, John von, and Oskar Morgenstern, *Theory of Games and Economic Behavior*, Princeton University Press, Princeton, NJ, 1944.

North, Douglass, "Institutions," *Journal of Economic Perspectives* 5, No. 1. Winter 1991.

———, *Institutions, Institutional Change, and Economic Performance*, Cambridge University Press, Cambridge, 1990.

Ohlin, Bertil, "1933 and 1977—Some Expansion Policy Problems in Cases of Unbalanced Domestic and International Economic Relations," *American Economic Review*, December 1993.

Persson, Torsten, ed., *Nobel Lectures: Economic Sciences, 1991–1995*, World Scientific, Singapore, 1997.

Phillips, A.W., "The Relation Between Unemployment and the Rate of Change of Money Wage Rates in the United Kingdom, 1967–1957," *Economica* 5, 1958.

Poundstone, William, *Prisoner's Dilemma*, Doubleday, NY, 1992.

Rawls, John, "Some Reasons for the Maximin Criterion," in *Readings in Public Sector Economics*, Samuel H. Baker and Catherine S. Elliott, eds., D.C. Heath, Lexington, Mass., 1990.

Romer, Thomas, "On James Buchanan's Contributions to Public Economics," *Journal of Economic Perspectives*, Fall 1988, pp. 165–179.

Samuelson, Paul, "Altruism as a Problem Involving Group Versus Individual," *American Economic Review*, May 1993.

———, "Interactions Between the Multiplier Analysis and the Principle of Acceleration," in *Readings in Business Cycle Theory*, The Blakiston Co., Philadelphia, 1951.

Sandmo, Agnar, "Asymmetric Information and Public Economics: The Mirrlees-Vickrey Nobel Prize," *Journal of Economic Perspectives*, Winter 1999.

———, "Buchanan on Political Economy: A Review Article," *Journal of Economic Literature* 28, No. 1, March 1990.

Schelling, Thomas C., *Strategy of Conflict*, Oxford University Press, London, 1960.

Scholes, Myron, S., "Financial Infrastructure and Economic Growth," in *The Mosaic of Economic Growth*, Ralph Landau et al., eds., Stanford University Press, Stanford, Calif., 1996.

Schultz, Theodore, *The Economic Value of Education*, Columbia University Press, NY, 1963.

———, "Investment in Human Capital," *American Economic Review*, March 1961.

Selten, Reinhard, "The Chain Store Paradox," *Theory and Decision* 9, 1978.

Sen, Amartya, "Economics and the Value of Freedom, *Civilization*, June/July 1999.

———, "Food, Economics, and Entitlements," in *The Political Economy of Hunger*, Jean Dreze, et al., eds., Clarendon Press, Oxford, 1995.

———, *On Ethics and Economics*, Basil Blackwell, NY, 1987.

Sharpe, William F., "Capital Asset Prices: A Theory of Market Equilibrium Under Conditions of Risk," *Journal of Finance* 19, No. 3, September 1964.

Simon, Herbert, "Altruism and Economics," *American Economic Review*, May 1993.

———, "Rationality as Process and as a Product of Thought," *American Economic Review*, May 1978.

Solow, Robert, "A Contribution to the Theory of Economic Growth," *Quarterly Journal of Economics* 70, No. 1, February 1956.

———, "Perspectives on Growth Theory," *Journal of Economic Perspectives* 8, No. 1, Winter 1994.

Stigler, George, "Basic Concepts in the Theory of Value," *Contemporary Economics: Selected Readings*," Reuben E. Slesinger et al., eds., Allyn & Bacon, Boston, 1967.

———, "The Case Against Big Business," *Readings in Economics*, Kohler, Heinz, ed., Holt Rinehart & Winston, NY, 1968.

Stone, Richard, "The Accounts of Society," *American Economic Review*, December 1997.

Szenberg, Michael, ed., *Eminent Economists, Their Life Philosophies*, Cambridge University Press, NY, 1993.

Thaler, Richard H., *The Winner's Curse,* Princeton University Press, Princeton, NJ, 1992.

Tinbergen, Jan, "Econometric Business Cycle Research," in *Readings in Business Cycle Theory,* The Blakiston Co., Philadelphia, 1951.

———, "The Use of Models: Experience and Prospects," *American Economic Review* 71, No. 6, December 1981.

Tobin, James, *Asset Accumulation and Economic Activity,* University of Chicago Press, Chicago, 1980.

———, "Inflation and Unemployment," *American Economic Review* 62, No. 1, March 1972.

———, "Liquidity Preference as Behavior Towards Risk," *Review of Economic Studies* 25, February 1958.

Townsend, Robert M., "Arrow-Debreu Programs as Microfoundations of Macroeconomics," *Advances in Economic Theory,* Truman F. Bewley, ed., Cambridge University Press, NY, 1987.

Vickrey, William, "Congestion Theory and Transport Investment," in *Public Economics,* Richard Arnott et al., eds., Cambridge University Press, Cambridge, 1994.

———, "Counterspeculation, Auctions, and Competitive Sealed Tenders," *Journal of Finance* 16, March 1961.

INDEX

ABOUT THE AUTHOR

Marilu Hurt McCarty, Ph.D., is Professor Emeritus of Economics at Georgia Institute of Technology. She has written or cowritten six textbooks in economics—with *Dollars and Sense* now in its eighth edition—and produced semiannual editions of *Applications in Microeconomics* and *Applications in Macroeconomics* for *The Wall Street Journal*. Dr. McCarty's work regularly appears in Georgia Tech's *Economic Digest*, and she is a popular speaker for civic groups and academic institutions.